"Bridge" is an apt description of the chapters in this book which work to connect the theoretical and academic with a variety of practical approaches to the spiritual formation of children ⸱ ⸱ ᵐ. Let these chapters become conversati  ne your own assumptions and practices re .th practices, spiritual formation, and inc :ds and differing abilities.

> Rev. Dr. Elizabeth F. Caldwell, adjunct faculty,
> Vanderbilt Divinity School and author of
> Wondering about the Bible with Children

This book builds a well-constructed bridge from biblical foundations and educational theories to a multitude of practices in which every person in a congregation is involved in the Christian discipleship of children. The team of diverse writers are bridge builders who have crossed this bridge many times as insightful teachers and well-tested practitioners. From engaging children with age-sensitive and creative ideas for dealing with the ABC's of the gospel to often-neglected areas of children's ministry like grief, disappointment, and racial prejudice, this book will help educators, teachers, leaders and volunteers in children's ministry give children a head start at lifelong discipleship.

> Dr. Robbie F. Castleman, professor emerita,
> theology & New Testament, John Brown
> University and author of Parenting in the Pew

Hats off to Keeley and Larson for compiling this welcome addition to the field of children's spirituality. For over fifteen years, the Children's Spirituality Summit has been gathering the best researchers and brightest practitioners, and this book is the fruit of their latest efforts. True to its promise, it blends theory and practice into a book that will fascinate the seasoned scholar and equip the frontline children's minister.

> David M. Csinos, assistant professor of practical
> theology, Atlantic School of Theology
> and founder of Faith Forward

The authors in this book represent a wide range of disciplines, providing the reader with insights into many aspects of child development and spiritual nurture. Based on these insights, they offer practical ways of ministering with children and their families. They also challenge the readers to broaden their awareness of children and families who are not in the church and to reach out and welcome them into the embrace of God's love through the church.

> *Dr. Catherine Stonehouse,* program director
> for PhD in Transformational Learning,
> Asia Graduate School of Theology

The title says it all! Keeley and Larson have masterfully crafted a volume that coalesces the theological, theoretical, and practical into a singular approach to childhood spiritual formation. It provides the reader access to not only some of the most current thoughts on child spirituality, but captures the essence of the Children's Spirituality Summit. Nowhere else will the academic and the practitioner find more common ground on this subject than in this one volume. It is beneficial to the student of education, the professor in the academy, and the pastor in the church.

> *James Riley Estep,* Jr., DMin, PhD, vice president of
> academics, Central Christian College of the Bible

This is a must-read for children's ministers and volunteers! Nowhere else can one find practical yet research-based explorations of spiritual direction, grief, trauma, and racially diverse spiritual experiences alongside more conventional discussions of biblical storytelling and spiritual play. Every congregation needs a copy (or two) of this book on its resource shelf!

> *Karen-Marie Yust,* ThD, Josiah P. & Anne Wilson Rowe
> professor of Christian education, Union Presbyterian
> Seminary and author of *Real Kids, Real Faith*

Bridging Theory and Practice in

CHILDREN'S
SPIRITUALITY

Bridging Theory and Practice in

CHILDREN'S SPIRITUALITY

NEW DIRECTIONS FOR EDUCATION, MINISTRY, AND DISCIPLESHIP

MIMI L. LARSON AND
ROBERT J. KEELEY,
general editors

ZONDERVAN REFLECTIVE

Bridging Theory and Practice in Children's Spirituality
Copyright © 2020 by Mimi L. Larson and Robert J. Keeley

Requests for information should be addressed to:
Zondervan, *3900 Sparks Dr. SE, Grand Rapids, Michigan 49546*

Library of Congress Cataloging-in-Publication Data

Names: Larson, Mimi L., 1966- editor. | Keeley, Robert J., 1954- editor.
Title: Bridging theory and practice in children's spirituality : new directions for education,
    ministry, and discipleship / Mimi L. Larson and Robert J. Keeley, editors.
Description: Grand Rapids : Zondervan, 2020. | Includes bibliographical references.
Identifiers: LCCN 2019046949 (print) | LCCN 2019046950 (ebook) | ISBN 9780310104919
    (paperback) | ISBN 9780310104933 (ebook)
Subjects: LCSH: Christian children--Religious life. | Church work with children. |
    Faith development.
Classification: LCC BV4571.3 .B75 2020 (print) | LCC BV4571.3 (ebook)
    DDC 248.8/2--dc23
LC record available at https://lccn.loc.gov/2019046949
LC ebook record available at https://lccn.loc.gov/2019046950

Cover design: John Hamilton Design
Cover photos: © Imgorthand / iStockphoto; © Hayati Kayhan / Shutterstock
Interior design: Kait Lamphere

To the students we have taught
and who have taught us.
We pray that God will bless you
in your work with children.

CONTENTS

SECTION 3:

The Importance of Story in a Child's Spirituality

SECTION 4:

Nurturing Children's Spirituality through Different Methods

SECTION 5:
The Future of Children's Spirituality

FOREWORD

I'm a father to three amazing daughters.

As parents, both Donna and I had at least two desires for our daughters. First, we wanted to raise them to be strong, confident women. Second, and more importantly, we desired to shepherd their heart towards Christ and raise them in a way that would cultivate Christian faith within their hearts and lives. I'm not sure I've ever met a Christian parent who didn't have a strong desire to see their children follow Christ and live out Christ-like values. But, as we all know, it's one thing to have a desire; it's another thing to act upon that desire. Desire requires intention; execution requires intentionality.

A Lifeway Research project on the predictors of spiritual health among young adults illuminates several positive predictors of spiritual health in children that continue into adulthood. Bible reading (most important), prayer, service in a church, mission trips, and listening to Christian music are intentional activities that cumulatively contribute to the spiritual health of young adults in their formative years in the Christian faith.

In itself, this illustrates several essential facts about ministry to children in our cultural moment.

First, it demonstrates how ministry to children has evolved significantly from a content-driven enterprise toward a modeling approach. What one will find is that children are more than simple recipients of spiritual goods; they are participants and contributors in their faith journeys. Along with several other significant trends, we see the increased importance of authenticity over spiritual authority. Those who actively live out a life of faith have greater credibility than those who speak about faith from a position of authority.

Second, it demonstrates that spiritual formation is no longer seen solely as an adult-to-child approach, but includes a peer aspect where children participate actively and frequently in gospel life with their parents. These experiences and the act of living out Christian faith with their parents shape their Christian foundation and identity for years to come. One thing is for sure, ministry *to* children, *for* children, *with* children, and *by* children—and their unique spiritual formation within the North American context—should be an essential aspect of the church's missional agenda. Truthfully, any serious missional intention should be built upon the foundation of a robust theology of children's spiritual formation within our cultural context.

This important collection of research describes the historical development of the spiritual formation of children and the main elements of a foundation to this process. It explores the various environments, contexts, and experiences that shape our children's lives in our world, alongside the power of stories and various methodologies that achieve a positive outcome for children's Christian formation. The aspects of formation presented here are essential for our consideration, especially in light of the broken world in which we live. In fact, this book asserts that faith, hope, and religious belief systems promote resilience in children who encounter hardship. This is an important consideration for missional ambassadors living in our fractured North American context.

I am thankful, for example, for the chapter which presents a "comparative views" approach that examines not only major theological traditions about children and their relationship with God, but also explores significant ministry efforts that flow out of those traditions in the life of the church. Kevin Lawson and Adam Harwood present five different Christian traditions and how they deal with several aspects that encompass children's spirituality and its development.

Another central aspect of this book is that it conveys to us the important role a child's environment plays in his or her holistic spiritual formation. Given this, the church and Christian parents should intentionally think through ways they can meaningfully equip, prepare, and support children in a world of brokenness, conflict, outrage, and tragedy. We are taught that essential aspects of the spiritual formation of children are their beliefs that are shaped by God's Word and their particular faith tradition. Therefore, it's important for children to root their growing faith in a healthy community driven by love. From such an environment, children's behavior takes form from what they see modelled and what they hear taught.

It is critical that we understand the seismic shifts that have taken place in various historical periods that have shaped the environments of both teaching and learning. Much of my own writing seeks to work toward contextual approaches in our current cultural moment that shape the contours of our culture for the good of the gospel. Much of my thoughts and writing—although not directly related—reflects the importance of what this book seeks to achieve. Any committed follower of Jesus would be remiss not to take note of the development of children's spiritual formation and its implications for current ministry among North American evangelicals.

I am confident that this book will be a tremendous resource to you and assist you in being more attentive to the children we encounter, allowing their journey, experiences, and faith to inform and shape ministry among them. What I believe this requires of us is an intentional missional posture that sees children as valuable co-partners in spiritual formation, which will lead to their faith being affirmed, embraced, and anchored within the turbulent waters of our era. If we are to see a new generation of wholly-devoted followers of Christ within the church, we need to embrace the change that is upon us and see another way.

Ed Stetzer, Billy Graham Center, Wheaton College

INTRODUCTION

Both of us have loved being in the academy, where we have time to think, time to write, and then time to think some more. Many amazing ideas come out of such places, and the world would be in worse shape without some of the best thinkers of each age being given time to think and time to teach. But in order to best serve the church, the ideas generated by these thinkers, especially in areas of ministry, need to get to practitioners. That's where we, the editors of this book, have spent a good part of our careers. Both of us have spent significant time in practical ministry, Mimi in churches, and Bob in teaching in middle and high school. As we both came to the academy a bit later in our lives, we have a love for practical theology—that place where theory meets the practice of being with kids in real settings.

The Children's Spirituality Summit is a place where this connection between theory and practice is at the center of the conversation. It is, in fact, at one of these meetings where we first met. This volume reflects some of the conversations and presentations that took place at the sixth Summit, held in June 2018 in Nashville, Tennessee, on the campus of Lipscomb University. We saw this particular gathering as a place where we heard a reflection of where the field of children's spirituality has been and where it should be going. There were both historical and prophetic voices from an array of denominations, representing some of the most important and most thoughtful people in the field. It has been our privilege to turn those conversations into a coherent message.

We did not want this book to be a collection of papers that merely reflect what happened that summer, however. In these pages, the chapters represent people who are listening to each other as well as bringing their own perspectives to these topics. You'll see, for example, that both Henry Zonio and Karen Williams reflect in different but powerful ways on the nature and importance of how children of color are represented in church school curriculum and how Mimi Larson pushes that conversation in yet a different direction. Marva Hoopes, Dana Kennamer, and Robert Keeley all reflect on the importance of story in helping children learn who God is. The chapters from Kevin Lawson and Adam Harwood and from Scottie May reflect conversations about how to characterize the work of those who came before us in children's ministry. Holly Allen, along with her students Megan Larry and Kaylee Frank, has learned from and extended the work of Shelly Melia. John Roberto, Lacy Borgo, Mimi Larson and Shirley Morgenthaler, Trevecca Okholm, and Erik Carter all look at the intersection of home and church. These conversations took place in workshops and in plenary sessions, but they also took place around the dinner table and in hallways. These chapters represent people who not only think well about these issues but have real-life experience in making things work in ministry.

We're grateful to our colleagues on the board of the Society for Children's Spirituality: Christian Perspectives, many of whom are represented in these chapters, for organizing and running the Children's Spirituality Summit and for encouraging us in our work. We're grateful to our colleagues at Wheaton College, Calvin University, and Calvin Theological Seminary for their support as we did our work on this book. Special thanks to the people at Zondervan who helped us in putting this book together, especially Ryan Pazdur and Harmony Harkema. They were a joy to work with. We're grateful to our congregations in Elmhurst, Illinois and Holland, Michigan for their ministry to us. We're grateful to Keith Larson and Laura Keeley, our spouses, for their continued love and support. We needed it. Finally, it is with gratitude to God that we offer this book as a thanksgiving offering. It is our prayer that this book will equip those who work with children to serve them well and help them recognize their place in God's big story as beloved sons and daughters of God.

Robert J. Keeley and Mimi L. Larson
May 2019

Foundations for

ENGAGING CHILDREN'S
SPIRITUALITY

CHAPTER 1

WHAT HAVE WE LEARNED?

Seventy-Five Years of Children's
Evangelical Spiritual Formation

SCOTTIE MAY

When we consider the spiritual formation of children, what, if anything, can we learn from the past? Are there ways history might help us move forward? The content of this anecdotal chapter is based on my own experiences and observations, in addition to historical and academic sources.

The phrase "spiritual formation" is relatively recent among evangelicals. Even more recent is the concept of the spiritual formation of children. "Discipleship" has been the long-standing term for helping new believers grow in their faith. Gradually it came to mean Bible study and prayer—good, essential things, but with a strong cognitive focus, which can be limiting.

Since the concept of spiritual formation is new to many, a working definition is in order: Spiritual formation involves all dimensions of a person—interpersonal, intrapersonal, and the interaction of the human spirit with God's Spirit. It is more than just knowing the Bible or the practice of spiritual disciplines. The apostle Paul addresses his aim for the people of the church of Galatia by saying that he is in the "pains of childbirth until Christ is formed in you" (Gal. 4:19). Simply stated, spiritual formation is the process of Christ being formed within his followers. It is a trinitarian process in which a person encounters the living God through the enabling of the Holy Spirit to become more like Jesus Christ. It is also an intentional, communal process in that believers need each other for this kind of growth to happen.[1]

A disclaimer is necessary at the outset of this chapter. What is represented here is an Anglo-American evangelical perspective.[2] No attempt is made to describe the spiritual formation of children of other ethnicities or from other Christian faith traditions. That important work falls to others. Yet the North American evangelical approach to ministry with children is especially significant because its advocates embrace the missional aspect of that tradition, which propels them to disseminate that approach far beyond their geographical borders rather than help other contexts develop their own approaches.

THE SIGNIFICANCE OF HISTORY

"[W]e must take into account how history influences our formation," writes Evan Howard in *A Guide to Christian Spiritual Formation*.[3] Significant cultural factors affect all of life—how we interact, communicate, parent, and worship. Thus, it is no wonder that historical context influences the ways discipleship and Christian formation happen.

Though not the focus of this chapter, a brief overview of the early history of formation begins with the Book of Deuteronomy, especially chapters 4 through 11, in which Moses describes ways children are to learn about God and his laws: in natural, informal ways in every aspect of life. Centuries later, during the exile, the process of passing on faith in the God of Israel became more formalized through synagogue schools, requiring

---

1. This definition is a compilation of the thoughts of Robert Mulholland and James Wilhoit. See Robert Mulholland, *Invitation to a Journey* (Downers Grove, IL: InterVarsity Press, 1993), 15, and James Wilhoit, *Spiritual Formation as if the Church Mattered* (Grand Rapids, MI: Baker Books, 2008) 23.

2. David Bebbington describes four distinctives that mark evangelicalism: a) personal "born-again" experience; b) demonstration of mission and social reform; c) the Bible as ultimate authority; d) emphasis on Jesus' sacrifice on the cross for people's redemption. See "What Is An Evangelical?" National Association of Evangelicals, www.nae.net/what-is-an-evangelical, accessed November 28, 2018.

3. Evan Howard, *A Guide to Christian Spiritual Formation* (Grand Rapids, MI: Baker Books, 2018), 35.

considerable memorization in order to recall God's commands and obey them. Subsequent to the establishment of the early church, catechetical schools arose for more systematized courses of study. Then in 1780, in Gloucester, England, Robert Raikes energized a fledgling movement called Sunday school. Through his publishing resources, word spread about how these schools for boys that began in the kitchens of a few women were accomplishing much in helping children know about God as they learned to read. Within a few years, over one million children in England attended Sunday school. Soon, Sunday schools began to appear in North American churches.

Then, in the late 1800s, Uniform Lesson Plans, published by Standard Publishing in Ohio, were made widely available so that scores of churches were teaching the same Bible passage every Sunday. These lesson plans enabled adult students to study the entire Bible in just a few years. Around that same time, the publishing industry expanded as printing presses became more efficient. In 1875, David C. Cook started publishing Christian literature in Illinois. The Southern Baptist Convention founded the Sunday School Board in 1891, now called LifeWay Resources. The number of independent publishing houses that were established during the twentieth century is noteworthy: Gospel Light (1933) and Scripture Press (1934)—both now part of David C. Cook, as is Standard Publishing—Urban Ministries Incorporated (1970), and Group Publishing (1974), among others. These two companies, Cook and LifeWay, who have published Sunday school lesson plans for well over a century, are now two of the largest suppliers of educational materials for Protestant churches.

Contemporary sociologist William Corsaro[4] believes that adults must become more reflective in their assumptions about children, because adults' perceptions of children have been the focus of what children need more than the perspectives of the children themselves. Although this has begun to change, vestiges are still evident in the sign-on-the-dotted line approach to the evangelism of children that has been around for over a century, as well as the heavily cognitive emphasis to faith formation. But the heart of this chapter is on more recent history.

---

4. William Corsaro, *The Sociology of Childhood*, 3rd ed. (Thousand Oaks, CA: Pine Forge Press, 2011).

PATTERNS IN THE PAST SEVENTY-FIVE YEARS

Now that I am in the sunset years of my academic and ministry life, I can reflect back over the many decades I have spent immersed in the Anglo evangelical church. That process has revealed three groupings of twenty-five years: 1940–1965, 1965–1990, and 1990 to the present. The divisions between these periods are not clean; they blur and even overlap. Nonetheless, patterns appear that differ from one period to the next.

John Westerhoff[5] implemented prepositions to describe ways children are perceived to learn: *to*—a production model; *for*—a garden model; and *with*—a "life" model. I find these prepositions helpful when comparing and contrasting the three periods I noted above, but I am nuancing them differently for our purposes in this chapter. The first period, 1940–1965, I characterize with the preposition *to*, because the consensus of many at the time was that children, being incomplete and non-productive, needed the help of adults in order to become disciples. Therefore, things were done *to* children to encourage that process. The period 1965–1990 may be viewed as the period in which adults did all they could *for* children to enable them to thrive and grow—as in, "bloom where they are planted." The main idea was that learning should be pleasant and enjoyable so that growth can happen naturally. There is validity in these two perceptions of the child, but the limitations are significant. The third period is notable in the emphasis on *with* as a guiding preposition. The relationship between the adult and child is key in this period.

Along with the differing prepositions, a pedagogical difference is also evident. The first period, designated as the TO period, focused on the *content*. The goal was to make sure the content was learned. The second period, the FOR period, was *student*-focused, making sure the child was enjoying Sunday school and the learning experiences of the church. The final period is the WITH period, which emphasizes the *process* by which learning takes place—that it requires holistic engagement by the learner in order to be formational. These delineations are tendencies, not clear absolute distinctions. See Table 1.

---

5. John H. Westerhoff III, *Will Our Children Have Faith?* 3rd ed. (New York: Morehouse Publishing, 2012), 102–103.

TABLE 1: *Primary Characteristics of Three Recent 25-Year Periods in the History of Children's Spiritual Formation*

Dates	1940–1965	1965–1990	1990–Present
Preposition	TO	FOR	WITH
Pedagogical Focus	Content-Centered	Student-Centered	Process-Centered

Having noticed the significance of prepositions in ministry approaches, it is noteworthy to consider the effect that metaphors have in shaping ministry. This effect is often implicit, and the volunteer is often unaware of it. As a figure of speech, a metaphor brings insight to an object or concept without directly explaining it. Metaphors can be small and detail-focused (micro-metaphors) as well as large and overarching in scope (macro-metaphors). Both types of metaphors will be taken into account in the following sections.

MICRO-METAPHORS

A micro-metaphor brings fresh understanding to a component of a larger concept by comparing it to an unrelated object. For our purposes here, the micro-elements of church-based formational education are the child, the teacher, and the subject or content. Table 2 represents these micro-metaphors.

THE CHILD

During the TO period, children were thought of as sponges, *tabula rasa* (Latin for blank slate), empty vessels, wet cement, or clay. Notice that these metaphors for children are passive, inanimate objects that must be acted upon. With the emphasis on the content, many assumed that cognitive knowing brought about Christian formation. The sponge was a very common metaphor, something that would soak up the material, similar to the way an empty vessel needs to be filled. Clay can be a lovely metaphor if used in the biblical sense: God, then, is the potter; we are the clay. This is very different, however, from children being clay molded by a human teacher's hands.

Later, during the FOR period, children were viewed as consumers, participants, explorers, or surveyors. The interests of the child played a significant role in the transition from Sunday "school" to events with names that reflected a new kind of experience, such as WonderLand, Kids' Exploration, or PromiseLand. This was a significant shift. Sunday morning classes began to include games and fun activities that helped bring home the aim of the lesson (but not always; sometimes it would be quite a stretch to see the connection). Children were actively involved in Sunday classes; they loved it. There were worship bands to lead the high-energy music, including lots of movement. In very large churches, ministry for children became elaborate, enthusiastic productions. Children even came to be seen as the catalyst for encouraging their parents to attend every week because the children did not want to miss out on the fun. Families sometimes "shopped" for the church that had the most fun children's ministry.

The next period has brought about more shifts in the view of children. Metaphors such as plant, sheep, scientist, and pilgrim are used to refer to children during the WITH era. Three of these metaphors are found in Scripture, each needing guidance or help. The plant needs a farmer to provide the environment for growth; the sheep needs a shepherd to protect and lead it to nourishment; a pilgrim needs a seasoned leader or companion who has traveled the same way before. A scientist, though not a biblical metaphor, captures children—even young children—beautifully. Always curious and questioning, a scientist investigates reality to find truth, just as a child does.

This WITH period of children's spiritual formation is burgeoning because of the work of scholars who study the spirituality of children and identify their remarkable ability to make meaning of life and experiences in ways that transcend cognitive learning. Young children make value judgments, sensing delight and despair. Because of their ability to wonder with a sense of awe, they are very aware of spiritual things—a spiritual "Other"—even though they cannot speak of these things until they are older. New findings in neurobiology reveal prenatal neural activity that was formerly unknown: learning happens before birth. The fetus is able to hear, taste, recognize the mother's language cadence, and even respond to visual stimuli.[6] These findings change the views and expectations of children in ways that were not available for the earlier periods.

THE TEACHER

There is notable consistency in the metaphors for the child and the teacher during each of the three periods. Because of the view of the child during the TO period, the teacher's role was seen as expert, boss, funnel holder, and evaluator. Those metaphors communicate that the teacher knows and the children do not. The metaphor of funnel holder vividly depicts the image of the child as an empty vessel with the teacher holding the means of pouring information into the child.

By the FOR period, since the child was more of the focus, the view of the teacher had shifted to these metaphors: coordinator, customer service representative, ringmaster, and planner. The teacher created ways to engage the children in more active learning. Sometimes the learning was so active that the teacher would feel it was a three-ring circus.

When it comes to the WITH period, there is a further shift in the metaphors for the teacher. There is more of a sense of partnership with the child. The teacher is shepherd, farmer, fellow pilgrim, co-learner. A shepherd leads the flock to green pastures and quiet waters, where the sheep find nutrition. The farmer prepares the soil, plants, waters, and weeds; but the farmer cannot make the seed grow. The farmer works to control the environment, but growth is within the seed itself. Fellow pilgrim and co-learner are similar; both require humility on the part of the teacher. As fellow pilgrims, both teacher and child are journeying toward Christlikeness, though the teacher is ahead on that journey. Co-learners realize that they can learn from each other. This rather revolutionary

---

6. Here are seven resources among many currently available that discuss these findings about children: 1) Jerome Berryman, *Godly Play* (San Francisco, CA: Harper, 1991). 2) Sofia Cavalletti, *The Religious Potential of the Child* (Chicago, IL: Liturgy Training Publications, 1992). 3) Steven Johnson, "Antonio Damasio's Theory of Thinking Faster and Faster: Are the Brain's Emotional Circuits Hardwired for Speed?" *Discover* 25, no. 5 (2004): 45–49. 4) Rhawn Joseph, "The Limbic System and the Soul: Evolution and the Neuroanatomy of Religious Experience," *Zygon* 36, no. 1 (2001): 105–135. 5) Andrew Newberg and Stephanie Newberg, "A Neuropsychological Perspective of Spiritual Development," in *The Handbook of Spiritual Development in Childhood and Adolescence,* eds. Peter Benson, et al. (Thousand Oaks, CA: Sage, 2006), 183–196. 6) Catherine Stonehouse and Scottie May, *Listening to Children on the Spiritual Journey* (Grand Rapids, MI: Baker, 2010). 7) Matthew Woodley, "The Wonder of It All," *Discipleship Journal* 119, (2000): 25–28.

thought recognizes that children can indeed teach adults something, including and perhaps especially spiritual insights, if the adults only have ears to
hear and eyes to see.

Having looked at metaphors for the child and for the teacher, one more
key component is left—that of the subject or content which, in a ministry
setting, is primarily the Bible.

CONTENT

In the TO period, the content of the Bible was usually approached sys-
tematically around theological themes with the goal that children should be
able to recall it. During the FOR years, the approach to the content was more
flexible, with options often provided by curriculum publishers so that teachers
could choose what and how to teach. Now with the explosion of research
and neurobiological data regarding infants and young children, especially
their spiritual responses, the teaching/learning process is being overhauled
in many ministries. In WITH settings, the focus is on helping the child to
encounter God and God's story in ways that form the child's character and life.

TABLE 2: *Micro-Metaphors for Three Recent 25-Year Periods in the History of
Children's Spiritual Formation*

Dates	1940–1965	1965–1990	1990–Present
Preposition	TO	FOR	WITH
CHILD	Sponge	Consumer	Plant
	Empty vessel	Participant	Pilgrim
	Wet cement	Explorer	Sheep
	Clay	Surveyor	Scientist
TEACHER	Expert	Coordinator	Fellow pilgrim
	Funnel holder	Customer service	Farmer
	Evaluator	Planner	Shepherd
	Boss	Ringmaster	Co-learner
CONTENT	Systematic	Flexible	Integrated
APPROACH	*Recall It*	*Choose It*	*Live It*

This progression of insights does not mean that earlier views were wrong or bad, it just means that they were less effective than was once thought. Though there is an increase in WITH approaches in churches, TO and FOR processes can still be found. The micro-metaphors for the three periods are represented in Table 2 so that comparisons and contrasts may be made.

MACRO-METAPHORS

Just as micro-metaphors reveal implicit meaning accompanying the components and processes in children's ministry, macro-metaphors reveal the overarching philosophy of the context. Even if this approach to ministry is not explicit, it is often palpable, i.e., the "feel" of the space. During the first twenty-five-year period, ministry with children was like a benevolent factory (although occasionally, benevolence was hard to find). The environment and pedagogical processes inherently did things TO the children to "make" them Christian. The major teaching time was called Sunday "school" and was organized and administered much like a traditional school, with age-graded classrooms, teachers, workbooks, attendance charts, departments, and even superintendents. Though the students were not given grades for their learning, they were often rewarded for good work with candy, stickers, and attendance pins. The ideal student would master the content of the Bible. By employing a transmissive approach with activities such as "Sword Drills," Bible memory contests, and quizzing, it sometimes felt like a training camp where, if you went through all the levels and mastered the content, you could feel confident that you were a maturing disciple of Jesus. This model served well for many, many generations.

The second twenty-five years saw a gradual shift to a FOR or student-focused emphasis that introduced helpful elements of fun and games designed to be developmentally appropriate, along with Bible stories. Creativity exploded on the scene in many churches in the activities as well as the décor, with elaborately designed spaces, sometimes cartoon-like, interactive puppet productions, musicians to lead singing, and well-crafted skits. Large, open spaces were preferred over classrooms with age-appropriate activity stations. Rather than the constraints of a factory-like model, the space felt more like a playground. Children were active through choreography as well as free movement. An agricultural metaphor, such as a meadow, is more appropriate to the FOR period than a mechanical one, such as a factory. These settings and experiences were designed FOR children to have fun, which was the number one value in many children's ministries. In these settings, children enthusiastically engaged in the high-energy activities as if they were dancing from one thing to another. The settings varied by age group so that the child's level of development was important in helping them be comfortable and grow in faith.

The third period, WITH, began slowly during the previous period. It is a shift to a more formational approach in which the entire person is involved—mind, emotions, attitudes, behavior, and relationships. The word *with* as a guiding philosophy changes the learning environment significantly. Growth in the learners is desired but in a carefully designed environment more like a cultivated garden than a meadow filled with wildflowers. The space for this growth is viewed as sacred; the pace has elements that are slow and gentle; the volume is joyful without being raucous, and voices are often soft. Observing a WITH environment is like being at a symphony where the various parts, adults and children, work together to make beautiful music. The leader and learners journey *with* each other, with the leader naturally being farther ahead on the journey; nonetheless, they are traveling together toward more personal and corporate Christlikeness. The WITH philosophical approach is one of formation—"Until Christ is formed" in the participants (Gal. 4:19).

Table 3 shows the macro-metaphors or contexts of the three twenty-five-year periods.

TABLE 3: *Macro-Metaphors for Three Recent 25-Year Periods in the History of Children's Spiritual Formation*

Dates	1940–1965	1965–1990	1990–Present
Preposition	TO	FOR	WITH
CONTEXT	Factory	Meadow	Cultivated garden
	Training camp	Playground	Symphony
	Reward club	Dance	Journey
PHILOSOPHY	Transmissive	Developmental	Formational

Significant insights unfold when we reflect upon the differences between these three twenty-five-year periods. In what ways, if any, is this analysis helpful for assessing your own ministry?

FACTORS THAT SHAPE THE CONTEXT

A multitude of factors contributes to the context in which we live. For the three time periods considered here, these factors differ in each period. What follows is a limited list of events and influences shaping ministry with children in these different periods. Events in one period bleed into the next, creating both continuity and reactions.

THE TO PERIOD: *1940–1965*
Influences:
- The final stages of World War II and its unspeakable horrors
- Renewed passion for evangelism because of the evil present in the war
- Behavioristic methods with clear, measurable results commonplace in learning environments
- Prayer and Bible reading in many public schools
- Sunday school was the primary outreach means to children, often through bus ministry
- Rewards and prizes viewed as motivators for obtaining desired behaviors

Events:
- Growing presence of television
- Contests of all sorts: attendance, "sword" drills, Bible memorization, and quizzing
- Sunday school conventions: thousands attend in Detroit, Chicago, and Los Angeles
- *Life* magazine, 1957, "Sunday school, the most wasted hour of the week."
- Booklets such as "Soul Winning Made Easy" help youth know how to evangelize

- Vietnam war and civil unrest (1955–1975)
- Availability of "the pill" (1960) and the beginning of the sexual revolution
- Onset of the church renewal movement and the small group movement

THE FOR PERIOD: *1965–1990*
Influences:

- Television now a powerful force
- Developmental stage theory widely embraced, first by schools, then by the church influencing curriculum development and church architecture
- Continuation of social and political unrest
- With a greater focus on the child, "fun" becomes a high value in many churches, inspiring *Time* magazine to write an article on Funday School.

Events:

- Lawrence O. Richards's Sunday School Plus, an ahead-of-its-time alternative curriculum to equip families to disciple their children
- *Mister Rogers' Neighborhood* begins, a sharp contrast to most children's TV programming
- Group Publishing brings more active forms of learning into curriculum
- Year of the Child declared by UNESCO in 1979, brings children out of the shadows.
- Children's Pastors' Conferences established and burgeon into the next period
- Prolific Christian media resources available; Christian bookstores thrive

THE WITH PERIOD: *1990–Present*
Influences:

- Post-Christian culture
- Media accessibility pervasive
- Electronics and hand-held devices ever-present

- Developments in brain research and neurobiology provide new knowledge of infants and children
- Evangelicals begin to emphasize formation in addition to education, an emphasis that had long been present in other Christian traditions.
- Recognition of the need for holistic—whole person—emphasis in ministry with children
- Ancient Christian spiritual practices increasingly seen as means of formation

Events:

- Experiential vacation Bible school materials
- Hands-on, Bible-time museum model[7]
- Downloadable curriculum; electronic hand-held Bibles
- Awareness that pre-birth learning takes place: language, sound, taste, even touch
- Awareness of the role of *wonder* in a child's spiritual formation is acknowledged.
- Bible-teaching media products such as "The Bible Project,"[8] "What's in the Bible?,"[9] etc.
- Resources focus on formation in addition to education

STRENGTHS AND WEAKNESSES OF EACH OF THE THREE PERIODS

Each of the three periods has both strengths and weaknesses. None of the periods is bad or wrong; they simply differ in significant ways—in philosophy, function, methods, and outcomes. That last difference is especially important. Leaders in ministry with children need to be aware of deficiencies while they critically retrieve the strengths of each period.

The weakness of the first period, the TO period, was the frequent

---

7. For a fuller explanation of this model, see Scottie May, et al., *Children Matter* (Grand Rapids, MI: Eerdmans, 2005), 246–281.
8. The Bible Project, thebibleproject.com.
9. *Buck Denver Asks . . . What's in the Bible?*, whatsinthebible.com.

employment of methods that tended to treat the learners as objects. But the strength of that period, which focused on Scripture, is *biblical literacy*, something that should matter to all Christians but in which interest has been waning ever since.

Church renewal happened early in the second, or FOR, period. Emphases in this period were on building relationships through small groups and making learning fun. Attention was paid to the needs of learners of all ages, and experiences were created to make learning meaningful and enjoyable.

Now, during the WITH period, effort is being made to bring about "authentic engagement" with the biblical story and with God through his Spirit. Has some of the energetic, enthusiastic delight of the earlier periods been lost in this latest shift? Are reflective engagement and authentic experiences enough to help children consider the church as their faith family?

I find it helpful to consider the three periods as building on each other rather than replacing one another. Culture and context shift and develop; so do approaches to formation. Howard views spiritual experiences as shaped by culture: "The *intention* of formation must be balanced with the *wisdom* of formation, the latter of which attends to context."[10] He encourages openness to the unfamiliar, which may be formational, much in the way that first-century Jewish followers of Jesus had to be open to welcoming gentiles.

Recent scholarly work is enabling children's voices to be heard, demonstrating that they are significant actors in events, making contributions that often facilitate contextual change. A prime methodology for this research, particularly with young children, is to watch and listen.

BIBLICAL FOUNDATIONS

Scripture provides much guidance for formational ministry. There is evidence that components of all three periods are needed. That evidence comes from observation *and* Scripture. Table 4 shows one of the relevant passages for each period.

---

10. Howard, *A Guide to Christian Spiritual Formation*, 65.

TABLE 4: *Biblical Evidence for Each Period*

Dates	1940–1965	1965–1990	1990–Present
Preposition	TO	FOR	WITH
	Content-focused	Student-focused	Process-focused
TEXT	Psalm 119:11	Exodus 13:14	Ephesians 3:17
PRINCIPLE	Hide God's Word in your heart	When the child asks, teach	Be rooted in love; abide

What might it look like to have all three forms—TO, FOR, and WITH—present in one setting? There are few, if any, models for this. Even though the periods are like three bell curves, each with very long tails, how do we balance and integrate all three, if indeed we should? This work awaits those younger than I.

Edesio Sanchez proposes some helpful principles that can be applied to current children's ministry.[11] Family units should be part of curricular planning since the centrality of the family (household) is so prominent in Deuteronomy. The church should help parents create an ecology of the home in which they see themselves as co-pastors, because the Christian formation of children is more than creedal assent; it is lived-out obedience, best seen in daily living. Generational and intergenerational commitment helps accomplish this. Perhaps part of holistic spiritual formation means getting rid of many of our age-related ministry silos and bringing the generations together more often in order to learn God's story from each other and share stories of his faithfulness with each other.

LOOKING FORWARD

We church leaders and educators must learn better in this twenty-first century to submit to the whole counsel of God in the context in which God has placed us. Consider passages such as Isaiah 41:17–20. The Lord is

---

11. Edesio Sanchez, "Family in the Non-narrative Sections of the Pentateuch," in *Family in the Bible,* eds. Richard S. Hess & M. Daniel Carroll R. (Grand Rapids, MI: Baker Academic, 2003), 57–58.

speaking encouragement to the Israelites through the prophet Isaiah after they have endured discouragement, loss, and hardships. He says:

> "The poor and needy search for water,
>   but there is none;
>   their tongues are parched with thirst.
> But I the LORD will answer them;
>   I, the God of Israel, will not forsake them.
> I will make rivers flow on barren heights,
>   and springs within the valleys.
> I will turn the desert into pools of water,
>   and the parched ground into springs.
> I will put in the desert
>   the cedar and the acacia, the myrtle and the olive.
> I will set junipers in the wasteland,
>   the fir and the cypress together,
> so that people may *see* and *know*,
>   may *consider* and *understand*,
> that the hand of the LORD has done this,
>   that the Holy One of Israel has created it."
> (italics added)

Verse 20 jumped out at me. God says he will do these things for the Israelites so that they might see, know, consider, and understand who he is and how he provides. As a curriculum developer, I find the sequence of these four verbs captivating.

1. See: begin with a concrete experience (sensory)
2. Know: help learners relate to that experience, get to know it, really know it (relational/emotional)
3. Consider: then have them reflect on the experience, think about it deeply, which requires time and quiet (cognitive/reflective)
4. Understand: finally, in response time, comes the AHA!

What if we took this sequence seriously? What might we need to do differently on Sunday mornings?

THE NEXT PERIOD: BY

My prayer is that when we see where we have come from and where we are now, we will realize that not only can we be spiritually formed *with* children, we can also be formed *by* them. There have been many times when I have been ministered to *by* children, but it has usually happened unintentionally. What if we made it intentional?

A poignant example for me comes from the life of Mr. Rogers. Yes, *that* Mr. Rogers, the TV personality of yesteryear. He was in California for an event, and a profoundly disabled young person wanted to meet him. After engaging the youth in conversation that was challenging to understand, Mr. Rogers asked the boy to pray for him. Afterwards, Tom Junod commended Rogers for his kindness. Mr. Rogers responded, "Oh, heavens no, Tom! I didn't ask him for his prayers for *him*; I asked for me. I asked him because I think that anyone who has gone through challenges like that must be very close to God. I asked him because I wanted his *intercession*."[12] Wouldn't it be wonderful and spiritually formational for all of us if we asked to be ministered to BY children?

Most of us are not there yet. Maybe we will be soon, though, because we need the ministry of children. In the meantime, I take encouragement from the words of Marjorie Thompson that "whether a family's impact is constructive or destructive, it is not ultimate."[13] Whether the ministry with children at my church is constructive or destructive, it is never ultimate. I praise God that through his Spirit, he is ultimately the one in charge of the spiritual formation of every child. I am simply responsible to align myself with him the best way I am able, and then get out of the way so the Spirit can do his work. Whew! What a relief.

---

12. Tom Junod, "Can You Say . . . Hero?" *Esquire*, April 6, 2017, www.esquire.com/entertain ment/tv/a27134/can-you-say-hero-esq1198/.

13. Marjorie Thompson, *Family: The Forming Center* (Nashville, TN: Upper Room, 1998), 12.

SUMMARY TABLE: *Primary Characteristics of Three Recent 25-Year Periods in the History of Children's Spiritual Formation*

Dates	1940–1965	1965–1990	1990–Present
Preposition	TO	FOR	WITH
Pedagogical Focus	Content-Centered	Student-Centered	Process-Centered
View of the Child	Sponge Empty Vessel Wet Cement Clay	Consumer Participant Explorer Surveyor	Plant Pilgrim Sheep Scientist
View of the Teacher	Expert Funnel Holder Evaluator Boss	Coordinator Customer Service Planner Ring Master	Fellow Pilgrim Farmer Shepherd Co-Learner
Content Approach	Systematic *Recall It*	Flexible *Choose It*	Integrated *Live It*
Context	Factory Training Camp Reward Club	Meadow Playground Dance	Cultivated garden Symphony Journey
Philosophy	Transmissive	Developmental	Formational
Biblical Evidence and Principle	Psalm 119:11 Hide God's Word in your heart.	Exodus 13:14 When the child asks, teach.	Ephesians 3:17 Be rooted in love; abide.

CHAPTER 2

COMPARING FIVE THEOLOGICAL VIEWS AND MINISTRY PRACTICES

KEVIN E. LAWSON AND ADAM HARWOOD[1]

———————— ┼┼┼ ————————

Children are a heritage from the LORD,
offspring a reward from him.

—PSALM 127:3

Within the Christian faith we affirm the truth of this psalm, and yet we wrestle with its implications for the ministry of the church. Over the last hundred years, churches of all denominations have posed theological questions related to children and childhood, seeking guidance in the development of the church's ministry to the "heritage" God has given them. They ask questions like:

- What is the spiritual condition of children when they are born and as they grow? How can and should they relate to God during this early phase of life?
- In what ways should Christians include young children within the fellowship and community of the church?

---

1. This chapter, and the conference presentation it is based on, are adapted, with permission from the publisher, from Adam Harwood and Kevin E. Lawson (Eds.), *Infants and Children in the Church: Five Views on Theology and Ministry* (Nashville, TN: B&H Academic, 2017), 1–9, 195–206.

- In what sacraments or ordinances should children participate at particular ages or stages, and what does their participation mean to them and to the church?
- How might believers effectively raise children toward a vital love and faith in God, toward trusting reception of God's grace through faith in Christ, and toward spiritual maturity?
- What responsibilities should the church in general, and parents or caregivers in particular, take in the spiritual instruction and nurture of children?
- How can Christians work together for our children's good?

Though most believers would express a desire to be faithful in the care and spiritual training of God's gift of children to us, answering questions like these proves difficult for many. We simply have not invested enough study on theological issues surrounding children, their relationship with God, and their place in the church. Marcia Bunge, reflecting on the current state of theological thought on issues regarding children, observes that this has had some negative consequences:

> The absence of well-developed and historically and biblically informed teachings about children in contemporary theology helps explain why many churches often struggle to create and to sustain strong programs in religious education and in child-advocacy ministry.[2]

This is a struggle we have sought to address through a writing project on theologies of childhood and the church's ministries that flow from these varying beliefs.

BACKGROUND ON THE PROJECT

This project began with a conversation between the coauthors at the 2007 Evangelical Theological Society conference, where Adam presented a paper on theological issues regarding young children. Together we decided to

---

2. Marcia J. Bunge, Ed., *The Child In Christian Thought* (Grand Rapids, MI: Eerdmans, 2001), 4.

pursue a "comparative views" book that examined not only major theological traditions about children and their relationship with God, but also discussed the ministry efforts that tended to flow out of those traditions in the life of the church. We selected five historical Christian theological traditions for comparison: Orthodox, Roman Catholic, Lutheran, Reformed, and Baptist. Over the next few years, we developed and refined the proposal, recruited the contributing authors, found a publisher, and developed the chapters.

As part of the project, in April 2015, New Orleans Baptist Theological Seminary hosted a conference on this topic, co-sponsored by its Baptist Center for Theology and Ministry and Christian Education Division. At this event, the five authors presented drafts of their chapters and interacted with one another and those in attendance. It was an enlightening time together, and the spirit of the interactions was earnest but respectful. Following the conference, the authors revised and completed their chapters and wrote responses to one another's chapters. Adam contributed a chapter, and Kevin contributed an introduction and a final chapter reflecting on ministry with children in light of our theological convictions. The resulting book, *Infants and Children in the Church: Five Views on Theology and Ministry* (Broadman & Holman), was released in November 2017. Contributors to the volume representing the five different theological traditions include:

EASTERN ORTHODOX: Jason Foster (Ph.D., Durham University), priest of Holy Nativity of Our Lord Orthodox Church, Bossier City, Louisiana

ROMAN CATHOLIC: David Liberto (Ph.D., Marquette University), professor of historical and dogmatic theology at Notre Dame Seminary and Graduate School of Theology in New Orleans, Louisiana

LUTHERAN: David P. Scaer (Th.D., Concordia Seminary), professor of systematic theology and New Testament at Concordia Theological Seminary in Fort Wayne, Indiana

REFORMED: Gregg Strawbridge (Ph.D., University of Southern Mississippi), pastor of All Saints Presbyterian Church in Lancaster, Pennsylvania

BAPTIST: Adam Harwood (Ph.D., Southwestern Baptist Theological Seminary), associate professor of theology at New Orleans Baptist Theological Seminary in New Orleans, Louisiana

SUMMARY OF THE VIEWS IN INFANTS AND CHILDREN IN THE CHURCH

	How are infants and children impacted by sin?	How does God treat people who die in infancy or childhood?	When and how are they considered members of the church?	When and how are they instructed in Christian doctrine?
Orthodox	They inherit a fallen condition (mortality and propensity to sin) as victims, not as perpetrators.	Baptized infants are received by Christ and granted rest in the kingdom of heaven; unbaptized infants will not be in hell.	Infants are brought into the church where the faith of Christ is present by baptism.	They are educated by participating in the liturgy at church and home through icons, incense, the Bible, songs, confessions of faith, prayers, and Holy Communion.
Roman Catholic	They are deprived of their original holiness and justice. Their fallen nature leads to a darkened intellect and a weakened will.	Baptized infants are in a state of grace; no dogmatic statement of the church definitively addresses the final destiny of deceased unbaptized children.	A child is incorporated into the church in and through baptism.	Parents should model and teach their children about the faith. Children are taught doctrine in confirmation classes. Also, the church has established schools to educate children.

Lutheran	From conception all are overcome by sin, are under the power of Satan, and cannot believe in God; thus, they are condemned to God's wrath.	Baptized infants are included in God's kingdom by faith, which can be created in baptism, or by the spoken gospel before or after birth. Unbaptized infants will not be condemned.	They are members of the church as soon as they are baptized. Baptism works the forgiveness of sins, delivers from death and the Devil, gives eternal salvation, and incorporates people into the body of Christ.	In Sunday school, parochial school, and at home, they hear the Bible stories, learn the Ten Commandments, recite the Creed and pray the Lord's Prayer. Also, they are taught prior to confirmation.
Reformed	All people are born guilty of Adam's sin. They participated covenantally in Adam, die in Adam, and are alienated from God. Human nature is corrupt because of Adam's fall.	The Reformed tradition affirms the salvation of covenant children (those with at least one believing parent) who die in infancy. This affirmation is not made about the infants of unbelievers.	The children of believing parents are included as members of the church due to the Abrahamic covenant. Baptism does not make a child a member of the covenant; rather, it is a sign and seal of the covenant.	Covenant succession (training Christian children as a chief means of salvation being realized in their lives) through congregational worship, catechism, and Christian education.
Baptist	Baptists affirm two views of original sin. One view affirms that all people inherit both a sinful nature and guilt, but the other view affirms that people are born with a sinful nature only.	All who die prior to attaining moral capability are safe with God in heaven because of his grace and the atoning work of Christ on the cross.	Anyone who repents of sin and confesses personal faith in Jesus through immersion baptism—which excludes infants—should be welcomed as a member of a local church.	They should be taught to love and follow Jesus at the earliest possible age through Scripture and example at home and church as well as through witnessing the ordinances.

FOUR CRITICAL QUESTIONS ADDRESSED

Each of the contributing authors was asked to represent his theological tradition and how it tended to answer the following kinds of questions:

- IMPACT OF SIN: How are infants and children impacted by sin? How does this affect their ability to be in relationship with God?
- DEATH OF CHILDREN: How does God treat people who die in infancy or childhood? Are children held to a different standard than adults in their relationships with God? Is there an "age of accountability" that marks a transition in responsibility for one's sinful actions?
- CHURCH MEMBERSHIP: When and how are children considered members of the church? What is the church? Who belongs to it? What is required in order for a person to be counted as a part of it? Connected to this: what is the meaning of Christian baptism? What is the requirement for baptism? What does it accomplish in the lives of those who are baptized? Are infants proper candidates for baptism? If so, why? If not, why not? How else might or should children participate in the life of the church?
- INSTRUCTION IN THE FAITH: When and how are children instructed in Christian doctrine? Who bears the responsibility for instructing children in the Christian faith? When and how should little ones receive this instruction?

We are very grateful to each of the authors for carefully working through these issues and offering a summary of their theological tradition's beliefs and practices regarding children. Space does not allow a full presentation of each of the five traditions, but the chart on pages 42 and 43 is a brief overview of their positions and practices on each of the key issues.

CRITICAL DIFFERENCES AND AREAS OF COMMON GROUND

It is easy to see some significant differences both in the theological perspectives offered and in the practices with children in each tradition. Clearly, our understanding of baptism, who it is for and what it accomplishes, is a critical issue in how we think about ministry with children. Tied to this are our differing practices regarding the use of catechisms in a confirmation experience as children grow into adolescence. A particularly difficult issue we all wrestle with is how God relates with children outside the church, given the impact of sin in their lives. It is an area in which we recognize more theological work needs to be done. These issues and others distinguish our understandings of the nature of children, how God relates to them, their place in the church, and appropriate children's ministry practices.

Recognizing and reflecting on these differences and the reasons behind them will sharpen our own thinking about why we hold the views we do and why we carry out the practices we think are important. In spite of these differences, it was heartening to recognize a number of areas of agreement across these traditions. Here are some areas we hold in common that can help guide our ministry efforts with children:

1. **God loves children and desires for them to know him.** We all understand that God's heart is for children and that he desires them to come to faith in Christ Jesus. As ministry leaders, we need to reflect that same love and care as we interact with children and point them to their Heavenly Father, who created them and loves them deeply.

2. **Children are negatively impacted by sin.** While we disagree on the nature of the impact of sin, we recognize that because of Adam and Eve's fall, sin's curse is felt by all creation (Rom. 8:19–22). But that is not the end of the story!

3. **God has made provision for addressing the impact of sin.** Again, while we strongly disagree on how God's saving grace through the sacrificial death and resurrection of Jesus Christ may be received by children, we recognize that children can be included in God's redemptive plan. Ministry leaders need to carefully consider how we can best promote and facilitate children's response to the gospel of God's grace.

4. **Children are capable of a genuine spiritual walk with God.** God, through the Holy Spirit, is able to work in the lives of children to experience his presence for their good. They do not have to wait until they are grown to be able to pray, benefit from learning the

Scriptures, and recognize God's work of conviction and encouragement in their lives. Ministry leaders need to see themselves as partners with God in the spiritual nurture of children and be attentive to what God may be doing in their lives.

5. **In children, God sees qualities of faith that should characterize adults who would be part of his kingdom.** In the Gospels, Jesus lifts up children as examples of the kind of trust and dependence that should characterize us all in our walk with God, regardless of age (Mark 10:13–16). Children are God's gift to us to remind us of the posture we should all have in our relationship with him. We need to recognize God's gift to us in the children in our midst.

6. **Parents should be equipped and supported in their critical role as children's primary instructors and models of the Christian faith.** All theological traditions agree on this: the church's ministry with children is significant, but parents have the primary responsibility for instructing and nurturing children in the faith. Ministry leaders must develop ministries to equip and support parents in this critical role.

7. **The church as a whole has a responsibility to help in the spiritual nurture and instruction of children.** Along with equipping and supporting parents in their roles, the church as the body of Christ is gifted by God for the spiritual growth of the entire body (1 Cor. 12; Eph. 4:11–16). This includes teaching times such as Sunday school and other teaching ministries.

8. **We need to include children in beneficial ways in the life and practice of the church as they grow.** Each of the theological traditions represented in this project understands that the church's ministry for and with children goes beyond times of instruction to include children in the life of the church in ways that instruct them and form their faith. Worship services, weddings, funerals, fellowship times, ministry involvement, and relationships with other caring adults all contribute to our spiritual growth, and children benefit from this as much as adults, maybe even more so.

9. **Children are to grow to own their faith, not simply rest on the faith of their parents.** All of the theological traditions share a common goal of raising our children to embrace the Christian

faith as their own and to live their lives as an authentic expression of their personal responses to God's grace. While we disagree about how we think this is best accomplished, particularly regarding the role of baptism in this process, the end goal is one we all affirm.

In reflecting on these common understandings and priorities, we affirm the necessity of teaching our children about the God who made them, loves them, and calls them to respond to his grace in Christ. We read the words of Asaph in Psalm 78:1–8 and are convicted of our responsibility to exhort children to set their hope in God:

> My people, hear my teaching;
>> listen to the words of my mouth.
> I will open my mouth with a parable;
>> I will utter hidden things, things from of old—
> things we have heard and known,
>> things our ancestors have told us.
> *We will not hide them from their descendants;*
>> *we will tell the next generation*
> *the praiseworthy deeds of the LORD,*
>> *his power, and the wonders he has done.*
> *He decreed statutes for Jacob*
>> *and established the law in Israel,*
> *which he commanded our ancestors*
>> *to teach their children,*
> *so the next generation would know them,*
>> *even the children yet to be born,*
>> *and they in turn would tell their children.*
> *Then they would put their trust in God*
>> *and would not forget his deeds*
>> *but would keep his commands.*
> They would not be like their ancestors—
>> a stubborn and rebellious generation,
> whose hearts were not loyal to God,
>> whose spirits were not faithful to him.
> (italics added)

KEY THEOLOGICAL AND MINISTRY ISSUES
NEEDING FURTHER STUDY AND PRIORITIZATION

As we entered into this project, our primary goals were to better understand each of the five theological traditions, the reasons for their positions regarding the spiritual life and nurture of children, and their churches' ministry approaches and practices, which flowed out of those positions. Our five theologians accomplished these goals. Also coming out of this time of interaction, we were able to identify two important theological issues that need further exploration and two ministry implications that need to be pursued by all of our churches. We recognize that there is more work to be done to guide the church in its ministry practices with children, and this work is rooted in some foundational theological issues.

THEOLOGICAL ISSUE 1: *Understanding the Transition from Infancy to Responsibility, the Age of Accountability, Reason, or Discretion*

All five theological traditions see some kind of difference between young children and adults in their responsibility for sin or for their sin nature. All traditions attempt to discern whether children are innocent, guilty but not held accountable, guilty but already covered in some way, or guilty but potentially saved through baptism. In the Scriptures, God's treatment of children compared to his treatment of adults is shown in his judgment of the adult generation of Israel for not entering the Promised Land when he commanded them. Therefore, he does not allow them to enter it during their lifetimes, but allows their children to enter: "And the little ones that you said would be taken captive, your children who do not yet know good from bad—they will enter the land. I will give it to them and they will take possession of it" (Deut. 1:39). In the Gospels, we also see Jesus welcoming and blessing children, using them as exemplars of those who would receive the kingdom (Mark 10:13–16).

We need more theological research and writing on the status of children before God and how they grow and change in their responsibility for sin and their relationship with God. What marks the transition from innocence or a lack of accountability to being accountable? Is there a transition at some age or stage of accountability, reason, or discretion? These concepts have been discussed by theologians and ministry practitioners, but they tend to be stated in a vague or general way, and this hinders our careful thinking and discernment in developing ministries for children of different ages.

THEOLOGICAL ISSUE 2: *The Fate of Children Outside the Community of Faith*

Christians wrestle with the implications of our theological positions as we think about those who are born into this world apart from the Christian community. Some of our traditions focus a lot of attention on the status and fate of those who are born within Christian families, viewing these children as proper candidates for baptism due to the faith of their parents. But our conference interaction in 2015 showed the great reluctance of some to discuss the fate of children outside the Christian community, who die before either baptism or an opportunity to hear and respond to the gospel message. We must not be content to be concerned only about the needs of our own children in the church, a kind of "tribal theology" that does not concern itself with the rest of the world. We must better understand the needs of all children, what God has done for them, and what needs to be done to guide them toward receiving the grace of the gospel (if any action on our part is needed). As we do this needed theological work, we then need to understand the implications for compassionate ministry for the sake of children. We're afraid that God will hold us accountable for our current discomfort and resulting avoidance in thinking more carefully about and responding to these issues.

MINISTRY ISSUE 1: *Ministry for Fostering an Owned Faith*

In each of the five traditions represented in this project, we share a desire to raise our children to grow into adults who embrace the Christian faith as their own and take responsibility for their walks with God. None of us wants to see our children attend worship events as nominal Christians. Rather, we desire them to have a vital and growing faith commitment. We too often see children grow into young adults who no longer participate in the church. Some reject the teachings of their faith community and others simply drift into a nominal faith that has little impact on their lives.[3] We need to continue to study and understand from Scripture, from the history

---

3. For a research study on these issues from an international perspective, see Eddie Gibbs, *In Name Only: Tackling the Problem of Nominal Christianity* (Pasadena, CA: Fuller Seminary Press, 2000).

of the church, and even from contemporary social science research what contributes effectively to the growth of children into adults who fully own their faith.

MINISTRY ISSUE 2: *Prioritizing Ministry For/To/With/By Children*

If children are loved by God (and they are), and children are given as a reward to his people (and they are), and children are to be brought to Jesus (and they are), then why are children so often neglected in Christian communities? Too often, our churches focus their ministry efforts primarily on adult ministry and worship, and children are basically seen as some kind of distraction from more important ministry efforts. Too often, church leaders put major financial and personnel investments into the facilities and programs for adult worship, instruction, outreach, and service, but give little thought or attention to the children with whom God has gifted them—their "heritage." More careful theological study and reflection on the status and needs of children in our congregations and our communities should lead us to invest more thoughtfully and intentionally in ministry for their sake. We challenge and encourage all who care about the spiritual life and nurture of children to consider this fourfold vision for prioritizing ministry with children:[4]

- MINISTRY TO PARENTS AND OTHER CAREGIVERS FOR CHILDREN: If parents have primary responsibility for the instruction and spiritual nurture of their children, we need to invest heavily in equipping parents, and other caregivers in the lives of children, to do this well. What is your church doing to equip and support parents for this critical ministry? What training, resources, and encouragement are offered to them?
- MINISTRY BY THE CHURCH TO CHILDREN: As communities of believers called to share life together, and as the body of Christ with different gifts for ministry, it is appropriate for local churches to provide focused ministries to nurture the faith of children. Churches need to offer foundational teaching of the faith geared to the understanding and interests of children and relating it to the life challenges they face.

---

4. This model is adapted from one shared by John H. Westerhoff, III, in a plenary session he offered at the June 2006 conference of the Society for Children's Spirituality: Christian Perspectives, held at Concordia University, Chicago. This was later published as John H. Westerhoff, III, "The Church's Contemporary Challenge: Assisting Adults to Mature Spiritually with Their Children," in *Nurturing Children's Spirituality*, ed. Holly Catterton Allen (Eugene, OR: Cascade Books, 2008), 356–61.

- MINISTRY TOGETHER WITH CHILDREN: Children benefit from being a part of their church communities, experiencing firsthand the reality of how faith impacts the lives of others. This supports a growing sense of identity and a recognition of the need for God's grace and work in their lives as they seek to know and follow him. Having children participate in times of corporate worship, intergenerational learning and fellowship opportunities, and ministry with adults for the sake of others are all influential experiences in the spiritual lives of children.
- MINISTRY BY CHILDREN TO OTHERS: One mistake we sometimes make is viewing children simply as recipients of the ministry and guidance of others. Many active adult church members fondly recall that their own involvement in ministry both in and outside the church began when they were young. Because of those experiences, ministering to others has been a priority in their lives ever since. Projects like supporting other children through World Vision or Samaritan's Purse, for example, can open a child's eyes to the needs of others and God's ability to use them to bless others. Opportunities to help care for the needs of others in their church and community can help them see how God has gifted them and can use them as his hands and feet. In turn, God can use these experiences to help them grow spiritually, encouraging them to seek to follow God more fully in their lives of service.

All four of these aspects of ministry are needed to encourage children to know, love, and follow God, enabling them to grow into youth and adults who treasure their relationship with God and respond in obedience to him, living as salt and light in this world. May our theologies of children always lead us to more faithful ministry for them, to them, with them, and by them.

In this chapter, we have attempted to summarize our work of gathering academics with pastoral experience from various Christian perspectives to answer the same set of theology and ministry questions concerning infants and children in the church. The conversation which first occurred at a conference was refined and captured in a book. The result reflected the unique perspectives within the church which share some of the same concerns about the little ones entrusted to our care. Although differing answers to theological questions regarding the nature of and entrance into the church result in differing practices concerning baptism and the Eucharist, similar concerns focus our attention on shepherding infants and children and pointing them toward the Good Shepherd. May faithful ministry for, to, with, and by children continue in the distinct Christian traditions, and may the conversation continue among those different theological traditions so we can all learn from and be sharpened by one another as we seek to be faithful to the triune God.

A RECOMMENDED READING LIST ON THEOLOGICAL VIEWS ON CHILDREN

Harwood, Adam and Kevin E. Lawson, ed. *Infants and Children in the Church: Five Views on Theology and Ministry.* Nashville, TN: B&H Academic, 2017.

ORTHODOX VIEW

Koulomzin, Sophie. *Our Church and Our Children.* Crestwood, NY: St. Vladimir's Seminary Press, 2004.

Magdalen, Sister. *Reflections on Children in the Orthodox Church Today*, 5th ed. Essex, England: Stavropegic Monastery of St. John the Baptist, 2014.

Schmemann, Alexander. *Of Water and the Spirit: A Liturgical Study of Baptism.* Crestwood, NY: St. Vladimir's Seminary Press, 1974.

ROMAN CATHOLIC VIEW

Catechism of the Catholic Church, 2nd ed. Washington, DC: United States Catholic Conference, 1997.

Code of Canon Law: Latin-English Edition. Washington, DC: Canon Law Society of America, 1999.

International Theological Commission, "The Hope of Salvation for Infants Who Die without Being Baptised," available at http://www.vatican.va /roman_curia/congregations/cfaith/cti_documents/rc_con_cfaith_doc _20070419_un-baptised-infants_en.html.

LUTHERAN VIEW

Book of Concord (1580)

Boyle, Geoffrey R. "Confirmation, Catechesis and Communion: A Historical Survey." *Concordia Theological Quarterly* 79, (2015): 121–42.

Scaer, David P. *Baptism.* St Louis: Luther Academy, 1999. Confessional Lutheran Dogmatics 11.

Scaer, David P. "Lutheran View: Finding the Right Word." In *Understanding Four Views on the Lord's Supper,* edited by John H. Armstrong. Grand Rapids, MI: Zondervan, 2007.

REFORMED VIEW

Heidelberg Catechism (1563)

Westminster Confession of Faith (1646)

Strawbridge, Gregg, ed. *The Case for Covenantal Infant Baptism.* Phillipsburg, NJ: P&R, 2003.

Strawbridge, Gregg, ed. *The Case for Covenant Communion.* Monroe, LA: Athanasius, 2006.

Venema, Cornelis P. *Children at the Lord's Table?: Assessing the Case for Paedocommunion.* Grand Rapids, MI: Reformation Heritage, 2009.

BAPTIST VIEW

"The 2000 Baptist Faith and Message", Southern Baptist Convention, www .sbc.net/bfm2000/bfm2000.asp.

Ingle, Clifford, ed. *Children and Conversion.* Nashville, TN: Broadman, 1970.

Harwood, Adam. *The Spiritual Condition of Infants: A Biblical-Historical Survey and Systematic Proposal.* Eugene, OR: Wipf & Stock, 2011.

Sanders, Thomas. *When Can I?: Questions Preschoolers Ask in Their 1st Steps toward Faith.* Nashville, TN: Broadman & Holman, 2002.

CHAPTER 3

COLORING OUTSIDE THE LINES

A Conversation about Racial Diversity and the Spiritual Lives of Children

KAREN F. WILLIAMS

———————┼┼┼———————

God forgives *murder*
and he forgives *adultery.*
But He is very angry
and He actually *curses*
all who do integrate.[1]
—WHITE WOMAN IN THE SOUTH

All the fourth graders' eyes at North Harnett Elementary School were fastened on Mrs. Atkins. No one moved. On this day Mrs. Atkins was not explaining a math problem or preparing us for a spelling test. She was preparing us for a test of a different sort.

It was 1969. The school year was ending, and the upcoming year would bring a pivotal change to our segregated African American school. Mrs. Atkins was preparing us for school integration. For the first time in our nine years of life, we would be bussed to a new school—an all-White school. Her tone was stern:

---

1. James Baldwin, *I Am Not Your Negro* (New York: Vintage International, 2016), 11.

When you go to their schools, some White students are going to think they're better than you just because they're White. But they're not. Some aren't going to like you. Be proud of who you are because you are just as smart as they are. Your opinion is important. Stand on your opinion and what you believe, no matter what.

Mrs. Atkins urged us to ask questions as she spoke to our class of nearly thirty fourth graders. I don't remember if I asked any questions. But I vividly recollect my mind being filled with ambivalence. I not only felt the warm encouragement from one of my favorite teachers but also had anxious thoughts about going to a school where I was not wanted. *Will any of my friends from North Harnett be in my class at the White school?* I wondered.

In retrospect, I see an African American teacher deeply concerned not only about the mental well-being but also the spiritual well-being of her innocent, young African American students. Her talk that day was a straightforward conversation. It was a crossing-the-color-line conversation.

This chapter, too, is a conversation. It is a conversation about the impact of racial diversity[2]—or the lack thereof—on children's spirituality. Part one, "Toeing the White Line," which draws on the scholarly works of Willie Jennings,[3] presents the social construction of whiteness and its entanglement with Christianity.[4] Part two, "Racial Diversity and Children's Spirituality,"[5] shows the value of placing children in diverse settings. The last section, "Sunday School Curriculum and Racial Diversity," focuses primarily on biblical illustrations within children's Sunday school curriculum. In this chapter, you will hear the voices of persons I invited to join this conversation by telling about their experiences or by responding to questions I presented to them. I am thankful for these gracious individuals who, for the sake of anonymity, are mentioned by first name only.

---

2. Racial diversity is the representation of persons from different races and ethnic groups.

3. Willie J. Jennings, *The Christian Imagination: Theology and the Origins of Race* (New Haven, CT: Yale University Press, 2010), and Love L. Sechrest, et al., *Can "White" People Be Saved: Triangulating Race, Theology, and Mission* (Downers Grove, IL: IVP Academic, 2018).

4. I strongly suggest you read Jennings' works, as I have provided only an abbreviated perspective.

5. The definitions of children's spirituality abound, but this is one that I think is well stated: "the child's development of a conscious relationship with God, in Jesus Christ, through the Holy Spirit, within the context of a community of believers that fosters that relationship, as well as the child's understanding of, and response to, that relationship" from Holly C. Allen, "Exploring Children's Spirituality from a Christian Perspective," in *Nurturing Children's Spirituality: Christian Perspectives and Best Practices*, ed. Holly C. Allen (Eugene, OR: Cascade Books, 2008), 11.

Toeing the White Line: The Interwovenness of Whiteness and Christianity

Sometimes, as in the Bible when the demon is named, it loses its power and we gain mastery over it. Sacred conversations may help the demon of racism lose some of its power and to set the children of God free.[6]
—BISHOP MICHAEL CURRY

Beginning this conversation by providing the benefits of racially diverse settings is appropriate. But I think it is critical to begin by first naming the demon: racism.[7]

Discourses on race and racism are always difficult. Yet it is imperative that People of Color[8] and White people have an authentic conversation. Why did a fourth-grade teacher have to warn her nine-year-old students about the perils of being with and in the same academic space with White students and White teachers? The answer leads us back to colonial imperialism and Christianity. In fact, the words of the southern White woman who declared that God is angry and curses those who integrate are a historical expression of the deep-seated entanglement of Christianity and the imperialist mindset of colonists.

In *The Christian Imagination*, Willie Jennings speaks to this interwovenness and expounds on how Christianity bought into the imperialist mindset. Both invaded the spaces of native peoples and normalized the order of those spaces: "Christian theological imagination was woven into the processes of colonial dominance . . . It claimed to be the host, the owner of spaces it entered and demanded native peoples enter its cultural logics, its ways of being in the world, and its conceptualities."[9] Not only

---

6. "Spirituality and Racial Justice Course, Lesson One: Conversation," *ChurchNext*, www .churchnext.tv/home/.

7. One definition of racism is "an institutionalized system of economic, political, social, and cultural relations that ensures that one racial group has and maintains power and privilege over all others in all aspects of life." Louise Derman-Sparks and Carol B. Phillips, *Teaching/Learning Anti-Racism: A Developmental Approach* (New York: Teachers College Press, 1997) 2.

8. People of Color (also Children of Color) refers to all non-White persons, especially those who have historically experienced systemic racism.

9. Willie J. Jennings, *The Christian Imagination*, 8.

was this an appropriation of space and culture, but also the dehumanization of non-White peoples. These early Europeans placed people in racial categories: some people became not quite White, almost White, not quite Black, almost Black, and the delineations go on.[10] And the Europeans were considered White. According to Jennings, this created a viral world of designation between White and Black and captured all people in racial identity.[11] This social construction of racial identity placed Black persons as inferior beings, enslaved chattel property, and impure. At the same time, White persons epitomized purity making *whiteness* "a representative of spiritual purity within the Christian context."[12] Jacqueline Battalora explains that "whiteness" goes beyond white people and includes "ideological underpinning that sustains them and the social structures that support the idea of 'white' people, what they represent, and their position within society."[13]

So, it is colonial imperialism (white supremacy) joined with this social construction and normalization of whiteness (along with all its privileged benefits[14]) and "parasitically joined to Christianity"[15] that has marginalized People of Color, creating the racial divide and amplifying the need for a racial diversity conversation written on behalf of the most "vulnerable of God's creation—children."[16] My hope is that this frank conversation will assist with lessening our racial divide so adults who nurture the children will see all these precious little ones as God's wonderful creation.

---

10. Willie James Jennings, "Can White People Be Saved?" in *Can "White" People Be Saved: Triangulating Race, Theology, and Mission*, eds. Love L. Sechrest, et al. (Downers Grove, IL: IVP Academic, 2018), 31.

11. Ibid.

12. Jacqueline Battalora, *Birth of a White Nation: The Invention of White People and Its Relevance Today* (Houston, TX: Strategic Book Publishing, 2013) 44.

13. Ibid., 47.

14. White privilege is not connected to a White person's financial status. Rather it is the "unquestioned and unearned set of advantages, entitlements, benefits and choices bestowed on people solely because they are [W]hite." *Racial Equity Tool*, Justice Grantmaking Assessment Report references Peggy McInsoh's "White Privilege and Male Privilege: A Personal Account of Coming to See Correspondences Through Work in Women Studies," 1988. Also see Peggy McIntosh, "White Privilege: Unpacking the Invisible Knapsack," *Peace and Freedom Magazine*, July 1989, 10–12. While the term *white privilege* was in use prior to McIntosh's papers, her work became the impetus for its widespread use.

15. Love L. Sechrest, et al., *Can "White" People Be Saved*, 27.

16. Alicia Reyes-Barriéntez, "A White Jesus Can't Save a Brown Child," *Baptist News Global*, March 27, 2018, baptistnews.com/article/a-white-jesus-cant-save-a-brown-child/.

COLORBLINDNESS AND RACIAL DIVERSITY

Colorblindness justifies withdrawal from social action
by assuming that racism will cease to exist when people
stop noticing racial and cultural differences.[17]

Saying, "I am colorblind; I don't see race," sounds commendable on the surface. But this ideology has many blind spots. Someone who is diagnosed as colorblind *does* see color; they have challenges *distinguishing* between colors. It is a vision deficiency. Using the colorblindness analogy to address race is deficient as well. Susan Derman-Sparks and Carol B. Phillips point out this weakness of the colorblindness analogy: "Not noticing that someone is Black, for example, denies that person a history and culture, just as only noticing that someone is Black denies individuality."[18] Encouraging children to be colorblind is telling them that we do not applaud difference in others. As Miles McPherson says, "It shuts down attempts at engaging in a meaningful conversation about race. It sends the message that a tan received in Hawaii is celebrated, but a tan received in the womb is invalidated."[19]

One place to start the conversation about race with children is to help them appreciate differences in others. As children begin to notice differences in skin tones, we should talk with them about how God made each of us different and help children celebrate these differences. But when do children begin to notice race? The response varies. Some educators believe that children notice race around the ages of three to four. Louise Derman-Sparks and Julie Olsen Edwards support the fact that three-year-olds notice physical differences like the shape of facial features, hair texture, and skin color.[20] Other researchers believe children notice race much earlier.[21]

---

17. Louise Derman-Sparks and Carol B. Phillips, *Teaching/Learning Anti-Racism: A Developmental Approach* (New York: Teachers College Press, 1997), 52.

18. Louise Derman-Sparks and Carol B. Phillips, *Teaching/Learning Anti-Racism*, 52.

19. Miles McPherson, *The Third Option: Hope for a Racially Divided Nation* (New York: Howard Books, 2018), 11.

20. Louise Derman-Sparks and Julie Olsen Edwards, *Anti-Bias Education for Young Children and Ourselves* (Washington, DC: National Association for Education of Young Children, 2010), 77–89.

21. In Erin N. Winkler, "Children are Not Colorblind: How Young Children Learn Race," PACE: Practical Approaches for Continuing Education 3, no. 3 (2009):1–8. Winkler writes an interesting article that draws on the works of researchers P. A. Katz and J. A. Kofkin who espouse that infants as young as six months have the ability to nonverbally categorize people by race and gender. (P.A. Katz, and J.A. Kofkin, "Race, Gender, and Young Children, in *Developmental Psychopathology:*

Dr. Stacy Chapman affirms that the information children are process-ing as they notice skin color does not lead to prejudice but is an early stage of informing them that people have identities, and that there are categories of people, with some people being treated a certain way because of those identities.[22] Chapman explains that the pre-prejudiced stage (ages two to six) is key, as it can develop into prejudice as children grow older because no one is "informing them differently about all of those identities and all those groups of people."[23] Therefore, ages two to six is the perfect time to begin talking with children about skin color and acknowledging that people have different skin tones. Reading books to and with children that feature children of Color as the main character is important.

Dorena Williamson's book, *Colorfull: Celebrating the Colors God Gave Us*, is a delightful children's book that highlights the beauty of diversity and the fallacy of colorblindness. The book concludes with questions readers can explore and discuss with children. I contacted Williamson and invited her to respond to a question about faith communities talking with children about racial issues.[24] She said:

I believe faith communities should play a pivotal role in talking to children about racial issues. Psalm 139:14 says we are wonderfully made, but Christians have not always lived out this powerful truth. With the growing racial diversity of our world today, it is a ripe time to shape young minds with God's heart for justice.

I encourage organizations to use curriculum with diverse eth-nicity rather than adopting a colorblind approach. Children need to see that God has included all people in his redemption story. Consideration should also be given to not whitewash our shameful history. The sin of racism is still a reality today, and we leave children

Perspectives on Adjustment, Risk, and Disorder, eds. S. S. Luthar, J. A. Burack, D. Cicchetti, & J. R. Weisz (New York: Cambridge University Press, 1997), 51–74.

22. Melissa Giraud, "Recording and Resources: Understanding Racial-Ethnic Identity Development," webinar, *embracerace.org*, June 1, 2017, https://medium.com/embrace-race /understanding-racial-ethnic-identity-development.

23. Ibid.

24. Williamson responded to the following question: "Do you think it is important for faith communities to talk with children about racism, racial diversity, and/or racial justice? Why or why not? If yes, what tools do you feel faith communities should be employing to discuss these topics with children?"

open to prejudicial philosophies by minimizing the pain of the past and present. As leaders constantly evaluate their own biases, they can humbly teach that every human has dignity because we are made in the image of God.

Another helpful resource on race and colorblindness is *The Gospel in Color: A Theology of Racial Reconciliation for Kids* by Curtis Woods and Jarvis J. Williams. Parents can read this book with and to their children. The book includes discussion questions and can assist parents in talking about race with children. The authors have also written an accompanying book (by the same title) just for parents.

Settings bereft of racial diversity affect children spiritually. Twenty-seven-year-old Courtney, a White graduate student, states that she didn't know how a lack of diversity was impacting her spiritual life when she was younger. In retrospect, she says, "I think it really meant that I wasn't getting a full picture of the Gospel."[25]

Courtney grew up in a predominately White church and attended a predominately White Christian school from kindergarten through eighth grade. Courtney explains:

My young spirituality was very personal—Jesus and me, a personal relationship with my Lord and Savior. I think that was a good thing, but what I missed was interaction with and understanding of the broader kingdom of God—brothers and sisters with different cultural traditions and histories than mine.

Since high school, my "settings" have diversified during certain seasons and then become whiter again in other seasons. As I've reflected on this, two things I've learned during seasons of more diversity in my life that I didn't learn as a child stand out to me: (1) that lament for the marginalized and oppressed is part of a healthy and whole spirituality, and (2) in more diverse communities, I experience more of the wonder of God—his creativity, his love, and his power.

---

25. Courtney responded to this question: As a child what role, if any, did the faith community play in helping or hindering an appreciation for racial diversity and/or racial justice? How did this role affect you as a child? Talk about your perspective of this role as an adult. How are you engaging or disengaging it?

Courtney's response is insightful. Being in a setting devoid of racial diversity only gives children a partial vision of the kingdom of God. Each child is unique, so children's experiences can be enriched as they learn from one another in a racially diverse setting. They can see that God's kingdom is not just for one group of people but for everyone.

Reggie, a forty-one-year-old African American youth pastor and director of a nonprofit organization, affirms the value of racially diverse worship settings:

Black churches need to invite others, including Caucasians, into our space to expose different racial groups to our experiences. For too long we have had to go into their spaces and have been receptive to their culture and modes of worship. But others need to experience our style of worship, the role of God in our lives and in our corporate experience, etc. This racially diverse exposure and involvement provides room for justice and helps everyone to see people as people, as individuals who come with an array of experiences, cultures, styles, and personalities, and not as just stereotypes.

Reggie's point about stereotypes is helpful. Viewing a child only in a racialized stereotypical manner creates judgmental false assumptions about that child that hinders an adult from knowing who the child really is and can lead to racist behaviors and actions.

In reference to faith communities discussing racial concerns with children, Wanda, a fifty-two-year-old African American corporate trainer and a Christian education director at her church, feels these conversations are critical, especially in the African American community.[26] She asserts:

Dialogue is the way to raise awareness. If our youth could hear someone's personal story of mistreatment and then that same person explains why, paraphrasing Michelle Obama, "they went high when their detractors went low," it may speak volumes and have a lasting positive impact. More importantly, it would prompt questions about

---

26. Wanda responded to this question: Do you think it is important for faith communities to talk with children about racism, racial diversity, and/or racial justice? Why or why not? If yes, what tools do you feel faith communities should be employing to discuss these topics with children?

how this world came to be so chaotic and what can be done or what they can do to change it for the better. The Word does say, "And a child shall lead . . ."

While racial diversity is vital to a child's spirituality, these diverse settings must engender justice. In fact, *justice* was one of Merriam Webster's words of the year in 2018, which means it was one of the most frequently searched words that year.[27] With issues of economic justice, social justice, criminal justice, and racial justice making daily headlines that year, it is no surprise *justice* had top ranking. The word *justice* also has a prominent place in the Bible. Throughout the Scriptures, we can see God advocating for justice (especially for the poor and marginalized) as well as commanding us to be people of justice (see Ps. 33:5; Mic. 6:8; Amos 5:24; Matt. 7:12; 26:35–40)[28]

Racial justice and racial diversity are two sides of the same coin. One definition of racial justice is "the proactive reinforcement of policies, practices, attitudes and actions that produce equitable power, access, opportunities, treatment, impacts, and outcomes for all."[29] While this compact definition provides a potent redress to racism, these words must be connected to praxis. When it comes to words and praxis, philosopher Paulo Freire said that "the word" is the essence of dialogue with every word having two dimensions: action and reflection.[30] A word without action is "idle chatter," "an empty word," and "cannot denounce the world."[31] A word that excludes reflection and emphasizes action only results in action for action's sake.[32]

Too often, the praxis of racial justice is missing, making racial diversity incomplete. And racial diversity becomes empty words when the evils of racism have not been denounced. Faith communities and organizations can tout being racially diverse but still have systems of racial oppression.

---

27. "Word of the Year: Justice." *Merriam-Webster*, 2019, https://www.merriam-webster.com/word-of-the-year-2018.

28. There are more than 2,000 Scriptures on poverty and justice in the Bible. See *The Poverty and Justice Bible: Contemporary English Version*, ed. The British and Foreign Bible Society (Swindon, UK: Bible Society, 2008).

29. "Glossary." *Racial Equity Tools*, www.racialequitytools.org/glossary in Justice Grantmaking Assessment Report, Philanthropic Initiative for Racial Equity and Applied Research Center, 2009.

30. Paulo Freire, *Pedagogy of the Oppressed: 50th Anniversary Edition*, Fourth ed. (New York: Bloomsbury Academic, 2018), 87.

31. Ibid.

32. Ibid.

As such, placing children in racially diverse settings devoid of racial justice engenders an environment of oppression, racism, and microaggressions.[33] So how can this dialogue on racial diversity and the spiritual lives of children truly be transformative? This transformation can only take place by employing "true words," as Freire calls them. For Freire, a true word is praxis: "There is no true word that is not at the same time a praxis. Thus to speak a true word is to transform the world."[34] This transformation takes place by merging the praxis of racial diversity with the praxis of racial justice. Such action set in motion then *can* denounce the world—the evil world of racism and racial injustice—creating equitable power, equitable access, equitable opportunities, equitable treatment, and equitable impacts and outcomes for all our children.

SUNDAY SCHOOL CURRICULUM AND RACIAL DIVERSITY

Normalizing Jesus as white in Sunday school literature perpetuates a twisted gospel of white supremacy, wounding the most vulnerable of God's creation—children.[35]

—ALICIA REYES-BARRIÉNTEZ

During a discussion on a Black versus a White Santa Claus, Fox News anchor Megan Kelly insisted that Santa was White.[36] She further stated, "Jesus was a White man, too." She deservedly received public backlash. But before we criticize her, we must recognize that the idea of a White Jesus did not originate with Kelly.

---

33. L.V. A. Tolbert and S.D. Little address some of these microaggressions in S. D. Little and L. V. A. Tolbert, "The Problem with Black Boys: Race, Gender, and Discipline in Christian and Private Elementary Schools," *Christian Education Journal 15, no.* 3 (2018): 408–421. Also the following webinar speaks to the impact of racism on children: Donielle Prince, "APHA Webinar: Racism and Its Impact on Children's Health," *ACES Connection,* October 25, 2015, https://www.acesconnection .com/blog/apha-webinar-racism-and-its-impact-on-children-s-health.

34. Freire, *Pedagogy of the Oppressed: 50th Anniversary Edition,* 87.

35. Alicia Reyes-Barriéntez, "A White Jesus Can't Save a Brown Child," *Baptist News Global,* March 27, 2018, baptistnews.com/article/a-white-jesus-cant-save-a-brown-child/. The retelling of Alicia Reyes-Barriéntez and selected excerpts have been used with permission.

36. "Aisha Harris; Santa Claus Should Not Be a White Man Anymore," Hosted by Megan Kelly, *The Kelly File,* Fox News, December 12, 2013, www.youtube.com/watch?v=7XYlJqf4dLI.

The perpetuation of a White Jesus goes back to his portrayal as European during the medieval and Renaissance periods. One revealing document circulating in Western Europe during the fourteenth century was the Letter of Publius Lentulus.[37] This was supposedly a long-lost letter from Jesus' trial written by a Roman official.[38] The letter describes Jesus thus: "He has hair of the colour of an *unripe hazelnut* and it falls smoothly about his ears, then from his ears in curling locks . . . He has a parting at the middle of his head. . . . a face without a wrinkle or any spot, which a slightly *reddish hue* beautifies."[39] Reddish hue? No doubt many artists used the Lentulus description to depict Christ. This letter, later discovered to be a complete fabrication due to its many historical inaccuracies, was circulated to assure that Jesus was not represented as Jewish-looking.[40]

One iconic painting of White Jesus is Warner Sallman's *Head of Christ*. Popularized in the 1940s, this blue-eyed Jesus hung in the homes of both Black and White Americans. Joan Taylor says of Sallman's image, "While it is a beautiful image, it has nothing to do with any evidence about what Jesus looked like, and—like so many other paintings—it misrepresents his ethnicity."[41]

In the twenty-first century, the iconic European Jesus is still prevalent. Some publishers are intentional about presenting multicultural biblical images, and so there are some wonderful racially diverse Bible storybooks on the market. Yet there is still a dearth of such books, and some people still raise their eyebrows if they see an image of Jesus with skin a shade too dark for their liking.

An artist friend of mine, Carol Ann, can attest to this. Carol Ann, who is White, completed her first mural in a church in North Carolina. She was intentional about including multicultural biblical images in the painting. During the painting process, Carol Ann said, people would often stop by and comment on her work. She tells about one of many comments she received related to skin color: "An older White woman stopped by, and seeing the six-and-a-half-foot angels, one with dark golden skin (Hispanic),

37. Joan E. Taylor, *What Did Jesus Look Like?* (New York: Bloomsbury T&T Clark, 2018), 16–17.
38. Ibid. 17.
39. Ibid., italics mine.
40. Ibid., 16–17.
41. Ibid., 24.

the other with rich brown skin (African American), and the four-foot-tall, deep brown Jesus, asked tentatively, 'Are the people going to stay dark?'"

Coloring outside the lines, then, means confronting this "diseased imagination"[42] of Whiteness representing what is pure, holy, and good. This normalization of the White Christ and all White biblical characters does have an effect on a child's spirituality. Alicia Reyes-Barriéntez is an example. Reyes-Barriéntez recounts her childhood experience in central Texas.[43]

She attended a Brown[44] evangelical church consisting mainly of poor, uneducated migrants from rural Mexico. The "mother" church, First Baptist Church (FBC), was White. Reyes-Barriéntez remembers the explicit and implicit racism the White Baptist Christians exhibited toward her community, all in the name of evangelizing them. She recalls how an FBC member exploited the labor of the migrants, paying them meager wages. For eighteen years, the only portrayal of Jesus in the Sunday school curriculum was White. Since Reyes-Barriéntez's community was the target of oppression, for her, the association of Jesus with whiteness was oppressive. She concluded that a White Jesus is racist and a false idol: "A [W]hite Jesus can't save a [B]rown child, and a Jesus that can't save all, liberate all, and redeem all is no Jesus at all." Reyes-Barriéntez's story clearly reveals not only the negative impact of a lack of racial diversity on a child's spirituality, but also the interwovenness of Whiteness and Christianity.

I had the opportunity to contact Reyes-Barriéntez regarding her story, and she provided this commentary:

One of God's greatest gifts to children is the enhanced ability to imagine. Our responsibility as adults is to encourage children as they discover God through their unsullied imagination of the Divine. Normalizing Jesus as White disrupts the creativity of children, inculcating in their developing minds a false and oppressive portrayal of

---

42. Frederick Douglass spoke about racism as painting "a hateful picture according to its own diseased imagination" in Frederick Douglass, "The Color Line," *The North American Review* 132, no. 295 (June 1881): 567.

43. Alicia Reyes-Barriéntez, "A White Jesus Can't Save a Brown Child." The retelling of Alicia Reyes-Barriéntez and selected excerpts have been used with permission of *Baptist News Global*. I am grateful to have been in communication with Dr. Reyes-Barriéntez and to receive her support regarding the retelling of her story.

44. Brown in this context refers to persons of Mexican descent.

Christ and ultimately disobeying the Lord's commandment to let the children come to Jesus. Let us encourage children to freely seek the kingdom of God without imposing on them whitewashed representations of Christ—for, after all, the kingdom is theirs.

Reggie, the previously mentioned youth pastor, also speaks to the importance of diverse biblical images:

African American and other minority children may have a difficult time connecting with a personal God through Jesus Christ if they are not sufficiently exposed to stories and images depicting biblical characters and faith stories from multiple ethnic backgrounds. The potential lack of exposure to racial diversity when children watch media programming and listen to stories retold in a White context can contribute to a notion that Christianity is something to which White America has closer access.

The bottom line is that all children need to see themselves reflected in Sunday school curriculum. As I think about children seeing themselves reflected in images, something my older sister Ann taught me about coloring when I was six years old, comes to mind. I had just finished coloring the picture of a little girl in a coloring book. Ann picked up a brown crayon and said, "Karen, you are not White. Your skin is brown, so you need to color her skin brown." And I did! Revolutionary! I thought the little girl on the coloring page had to remain White. With brown skin, that little girl became *me*. I connected with her. Later, at age seven, when I started wearing glasses, I even began drawing eyeglasses on the faces of little girls in coloring books. For me, this was coloring outside the lines. This was my Emily Style "mirror" moment.

More than thirty years ago, Emily Style spoke about curriculum functioning as windows and mirrors, a way of seeing that is both a reflection and revelation of a multicultural world and the student.[45] Style said that windows help children to see the realities of others, while mirrors help children to see their own reality. Sunday school curriculum writers and

45. The National Seed Project, *Listening for All Voices* (Summit, NJ: Oak Knoll School monograph, 1988), https://nationalseedproject.org/be-a-part/new-leaders-week.

publishers are biblical expositors responsible for telling Bible stories as well as making them applicable to the everyday lives of children. A curriculum is deficient if it only tells the story of Daniel in the lions' den (Dan. 6) and does not relay what the story means for today's children. Curriculum, too, is impaired if it does not see through a multicultural lens. Style says, "Knowledge of both types of framing is basic to a balanced education which is committed to affirming the essential dialectic between the self and the world."[46]

While the majority of this section has focused on the importance of multicultural biblical images in curriculum, I will emphasize that all images in curriculum should be multicultural. Any illustrations or photographs of children and adults should be multicultural as well. "All children deserve a curriculum which mirrors their own experience back to them."[47]

CONCLUSION

God must love color to have made all of earth's people with
such wonderful shades. That's something to celebrate![48]
—GRANNY MAC

I only recall parts of Mrs. Atkins's talk that day back in 1969, but it was a timely conversation. She was right about the racism we would face. That first year of school integration was my worst school year ever. I was relieved to see Linda, my close friend from North Harnett, in my class on the first day of school. I remember Linda and I always talking about some racist incident we had faced, whether it involved a student or the teacher. Our conversations were sacred. They were a means of support and helped us deal with, as well as confront, our challenges.

Conversations are important. Talking with children about race and racism as well as exposing them to racially diverse settings is essential. Conversely, when they are not in diverse settings, I believe, as Courtney

---

46. Ibid.
47. Ibid.
48. Dorena Williamson, *Colorfull: Celebrating the Colors God Gave Us* (Nashville, TN: B&H Publishing Group, 2018).

stated earlier, "they miss the interaction with and an understanding of the broader kingdom of God." Coloring outside the lines is about seeing all children as being made in the image of God.

This consideration of racial diversity and the spiritual lives of children has been brief, so consider this chapter a preface to more discussions to come. I encourage you to pick up the conversation from here. My hope is that I have given you a few ways to begin.

CHAPTER 4

BELIEVING AND BELONGING

Embracing Children with Disabilities

ERIK W. CARTER

————————|╫|————————

There should be no asterisks in children's ministry, no footnotes or excep-
tions, no caveats or qualifiers, nothing that inadvertently or intentionally
invites some children in but leaves other children out. Yet asterisks are an
all-too-common theme in church stories of parents who have children
with disabilities.[1] Many parents struggle to find a church that will welcome
their child the first time and encourage them to come back a second time.
Many are unsure whether their church is really in it for the long haul,
even when promises are made at their child's dedication or baptism. And
many wonder whether proclamations that "*all* are welcome" really mean
that only *some* are welcome.

Yet the call to help children grow in their faith and spiritual lives is not
a narrow call. Those many verses that ask us to welcome, teach, serve, and
love children also come without asterisks. The Scriptures never include the
phrase "except for children with disabilities." Indeed, the opposite is true.

---

1. Erik W. Carter, "Spirituality and Supports for Individuals with Intellectual and Developmental
Disabilities and their Families," in *APA Handbook on Intellectual and Developmental Disabilities*, eds.
Laraine M. Glidden, Laura L. McIntyre, Len Abbeduto, Wayne Silverman, and Marc Tasse (American
Psychological Association, in press).

The Gospels are replete with the call to move the margins to the middle, to welcome the stranger, and to give special honor to those who are overlooked and undervalued. A thriving and effective children's ministry is designed with every child in mind; it provides a place of belonging for every child.

This chapter is an invitation for readers to reflect on the ways they are supporting the spiritual development and full participation of children with disabilities in their faith community. Although the accent within children's ministry is often on believing, I will emphasize the necessity of also addressing belonging. We grow in our knowledge and love of God when we live in a community that knows and loves us well. Belonging provides a context for believing.

Who Are Children with Disabilities?

Nearly seven million children in the United States are identified in their schools as having a disability.[2] Of course, the labels used to describe these disabilities are quite diverse. Some highlight the struggles children may have in the areas of reading or math while others highlight the areas of speech or communication. Some describe cognitive disabilities or emotional challenges while others address impairments related to vision or hearing. In other words, the impact of a disability varies tremendously from one child to the next—and every child is unique, even when a group shares the same label. What these children do have in common, however, is that they often experience real barriers to meaningful participation in the activities, relationships, and opportunities available within their schools and communities. And this often includes their faith communities.

We tend to get a few things wrong when we talk about children with disabilities. First, we sometimes assume that the disability label is the most important thing to know about a person. Although there is value in

---

2. Joel MacFarland, et al., *The Condition of Education* (Washington, DC: U.S. Department of Education, 2018), nces.ed.gov/pubs2018/2018144.pdf.

knowing something about the challenges a child experiences, each child also has stories, strengths, passions, and a personality worth discovering. All that makes up a person can never be captured by a single label. Second, we tend to get stuck on the things a particular child cannot do or struggles to do, rather than focusing on the many things they can do and the contexts in which they are most likely to shine. Children with disabilities have gifts and talents like anyone else. The difference is that those gifts and talents are more often overlooked. Third, we tend to think children with disabilities have only "special needs" rather than ordinary needs. But children with disabilities are, first and foremost, children. Like everyone else, they need to be known, needed, supported, and loved. Like everyone else, they need to belong.

WHAT DOES IT MEAN TO BELONG?

Every child with a disability should experience belonging within the church. Although this is easy to affirm in principle, it can sometimes seem daunting to put into practice. What does it mean to be a place of belonging for children with disabilities? What steps should we take to ensure every child encounters actions and attitudes that assure them that they really do belong? I suspect you already have some initial answers to these questions, because fostering belonging is not altogether different when disability is part of the conversation. Consider the following dimensions of belonging that were highlighted by young people with disabilities and their parents in a study that focused on faith, flourishing, and disability. We found that belonging is experienced when children with disabilities are *present, invited, welcomed, known, accepted, supported, cared for, befriended, needed,* and *loved.*[3] As we explore each of these areas in the remainder of this chapter, I invite you to reflect on the steps you are presently taking—or might begin taking—that address each of these ten areas. Use Figure 1 to guide your own reflection along the way.

---

3. Erik W. Carter, "A Place of Belonging: Research at the Intersection of Faith and Disability," *Review & Expositor* 113 (2016): 167–80.

FIGURE 1: *Reflection Tool for Fostering the Belonging of Children with and without Disabilities*

Are children with disabilities:	What are we doing well right now?	What could we do better or differently?
Present: Are they participating in all aspects and activities of our programs and ministry?		
Invited: Are we announcing our commitment widely and personally inviting families?		
Welcomed: Are we extending a warm—indeed extravagant—welcome whenever they arrive?		
Known: Do we know them personally and for the strengths and gifts they possess?		
Accepted: Are we receiving them without condition or caveat, with gratitude and grace?		
Supported: Are we providing the assistance they need to participate fully and meaningfully?		
Cared for: Are we extending care to them and their families the other six days of the week?		
Befriended: Are they developing and deepening relationships with other same-age children?		
Needed: Are we helping them discover, develop, and share their gifts with others?		
Loved: Is our entire community loving them deeply and unconditionally?		

TO BE PRESENT

Are children with disabilities already participating in all aspects of your ministries and programs? Presence is the starting point for belonging. Put simply, no one feels like they belong when they're looking in on a community from the outside. Many recent research studies indicate that children with disabilities often are absent from the ordinary experiences that take place in and through the local church—Sunday school classes, worship services, youth programs, retreats, social activities, service projects, and so much more.[4] *Ministry apart* from children with disabilities remains a common ministry model in the United States and around the world (see Figure 2).

Consider the children who are already present within your ministry. Nearly one in seven children attending the schools near your church has a disability. To what extent are these children present in your church? Of course, most disabilities are not visible or immediately apparent. And some disabilities may not substantially impact a child's participation or relationships at church. Other children may have autism, Down syndrome, intellectual disabilities, physical disabilities, sensory impairments, or other, more obvious, disabilities. I anticipate one or more children immediately came to mind. But consider whether other children might be missing. What may be standing in the way of the presence of children with disabilities? Is it where you gather? Is it how you gather? Is it when you gather? Is it what you do when you gather? Or is it something else altogether? Belonging requires presence, but being present is insufficient for belonging. We are called to go much deeper.

FIGURE 2: *Portraits of Different Ministry Models Currently Evident in Churches*

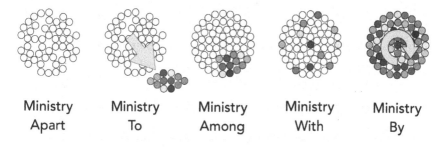

| Ministry
Apart | Ministry
To | Ministry
Among | Ministry
With | Ministry
By |

---

4. Melinda Ault, et al., "Congregational Participation and Supports for Children and Adults with Disabilities: Parent Perceptions," *Intellectual and Developmental Disabilities* 51 (2013): 184–211. Erik W. Carter and Thomas L. Boehm, "Religious and Spiritual Expressions of Youth with Intellectual and Developmental Disabilities," *Research and Practice for Persons with Severe Disabilities* 44 (2019): 37–52. Andrew

TO BE INVITED

The absence of children with disabilities is often inadvertent. As one pastor reflected, "It's not that we deliberately excluded [individuals with disabilities]. In fact, we weren't deliberate at all. That was the problem."[5] Increasing the presence of children with disabilities may require extending new invitations throughout your local community to a group of children and families who are rarely sought out. Invitations—whether passive and personal—communicate a critical message: We want you here.

Consider the language and imagery that you incorporate into your website, on your signage, in your mission and vision statements, and on your outreach materials. Do the words and pictures you use communicate to unreached families that you also have children with disabilities in mind when you say that "everybody is welcome"? Will they resonate with families who are wondering what response they will receive when they visit your church for the first time? The more specific you are about your commitment to including children with disabilities, the more confident families can be of the reception they will encounter.

Although passive announcements are important, personal invitations are likely to be much more powerful. For many children with disabilities and their families, broad promises of a warm reception have not always been honored. Know that announcements about your hospitality may not resonate with families who previously have been excluded. And there are more than a few. In one of our studies, we found that nearly one in three families (32 percent) had previously left their congregation because their son or daughter with an intellectual or developmental disability was not welcomed or included.[6] For these families, a personal invitation provides the sort of assurance they rarely receive from any other corner of the community. If you do not personally know families impacted by disability, others in your church certainly will. In addition, reach out to local disability organizations, parent networks, schools, and agencies to find out how you might connect with families in your area.

L. Whitehead, "Religion and Disability: Variation in Religious Service Attendance Rates for Children with Chronic Health Conditions," *Journal for the Scientific Study of Religion* 57 (2018): 377–95.

5. Erik W. Carter, *Including People with Disabilities in Faith Communities: A Guide for Service Providers, Congregations, and Families* (Baltimore, MD: Brookes Publishing, 2007), 82.

6. Melinda J. Ault, "Congregational Participation and Supports for Children and Adults with Disabilities: Parent Perceptions," 184–211.

TO BE WELCOMED

Every invitation must be matched with a warm welcome, perhaps even an extravagant welcome. Children with disabilities feel like they belong when they are welcomed well by leaders, by volunteers, and by their peers. In so many other aspects of community life, children with disabilities go unnoticed or overlooked; sometimes they are even avoided or ignored.[7] The response within our churches must be noticeably different. There is a rabbinic text suggesting that a procession of angels goes before every person proclaiming, "Make way for the image of God!"[8] Consider how you might join in that chorus through your actions and attitudes.

What does it look like to welcome children with disabilities? Begin by asking yourself what makes any child feel welcomed. Knowing their names, greeting them personally, asking about their week, encouraging their participation, anticipating their needs, showcasing their gifts, providing them ways to serve, creating a friendly and safe space, praying with them, and much more. Do these same things for children with disabilities. And then ask what additional or alternative steps you can take to make Sunday or Wednesday (or whenever you gather) the best day of the week for every child with a disability. Parents and other family members can help you discern what other steps you can take to make sure their children feel celebrated.

Let me emphasize that you do not have to have special expertise or experience related to any disability in order to welcome children with disabilities well. It involves ordinary, rather than extraordinary, gestures, but it does require intentionality. At the same time, it can be helpful to offer some training or information to leaders and volunteers who may be reluctant or uncertain about what to do. They may feel more confident extending hospitality when given some guidance on disability etiquette, person-first language, and available church resources.[9] They may also benefit from having information about how to interact with children who have complex communication challenges, who behave in unfamiliar ways, or who have extensive support needs.

---

7. Erik W. Carter, et al., "Being Present Versus Having a Presence: Dimensions of Belonging for Young People with Disabilities and their Families," *Christian Education Journal* 13 (2016): 127–46.

8. Deuteronomy Rabbah 4:4.

9. Terry A. DeYoung and Mark Stephenson, editors, *Inclusion Handbook: Everybody Belongs, Everybody Serves*, 2nd ed. (Grand Rapids, MI: Faith Alive, 2013).

To Be Known

Being known is an essential aspect of belonging, and yet it is common for children with disabilities to be present without having a presence and welcomed without really being known. In far too many places, these children are known by their disability labels but not by their names. They are seen as members of a larger group rather than as individuals. In other words, they are known *about* but not known *personally*. Every child—with or without a disability—is unique and remarkable. Invest time in getting to know every child individually and well.

It is also important that children with disabilities are known both by adults and by their peers. Sometimes the avenues through which we support the participation of children with more severe disabilities can inadvertently hinder regular interactions with peers. If we aren't careful, an exclusive reliance on adults as one-to-one supports (e.g., "buddies," "shadows," or "assistants") can sometimes crowd out opportunities for other children to meet, spend time with, and get to know children with disabilities. Emphasize shared activities that give children with and without disabilities the chance to come to know each other well.

As emphasized earlier in this chapter, *how* children with disabilities are known matters as much as *whether* and *by whom* they are known. Disability labels almost always and exclusively emphasize "deficits" or "challenges." This is an incomplete (and inappropriate) way to come to know someone within a faith community. Like anyone else, children with disabilities possess strengths, gifts, passions, and positive qualities worth encountering. For example, parents and siblings involved in our studies often described their family members with disabilities as having enviable qualities like kindness, optimism, courage, empathy, gratitude, and joy.[10] These children have skills, abilities, talents, and interests that could provide points of connection to peers and be of service within and through the church. What steps are you taking to come to know children with disabilities personally and positively?

---

10. Erik W. Carter, et al., "Known for My Strengths: Positive Traits of Transition-Age Youth with Intellectual Disability or Autism," *Research and Practice for Persons with Severe Disabilities* 40, (2015): 101–19. Erik W. Carter, et al., "Seeing Strengths: Young Adults and their Siblings with Intellectual and Developmental Disabilities," (*Manuscript submitted for publication*, 2019).

TO BE ACCEPTED

Acceptance always accompanies belonging. The parents in our studies talked about their children with disabilities being included fully, welcomed without condition, loved wholeheartedly, treated like family, and embraced for who they are.[11] Although societal attitudes toward people with disabilities have changed dramatically over the last fifty years, there is still no assurance of acceptance. This is also true within churches. When we explored the extent to which an attitude of acceptance was evident within local congregations, nearly one third (30 percent) of parents we surveyed indicated they were not very satisfied with how welcoming people in the church were to individuals with intellectual disability or autism.[12]

In his "5 Stages" framework, Dan Vander Plaats encourages reflection on whether prevailing attitudes in our churches reflect a posture of (a) *ignorance* about people with disabilities, (b) *pity* toward people with disabilities, (c) *care* for people with disabilities, (d) *friendship* with people with disabilities, and/or (e) *co-laboring* alongside people with disabilities.[13] Churches can undertake formal awareness activities as one avenue for fostering greater acceptance and elevating attitudes. This might include hosting a disability or inclusion awareness Sunday, incorporating information and activities into Sunday school classes, or identifying other ways children and adults can learn more about the gifts and lives of people with disabilities.[14] However, what is modeled may be as important as what is taught. When ministry leaders and volunteers model respectful interactions, hold high expectations, use affirming language, and demonstrate love and care, children are likely to follow their lead.

TO BE SUPPORTED

Children with disabilities need ordinary supports to participate fully in the educational, social, service, and worship experiences that will support

---

11. Erik W. Carter, et al., "Being Present Versus Having a Presence: Dimensions of Belonging for Young People with Disabilities and their Families," 127–46.

12. Erik W. Carter, et al., "Supporting Congregational Inclusion for Children and Youth with Disabilities and their Families," *Exceptional Children* 82, (2016): 372–89.

13. Dan Vander Plaats, *There is No Asterisk: Changing Attitudes about Disabilities through the 5 Stages* (Chicago: Elim Christian Services, 2016).

14. Kelly L. Leigers and Christine T. Myers, "Effect of Duration of Peer Awareness Education on Attitudes toward Students with Disabilities: A Systematic Review," *Journal of Occupational Therapy, Schools, & Early Intervention* 8, (2015): 79–96.

their faith formation and spiritual development. However, most of these children will also benefit from additional supports that are more individualized, intensive, and/or more lasting. Sometimes this support will be fairly minimal, and other times it will be more extensive. But it must always be intentional. In one of our studies, we found that almost half (46 percent) of parents of children with intellectual and developmental disabilities reported that they had *never* been asked by anyone in their church about how best to include their child in congregational activities.[15]

This is not the place for making assumptions; instead, ask good questions. *What can we do to make Sunday morning the best day of the week for your child? What goals and experiences do you consider to be most important right now? How can we support your family to be part of all we do in and through this church?* The answers you receive will vary widely. Some children will benefit from modifications or accommodations, such as large-print materials, visual schedules, additional prompts, specific room or seating arrangements, personalized feedback, or assistive technology. Others may need alternate ways of participating in lessons or activities that are responsive to their communication, learning, and behavioral needs. For example, parents told us that the following supports would be somewhat helpful to very helpful for their child with intellectual and developmental disabilities: a spiritual or religious support plan (59 percent), modifications to religious education programs (59 percent), someone to provide support during religious education (46 percent), and someone to provide support during worship services (38 percent).[16] Such individualized supports are what makes *ministry with* people with disabilities possible.

TO BE CARED FOR

Research addressing faith in the lives of children with disabilities and their families emphasizes the connection between care and flourishing.[17] Indeed, the relationships and activities that take place within faith communities are strongly associated with overall quality of life among individuals and

15. Melinda J. Ault, "Congregational Participation and Supports for Children and Adults with Disabilities: Parent Perceptions," 184–211.

16. Erik W. Carter, et al., "Supporting Congregational Inclusion for Children and Youth with Disabilities and their Families," 372–89.

17. Naomi Annandale, *Attending to Care: A Pastoral Theological Response to Families Facing Disabilities (PhD diss., Vanderbilt University, 2015).* Erik W. Carter, et al., "Being Present Versus Having a Presence: Dimensions of Belonging for Young People with Disabilities and their Families," 127–46.

families.[18] What might you do to help meet the spiritual, emotional, material, and other needs of children and families in your midst? As with identifying supports, it is important to find out firsthand from families what you can do to demonstrate care rather than making assumptions. The very same gesture can seem like caring to some people but feel patronizing to others.

Offering respite is one way to enable parents to attend worship services, participate in small groups, address personal needs (e.g., doctor's appointments, running errands, shopping), or enjoy a date with their spouse. We found that nearly two-thirds of parents (61 percent) thought that respite care would be especially helpful, yet only 8 percent said that their congregations offer such care.[19] Although some churches offer formal respite events—individually or in partnership with other churches—you should also commit to including children with disabilities in children's ministry programs without requiring their parents to be present or provide assistance. This frees parents to allocate their time elsewhere, even if only for a couple of hours. Other actions might include facilitating a support group for parents or siblings, connecting families to community resources related to disability, or providing needed financial, household, or other assistance. Whatever steps you choose to take, remember that the needs of families extend throughout all seven days of the week. Although much of our ministry happens on a particular morning or evening each week, it is the investments made beyond the walls of your building that will have the greatest impact on the well-being of children with disabilities and their families.

TO BE BEFRIENDED

We were created for community. We all need people in our lives who know us, accept us, need us, love us, and miss us when we are not there. Indeed, study after study affirms what we all know firsthand—people flourish most in the midst of friendships and other supportive relationships.[20] This includes children with disabilities. Belonging requires being befriended.

18. Thomas L. Boehm, et al. "Factors Associated with Family Quality of Life during the Transition to Adulthood for Youth and Young Adults with Developmental Disabilities," *American Journal on Intellectual and Developmental Disabilities* 120, (2015): 395–411.

19. Erik W. Carter, et al., "Supporting Congregational Inclusion for Children and Youth with Disabilities and their Families," 372–89.

20. William M. Bukowski, Brett Laursen, and Kenneth H. Rubin, editors, *Handbook of Peer Interactions, Relationships, and Groups*, 2nd ed. (New York: Guilford, 2018).

Yet many children with disabilities have friendship networks that are small and fragile. For example, one nationally representative study found that only 52 percent of youth with disabilities get together with friends outside school at least once a week compared to 66 percent of peers without disabilities.[21] For youth with intellectual disability or autism, these numbers were much lower (42 percent and 29 percent, respectively). Among elementary and middle school students with disabilities, only 66 percent get together with friends outside school at least once a week. Again, these social connections were more restricted for children with intellectual disability (52 percent) or autism (31 percent).[22] These relationships, which are so essential to belonging, are elusive for many children.

What steps might you take to nurture friendships among children with and without disabilities in your church? Friendships are most likely to develop when children with and without disabilities (a) participate in shared activities, (b) are connected on the basis of common interests, (c) have a reliable way to communicate with one another, (d) are assigned valued roles within ongoing activities, (e) are provided relevant information about each other, and (f) have just enough—but not too much—adult facilitation.[23] Consider how you might establish regular opportunities and individual supports that provide children the chance to spend time together and discover new relationships. Remember that your approaches to ministry also impact the extent to which children with disabilities will experience friendships and experience belonging. If ministry models for children with disabilities are largely separate or specialized (i.e., *ministry among* rather than *ministry with*), then the opportunity to be chosen as a friend by others becomes limited.

TO BE NEEDED

To belong is to be needed and to feel valued. When leaders and members throughout the church see children with disabilities as having gifts,

21. Stephen W. Lipscomb, et al., Preparing for Life after High School: The Characteristics and Experiences of Youth in Special Education (Washington, DC: U.S. Department of Education, 2017).

22. Jose Blackorby, et al., Engagement, Academics, Social Adjustment, and Independence: The Achievements of Elementary and Middle School Students with Disabilities (Menlo Park, CA: SRI International, 2005).

23. Elizabeth E. Biggs and Erik W. Carter, "Supporting the Social Lives of Students with Intellectual Disability," in *Handbook of Research-Based Practices for Educating Students with Intellectual Disability*, eds. Michael L. Wehmeyer and Karrie A. Shogren (Oxford: Routledge, 2017), 235–54.

faith, and friendship the community desperately needs, belonging is quick to follow. As John Swinton writes, "People need to be concerned when you are not there; your communities need to feel empty when you are not there. The world needs to be perceived as radically different when you are not there. Only when your absence stimulates feelings of emptiness will you know that you truly belong."[24]

More and more churches are investing in *ministry to* people with disabilities, but many still struggle to step into the place of *ministry by* people with disabilities. Children with disabilities are still viewed as the "designated recipients" of service and the focus of outreach. The roles of giver and receiver remain static and predetermined. Certainly children with disabilities and their families have much to gain from being woven into the fabric of their faith communities, but it also is true that a faith community has much to gain from the gifts these individuals have to bring. This portrait of a reciprocal community—one in which every member is indispensable—is depicted in Paul's letter to the church at Corinth (1 Cor. 12). A community marked by belonging sees itself as incomplete without the presence and participation of children with disabilities.

Consider the steps you might take to discern and develop the gifts and talents of children with disabilities in your church. Explore ways in which you might connect children with opportunities to share those gifts and talents with others in their community. And identify new avenues through which you can help children with disabilities assume valued roles in all aspects of congregational life.

TO BE LOVED

The Scriptures remind us over and over that all we do—and all we are—must be saturated with love. Children with disabilities, like all children, need to experience deep and lavish love from others in their faith community. And children with disabilities, like all children, need to encounter the expansive and endless love of God. As we strive to follow the greatest commandment (Matt. 22:36–40), we encourage and equip children with disabilities to do likewise.

---

24. John Swinton, "From Inclusion to Belonging: A Practical Theology of Community, Disability, and Humanness," *Journal of Religion, Disability, & Health* 16, (2012): 172–90.

MOVING FORWARD

The portrait of belonging depicted in this chapter provides a helpful framework for thinking about ministry involving children with disabilities. At the same time, it invites us to consider the steps we are taking to foster belonging for anyone in our community. How might your postures and practices aim toward each of these aspects of belonging? What steps might you take as a church to become known as a place where every child is invited, present, welcomed, accepted, cared for, known, supported, befriended, needed, and loved?

The Environments That
SHAPE A CHILD'S
SPIRITUALITY

CHAPTER 5

FAITH-FORMING ENVIRONMENTS FOR CHILDREN

JOHN ROBERTO

—————╫———————

We are all familiar with the trends and challenges inherent in nurturing the spiritual and religious growth of children: a new generation of millennial parents with much more diverse religious practices and engagement, the emergence of Generation Z (those who were born from about 1997 onward), new ways of learning in and interacting with the world, children living in multiple family structures and living arrangements, seemingly omnipresent internet and digital technology, declining church engagement among the younger generations, declining religious practices at home, the difficulty of finding volunteer leaders, and more. These challenges make it more and more difficult to engage children in robust, life-giving, vital, and vibrant Christian faith formation that will guide them in developing a loving relationship with Jesus, embracing the good news, and following Jesus in their daily lives.

THE IMPORTANCE OF CHILDHOOD FAITH FORMATION

Developing the religious and spiritual life of children has never been more important for religious congregations. In the National Study of Youth and Religion (NYSR), Christian Smith and his colleagues found that young people committing to live for God is one religious experience that is among the most important factors in leading teenagers into serious adult faith commitments. They found that almost 60 percent (58.8 percent) made their first commitment to live their lives for God before the age of fourteen. Most of these probably committed to God during the childhood years. Approximately 6 percent made a first commitment between fourteen and seventeen, and another 5 percent between eighteen and twenty-three. Thirty-one percent of young adults reported never committing to God as a teenager or emerging adult. Smith says few of them probably ever will. *So, 85 percent of young adults who have committed their lives to God appear to have made their first commitment before age 14.*[1]

It is clear from the findings of the NSYR that religious commitments and orientations of most people appear to be set early in life, that what matters most is what happens before the teenage years, and that early formative experiences shape everything that happens later. The flip side of the early commitment to live for God is that most Americans who leave behind their childhood religious identity and become unaffiliated generally do so before they reach their eighteenth birthday. More than six in ten (62 percent) religiously unaffiliated Americans who were raised in a religion say they abandoned their childhood religion before they turned eighteen. About three in ten (28 percent) say they were between the ages of eighteen and twenty-nine. Only five percent say they stopped identifying with their childhood religion between the ages of thirty and forty-nine, while just two percent say age fifty or older.[2]

The results from the *Exodus* study by the Public Religion Research Institute survey are affirmed by a 2017 study of Catholic youth and young adults in the book, *Going, Going, Gone*:

The median age for when formerly Catholic teens and young adults left the faith is 13. Nearly four in ten (39%) report leaving between the ages of 13 and 17. Only 5 percent say they left before age 5 and 18 percent between the ages of 5 and 9. About a quarter (24 percent)

1. Christian Smith with Patricia Snell, *Souls in Transition: The Religious and Spiritual Lives of Emerging Adults* (New York: Oxford University Press, 2009), 247.

2. Robert P. Jones, et. al., *Exodus: Why Americans Are Leaving Religion—and Why They're Unlikely to Come Back* (Washington, D.C.: Public Religion Research Institute, 2016), 5.

left between ages 10 and 12. Eleven percent left in the first few years of adulthood, between 18 and 22. Only 3 percent left from age 21 to 25.[3]

It should be pretty clear that what we do in faith formation with children *and* adolescents can make a huge difference when they are young and, therefore, as they grow into adults. Faith formation in the first two decades of life sets people on a trajectory toward adult faith. *What we do in faith formation and how we do it matters!*

A VISION OF MATURING IN FAITH

We want a robust, life-giving, vital, and vibrant faith formation for children and adolescents that develops them as disciples of Jesus Christ and equips them to follow Jesus. We want young people to develop loving relationships with Jesus, embrace his good news, and follow him in their daily lives as disciples. This type of faith formation is a way of the head, the heart, and the hands, as Jesus said: "'Love the Lord your God with all your heart and with all your soul and with all your mind.' This is the first and greatest commandment. And the second is like it: 'Love your neighbor as yourself'" (Matt. 22:37–39). Jesus presented faith as a whole way of life.

We can help form disciples and promote faith growth by focusing on characteristics of faith maturing that incorporate knowing and believing, relating and belonging, practicing and living. The following ten characteristics of faith maturing, drawn from the Christian tradition and research on faith growth, can serve as a guide for developing faith formation at every stage of life. They can form the foundation for creating faith-forming experiences, programs, and activities that nurture the spiritual and religious life of children and families. They provide a way to direct energy and attention to specific goals or outcomes. They provide a way to develop a seamless process of fostering faith growth from birth to nineteen years old.

---

3. Robert McCarty and John M. Vitek, *Going, Going, Gone: The Dynamics of Disaffiliation in Young Catholics* (Winona, MN: Saint Mary's Press, 2017), 11.

1. Developing and sustaining a personal relationship and commitment to Jesus Christ
2. Living as a disciple of Jesus Christ and making the Christian faith a way of life
3. Reading and studying the Bible—its message, meaning, and application to life today
4. Learning the Christian story and foundational teachings of the Christian faith and integrating its meaning into one's life
5. Praying together and by ourselves, and seeking spiritual growth through spiritual disciplines
6. Living with moral integrity guided by Christian ethics and values
7. Living the Christian mission in the world—serving those in need, caring for God's creation, and acting and advocating for justice and peace.
8. Worshipping God with the faith community at Sunday worship, ritual celebrations, and observing the seasons of the church year
9. Being actively engaged in the life, ministries, and activities of the faith community
10. Practicing faith in Jesus Christ by using one's gifts and talents within the Christian community and in the world

We can design faith formation using each characteristic by asking questions such as, *What do we need to do to help children [characteristic]? How can we engage children and their families in [characteristic]? How do we equip children and their families for [characteristic]?*

Focusing on characteristics of faith maturing reflects a significant shift from a provider-centered, program-and content-driven approach to a *person-centered* and *environmental* approach to faith formation. We need to focus on children (and adolescents) growing in faith and ask how we can accompany them relationally and programmatically. We need to utilize three environments for faith growth: the intergenerational faith community, the family, and age groups or peer settings. Instead of asking what program or textbook we need to adopt or what content we need to teach, we focus on the person growing in faith. We start asking how we promote growth in faith and discipleship from birth through the high school years—a faith that provides a foundation for adult faith.

These ten characteristics need to be contextualized within specific Christian traditions, within the specific ethnic-cultural traditions and identities of faith communities, and within the unique socio-cultural needs of faith communities.

A HOLISTIC APPROACH
TO FAITH FORMING

To promote maturing in faith, we need to think much more systemically and holistically about the spiritual and religious growth of children. We need Christian faith formation for children that integrates three primary faith forming environments: the faith community, the family, and age groups—by (1) engaging children in intergenerational relationships, activities, and church life and events (including Sunday worship), (2) equipping and supporting parents and families in sharing and practicing their faith at home, and (3) engaging young people in activities and experiences designed for Generation Z and the ways they learn and grow.

Every child, every year, needs to experience the faith-forming influence of all three environments. This new approach blends intergenerational, family, and age-group settings into a holistic approach to faith formation. This reflects a significant shift from the age-segregated or siloed approach wherein faith formation with children (and adolescents) is primarily age-group-based without significant intergenerational and family faith-forming experiences. This shift situates children within a broader "ecology" or "ecosystem" of faith formation that blends intergenerational, family, and age-group settings into a comprehensive approach to faith formation.

The following section highlights each environment with a special emphasis on the intergenerational environment. Many of the chapters in this book provide ideas for nurturing children's spiritual and religious growth and family faith formation (see especially Trevecca Okholm's chapter on family faith practices). At the end of this chapter is a simple process for designing faith formation using the faith maturing characteristics and the three environments.

INTERGENERATIONAL FAITH FORMING

We need to immerse young people in a multigenerational community of relationships informed by faith in Jesus Christ, where they get to know Jesus through the witness of believers and the life of the church. We make them feel at home in these safe and nurturing communities where their participation, energy, concerns, questions, and faith life are valued. We welcome them and expect them to participate and lead in church-wide ministries. We can do this in at least three ways:

First, we can **utilize** the intergenerational events and experiences of church life, community life events, worship, the seasons of the year, service and mission projects, prayer, and spiritual formation as a primary "content" in faith formation with young people by (1) *preparing* them with the knowledge and practices necessary to participate actively, (2) *engaging* them in the intergenerational experience, and (3) helping them *reflect* upon its meaning and discover how to *live* their faith.

There are opportunities throughout the year for making the events and ministries of the church life central to the faith formation of children and their families. One opportunity is Sunday worship: *prepare* children for Sunday worship and review the Scripture readings, *experience* Sunday worship with the faith community, and equip them to *live* the Sunday worship experience at home and in their daily lives. Another opportunity is connecting them to the service ministries of the church by focusing on a particular project: help children (and their parents) *learn* about a particular justice issue and the biblical and church teachings, *experience* the service project, and *reflect* on that experience and its connection to living as a disciple today. Where are the opportunities in your congregation?

Second, we can **infuse** intergenerational experiences and relationships into existing ministries and programs, bringing the other generations into children's (and adolescent) programs to serve as mentors and guides, and transforming age-group programs like vacation Bible school and service projects into intergenerational experiences by involving multiple generations. Think of all the possibilities for incorporating intergenerational relationship building and experiences into the programs and activities your congregation is already offering. Here are a few examples to spark your creativity.

- Include all generations in Sunday worship, and involve all generations in leadership roles—music, art, hospitality, reading Scripture, and more. While there may be time during the Scripture readings and sermon or homily when children have a separate experience, it's important to have children involved with the whole worship community for most of the service.
- Add other generations into current age-group programs, such as mission trips, service projects, retreat experiences, and vacation Bible school. Consider adding intergenerational experiences into VBS such as a grandparent component or redesigning the youth mission trip into an all-ages mission trip for adolescents through older adults.
- Incorporate intergenerational dialogues, interviews, and presentations into programming, providing opportunities for children and youth to experience the wisdom, faith, and interests of (older) adults, then reverse the process and provide opportunities for the (older) adults to experience the wisdom, faith, and interests of children or teens through presentations, performances, and discussions.
- Add a mentoring component, such as parent mentors for parents bringing their children for baptism, confirmation mentors, spiritual direction focused on prayer practices, and justice and service mentors, to name a few possibilities.
- Involve the whole community in praying for special moments and experiences, for example: the birth and baptism of a child, young people on a mission trip or retreat weekend, a milestone event such as first Communion or graduations.
- Add intergenerational relationship building and activities into social and recreational activities in the congregation, such as the church picnic and gatherings after Sunday worship.
- Develop a leadership or ministry apprenticeship for young people to serve in church ministries and leadership positions.

Third, we *connect* generations through intergenerational programs and experiences for learning, celebrating, praying, serving, working for justice, and worshipping. We offer intergenerational learning to educate the whole community, bringing all ages and generations together to learn with and from each other and to build community, share faith, pray, celebrate, and practice the Christian faith.

Intergenerational service benefits children, adolescents, families, and the whole church community. Intergenerational service helps narrow the generation gap between older and younger church members; recognizes that all people in the church, regardless of age, have talents to contribute that are valuable and important; assists young people in feeling a part of the church today, not just the church of tomorrow; connects the generations and builds relationships as people serve God by serving their neighbor; and communicates that it is the responsibility of all Christians, regardless of age, to serve people and work for justice as a follower of Jesus Christ.

Here are a few examples. Remember that there are local, national, and global organizations that provide educational resources and action projects your church can use to create new intergenerational programming.

- An annual church-wide service day: Create a four-week, church-wide campaign that culminates on a Saturday or Sunday where the entire congregation engages in service projects in the community. Select local and global projects already developed by a justice or service organization. Then develop a theme, such as poverty, care for creation, peacemaking. Prepare the whole community for the service engagement, including (1) worship and prayer experiences focused on the theme or project; (2) educational sessions exploring the theme and biblical and church teachings; (3) family activities; (4) a website with the resources, activities, action projects, and features to allow people to share what they are doing; and (5) special presentations by experts.
- A monthly intergenerational service project: Develop a monthly service project that addresses one particular need or issue (local and/or global) each month. Each month's project can include a short educational program on the topic, an action project, and reflection on the project. Themes for the service projects can correspond with calendar events and seasons, as well as church year seasons. Examples include Back to School (September) and school kits for students, Thanksgiving (November) and feeding the hungry, Lent (February or March) and serving the poor, and Earth Day (April) and caring for creation.

- Intergenerational service nights at church: Design programs featuring service activity stations that engage all ages in a simple project for the benefit of a group in need. At one station, people might create greeting cards for the elderly or for sick church members. At another booth, they might make blankets for a homeless shelter. At another booth, they might bake cookies or make sandwiches for a soup kitchen. Many organizations provide the organizational logistics a church needs for a service project. For example, Feed My Starving Children[4] provides the resources for people to pack food that will be shipped to people in need.

Intergenerational learning provides a way to educate the whole community, bringing all ages and generations together to learn with and from each other, build community, share faith, pray, celebrate, and practice the Christian faith. The key is that everyone is learning together—young and old, single and married, families with children and empty-nest families, and it involves the whole family—children, parents, grandparents—in a shared experience of the Christian faith.

We know from research studies that one of the most significant features of intergenerational learning is the way it builds community and relationships across ages and generations. Central to building relationships and community is creating an atmosphere of hospitality and welcoming where everyone feels a sense of belonging, acceptance, and respect. The intergenerational learning model creates an environment wherein people of all ages learn from each other and grow in faith together. Adults gain meaningful insights from their interactions with children and youth; and children and youth experience meaningful support from adults other than their parents. Participants feel safe to learn, ask questions, and grow in faith on a deeper level.

We also know that intergenerational learning strengthens parental and family faith by encouraging the whole family to participate—children, teens, parents, and grandparents. It equips parents (and grandparents) to be formers of their children's faith by developing their competence and confidence through such faith-forming experiences as sharing stories, celebrating rituals, praying together, reading the Bible, and more. Intergenerational learning

---

4. www.fmsc.org/en

includes activities that model the practices churches want parents and families to live out at home. The research findings also revealed that families *enjoy* opportunities to pray, learn, and be together (even if parents may resist participating initially).[5]

The *Generations of Faith* intergenerational learning model can be used in a variety of ways for all ages, for intergenerational faith formation or for family faith formation.[6]

1. Gathering and opening prayer (often including a meal).
2. All-ages learning experience: intergenerational learning begins with a themed multigenerational experience all generations can share in.
3. In-depth learning experience: structured learning activities with each generation—families with children, adolescents, and other adults—exploring the biblical and theological understanding of the topic, using one of three possible formats:
   - The *Age Group Format* provides parallel, age-appropriate learning for differentiated groups at the same time. Though age groups are separated, each one is focusing on the same topic, utilizing specific learning activities that are designed for their life cycle stage: families with children or children alone, adolescents, young adults, and adults.
   - The *Whole-Group Format* provides a series of facilitated learning activities for everyone at the same time, using intergenerational or age-specific small groups or table groups.
   - The *Learning Activity Center Format* provides structured intergenerational and age-specific learning activities at a variety of stations or centers in a common area.
4. Sharing reflections and application: in intergenerational groups, participants share what they learned and prepare for applying their learning to daily life using resources and activities provided in print or online.
5. Closing prayer service.

---

5. See John Roberto, "Intergenerational Principles and Three Stories," in *Intergenerate*, ed. Holly Allen (Abilene, TX: Abilene Christian University Press, 2018).

6. See John Roberto, *Becoming a Church of Lifelong Learners* (New London, CT: Twenty-Third Publications, 2016) and Mariette Martineau, et. al., *Intergenerational Faith Formation* (New London, CT: Twenty-Third Publications, 2008).

Congregations are using the Generations of Faith intergenerational learning model to develop a faith formation curriculum for the whole community using intergenerational faith formation as the primary learning model, supplemented by age-specific faith formation and faith formation for people with similar interests or in similar life circumstances. They use the model to extend a topic featured in the faith formation program for children to the whole community through intergenerational learning, or replace a topic in the children's program with intergenerational learning on the same theme; conduct intergenerational festivals around church year seasons, such as Advent and Christmas, Lent, Holy Week, Pentecost, and more; and create intergenerational vacation Bible school, camp, or summer programs, or add intergenerational learning experiences to existing programs.

The *Logos* model of intergenerational learning, created by *GenOn Ministries*,[7] includes weekly intergenerational experiences for children and youth where all ages can learn about and practice the art of Christian relationships. In these cross-generational gatherings, everyone eats together, plays together, studies together, and prays together. These four parts, plus weekly congregational worship, make up the whole, providing everyone involved with a cross-generational arena in which to have a complete, holistic experience of Christian nurture. In addition, young people also lead congregational worship on a regular basis. The four-part learning model includes Bible study, worship arts, family time, and recreation.

The *Messy Church* model of intergenerational learning[8] was created for those outside the church and became church for them rather than being a stepping stone to Sunday morning church. Messy Church is church for families who may not find other forms of church appealing and who don't yet belong to a church. A typical Messy Church meets monthly and includes four parts: (1) a flexible, relaxed arrival time with drinks and snacks; (2) creative exploration of a Bible story or theme through multiple creative experiences for children and adults together; (3) a time of worship with story, music, and prayers that builds on the creative exploration; and (4) a generous welcome and hospitality expressed through an invitation to share a delicious, home-cooked, sit-down meal with others.

---

7. www.genonministries.org
8. www.messychurch.org.uk and messychurchaustralia.com.au

Cross+Gen Life, created by FaithInkubators,[9] blends learning, worship, and deep care across the generations into one hour in the same sacred space each week, then connects the weekly Bible themes with nightly faith acts in the home (known as FAITH5). Built around the simple "share, read, talk, pray, bless" liturgy of FAITH5,[10] the system connects highs and lows (context) to Sunday's preaching theme (text) in a way that's personal, meaningful, and fun. The process is modeled at worship, and then all ages take the Bible theme home for a week of deeper engagement.

Intergenerational vacation Bible school is an emerging model wherein all ages might participate for three or four evenings in the summer with food, fun, music, learning, and games. The program incorporates typical VBS Bible content and interactive learning, but everything is intergenerational. A typical evening design (three hours) could look like this: registration, light meal, opening /music, Bible story, outdoor activity/inside craft, snacks, and closing. A second approach begins each evening with a family-style meal, then the children participate in Bible stories and activities while the adults (parents, grandparents) participate in an adult-themed session. Families reunite in the church for music and prayer to close the evening.

Grandparent-grandchild camp is another emerging model designed in a summer camp format, usually lasting three or four days, and held at a camp site or church setting. Designed with familiar camp content and activities, the intergenerational camp includes shared activities everyone engages in together, as well as age-appropriate activities for children and for grandparents.

FAMILY FAITH FORMING

The primary mechanisms by which Christian identity becomes rooted in children's lives are the day-to-day religious practices of the family and the ways parents model their faith and share it in conversation, collaboration, and exposure to religious opportunities outside the home. Through the processes of religious socialization, young people with seriously religious parents come to think, feel, believe, and act as serious religious believers,

---

9. www.crossgenlife.org
10. www.faith5.org

and that training sticks with them even when they leave home and enter emerging adulthood.

Congregations can create family faith formation for each stage of life from birth to nineteen years old by focusing on three components:

- At home: discovering God in everyday life, forming faith practices (praying, reading the Bible, serving others), and celebrating milestones and rituals
- In the faith community: celebrating seasonal events, encountering God in the Bible, connecting families intergenerationally (learning, service, community life), and offering whole family gatherings for learning, worship, service, relationship-building that provide high quality family experiences and model the types of faith practices families can do at home
- With parents: developing a strong family life and empowering parents and grandparents as faith formers[11]

Congregations can develop a "curriculum for the family" designed around the faith practices that make a significant difference in nurturing the faith of young people: reading the Bible as a family; praying together as a family; participating regularly in Sunday worship; being involved in the life of a faith community; serving people in need as a family and supporting young people in service; celebrating holidays, rituals, and church year seasons at home; having family conversations; talking about faith, religious issues, and questions and doubts; ritualizing milestone experiences; and providing moral instruction.

An important element of family faith forming is preparing today's parents and grandparents to teach and live the faith practices at home. Every congregation can create a parent plan with a progression of workshops, webinars, courses, activities, support groups, and resources from infancy through the end of the adolescent years that provides parent faith formation, equips parents to be faith formers of their children, and develops the knowledge and skills for effective parenting. With new digital tools and

---

11. For ideas and strategies for family faith formation see Leif Kehrwald, et. al., *Families at the Center of Faith Formation* (Cheshire, CT: Lifelong Faith, 2016).

media, we have the ability to reach today's parents and families anywhere and anytime with engaging and interactive faith-forming content.

AGE-GROUP FAITH FORMING

Congregations can design faith formation specifically targeted to the ways that Gen Z young people learn. We can dramatically improve our effectiveness in promoting faith growth and learning by using the new approaches and methods that are being designed by educators for twenty-first century learners. We know today's younger generations learn best in environments that are relational, interactive, participatory, experiential, visual, and multi-sensory.

We address Gen Z's need for authentic and meaningful experiences where they can share with and co-create their learning with their peers. We engage Gen Z in immersive faith-forming experiences that are hands-on, relational, participatory, visual, and multi-sensory, using methods such as project-based learning, and activities that utilize Gen Z's creativity, such as artwork, video presentation, and more.

We can make use of the new digital tools and media to enhance and expand faith formation with young people and their families. We provide young people and parents online with faith-forming content and experiences at home 24/7. We blend faith formation in physical and online settings and use models, like flipped learning, where young people and their parents learn online through video or other digital media and then participate in gathered sessions that provide an interactive environment for experience, discussion, and application.

DESIGNING FAITH FORMATION USING THE FAITH-MATURING CHARACTERISTICS AND THREE ENVIRONMENTS

Every child, every year needs to experience the faith-forming influence of all three environments. The new children's "curriculum" blends intergenerational, family, and age-group settings into a holistic approach to faith formation. Here is a simple process for designing a faith formation plan that blends all three environments. You can focus your design on young children or grade school children or all children from birth to ten years old. (You can use the same process for young adolescents and older adolescents as well.)

STEP 1: *Develop a Profile of Current Faith-Forming Activities*

Develop an inventory of the current intergenerational, family, and age-group activities your congregation provides correlated to the ten faith-maturing characteristics (or your own set of characteristics). Write each characteristic into the chart and add your current programming: (1) intergenerational (or whole-church) faith-forming experiences (ministries, programs, activities), (2) parent and family faith formation activities, and (3) age-group programming. It's not important to "fill every box."

Faith-Maturing Characteristic	Intergenerational Faith Forming	Family Faith Forming	Age-Group Faith Forming

STEP 2: *Create New Ideas for Faith Formation*

Review your profile. What are the strengths in your current approach to promoting faith maturing using the ten characteristics? What are the areas that need improvement? What new initiatives can your church create to build upon strengths and address areas in need of improvement? Add these new ideas to your profile.

STEP 3: *Design an Integrated Plan of Faith Formation for the Year*

The goal of the plan is to provide a holistic year of faith formation that integrates all three environments. Think of this as creating a "menu" for the year with a variety of faith-forming experiences: intergenerational (including whole church experiences), family-centered at church and home, and age-group or peer activities. From this "menu" of faith formation, children and their parents can develop their own faith formation plan by selecting a variety of faith formation experiences in which they will participate. Set a minimum number of activities for participation in each of the three environments. Have each child or family create a portfolio of all the activities they experienced with printed materials and photos. (For a similar example of this "menu" or electives approach, go to Westwood U, developed by Westwood Lutheran Church in Minneapolis.[12])

Guided by the faith-maturing characteristics and a variety of experiences in all three faith-forming environments, we can address the challenge of engaging children and their parents in a robust, life-giving, vital, and vibrant Christian faith formation.[13]

---

12. www.westwoodlutheran.org/Westwood-U

13. For a complete presentation of the approach presented in this chapter see John Roberto, et. al., *Faith Formation with a New Generation* (Cheshire, CT: Lifelong Faith, 2018). In addition, there are resources online at www.LifelongFaith.com to help you design children and family faith formation.

CHAPTER 6

Reimagining the Role of Family in Twenty-First Century Family Faith Practices

TREVECCA OKHOLM

—————⊩————

The family is the primary venue for forming faith in the heads, hearts, and hands of children. If you are a Christian educator, pastor, or children's volunteer in your local congregation, then by now, I suspect you already know this in theory. However, translating this theory into practice within our current ministry paradigm is not all that simple. Why? For one thing, much more is required than simply purchasing the latest and greatest curriculum or designing the most attractive program.

BREAKING DOWN ROADBLOCKS TO EFFECTIVE SPIRITUAL FORMATION IN THE FAMILY

The reality is that there are several roadblocks standing in our way, which create challenges that hinder effective spiritual formation in a family setting, including the way we think about family in the first place. Let's consider the implications of a few of those roadblocks.

ROADBLOCK #1: *The Changing Face of the Family*

In the world in which we now find ourselves, it is difficult to begin a conversation on the family's role in children's spirituality without first taking a step back for a brief look at what we mean when we say "family." When a church proclaims its intention to uphold the "traditional family" and support "traditional family values," the first question we might ask is, *Which tradition and what values are we talking about?*

If we begin to answer this question by looking through the lens of mid-twentieth century we have a vision of the family as *nuclear*—defined as two parents, 2.5 children, and probably a dog, living in their own little house in the suburbs with dad going to work and mom as homemaker, a suburban vision of domestic tranquility with conflicts that are easily resolved within the thirty-minute episode of a 1950's situation comedy. On the other hand, if we look at the family through an historical lens, we see a very different *tradition*, a tradition that included extended clan-based support groupings that involved not only parents and grandparents but also aunts, uncles, and cousins, some of whom were not even blood relations. According to Frances and Joseph Gies, the sociological concept of "family" is a relatively recent development in the history of humanity. In fact, no European language had a term specifically for the mother-father-children group before the eighteenth century.[1]

When we tell Bible stories, we often picture those ancient families through our modern lens of nuclear family; however, the historical reality is that biblical family was clan-based and culturally polygamous, with little to no divide between public and private life.[2] Why does this matter? It matters for the way we live as families in the twenty-first century, and it especially matters when we make statements such as, "God ordained the family as the basic institution through which God works in the world."[3] We must consider which paradigm of family God has ordained and desires to work through to bring light and life to the world. It might mean a much bigger family than the nuclear family. Throughout much of history, people in the church called one another *brother, sister, mother,* or *father,* even up to

1. Francis and Joseph Gies, *Marriage and Family in the Middle Ages* (New York: Harper & Row, 1987), 4.

2. Ibid.

3. Rodney Clapp addresses this idea in Rodney Clapp, *Families at the Crossroads: Beyond Traditional and Modern Options* (Downers Grove, IL: InterVarsity Press, 1993).

the mid-twentieth century.[4] So when we encounter Scripture passages such as Mark 3:34–35; Matthew 12:46–50; or John 19:26–27, we are left to wonder exactly what Jesus intended family to become.

What does this historical, extended "family" look like when we engage in family ministry in our churches? For one thing, it could mean that the church does not place all the expectations and guilt on the nuclear family, but rather creates a more intentional intergenerational ministry so that all ages are placed in community-shaping proximity to *family* one another. If we think of *family* as a verb instead of as a noun, might that influence the way we see the family's role in the spiritual formation of the church's children? Such a paradigm shift in ministry focus holds the potential for not only strengthening the *nuclear family* but also strengthening everyone in the church community as we begin to take seriously the role of *familying* one another.[5]

Given the fact that there are more single-person and single-parent households in our current cultural context than ever before in history, what would it mean to begin to shift our perception of the Christian family to include singles, widows, orphans, foster children, empty nesters, blended families, and multigenerational groupings? The term *family* has diverse implications today within an acceptable variety of family structures— kindred families and non-kindred families who live in shared households with a depth of intimacy of relationships and support. Perhaps one of the first shifts the church might make toward empowering families is to reenvision who is included. By putting all our family enrichment eggs in the nuclear family basket, the church narrows the scope of the foundational community children desperately need for nurturing spiritual growth. This shift would mean reimagining church within the sociological reality of family in our twenty-first century ethos and beginning to create space for a community of belonging within all generations by putting emphasis on the process of belonging to one another instead of developing more programs to meet the needs of the nuclear family.[6]

---

4. There are, of course, churches that still refer to one another with familial names; however, the larger and more institutional our churches become the less we recognize this sense of familial belonging and the more we diverge into a more *consumerist* paradigm.

5. For examples of *familying* used as a verb, see the holistic ministry of *Vibrantfaith.org* and *Lifelongfaith.com*.

6. For further study and resources toward intergenerational faith formation in the church, see:

ROADBLOCK #2: *Cultural Influencers*

C. Ellis Nelson writes, "Culture influences our beliefs and habits because it becomes a part of our life the day we are born. Unless our cultural values are challenged by an alternative way to live, they will influence what we think and do throughout our lives."[7] When the surrounding (external) culture has more influence on families than the church, we may need to consider ways to strengthen our internal culture. The term "culture" simply refers to the core values an identifiable people group shares with one another.[8] In order to understand culture—both external and internal—we begin this section by taking a brief look at the context of Western family going back a couple hundred years.

From the beginning of the 1800s until the mid-1900s, the primary influencer on culture (both external and internal) was the church; thus, the church could make pronouncements, and the culture paid attention. The church had an enormous impact on family, government, public schools, colleges and universities, and mass media. Society was an agency to teach the church's moral code. This moral code included what came to be termed "blue laws" (also known as "Sunday laws")—strictly enforced laws created to impose moral standards, restricting or outright banning many cultural activities on Sundays, so essentially, societally imposed Sabbath rest. At that time in history, the church served the surrounding culture as the primary influencer of sexual activity, including how we viewed marriage. Also, during this period of church-imposed values, most Christian parents were both motivated and competent to explain their faith to their children and to share their faith with other adults in community.[9]

By the last decade of the twentieth century, and even more so by the second decade of the twenty-first century, the patterns of influence in society turned upside down as the church and the family became privatized.

Holly C. Allen and Christine Ross, *Intergenerational Christian Formation: Bringing the Whole Church Together in Ministry, Community and Worship* (Downers Grove, IL: IVP, 2012). See also Trevecca Okholm, "The Gentle Art of Moving Your Church's Family Ministry from Programs to Process," in *Story, Formation, and Culture: From Theory to Practice in Ministry with Children*, eds. Benjamin D. Espinoza, et. al. (Eugene, OR: Wipf & Stock, 2018), 208-217.

7. C. Ellis Nelson, *Growing Up Christian: A Congregational Strategy for Nurturing Disciples* (Macon, GA: Smyth & Helwys, 2008), 7.

8. Diana Garland, *Family Ministry: A Comprehensive Guide, 2nd ed.* (Downers Grove, IL: IVP, 2012), 283.

9. Nelson, *Growing Up Christian*, 13.

With privatization, the church found itself able to exert very little influence over the culture and even over Christian families living in the culture. The good news is that this shift in cultural influencers gives those of us in the church family an opportunity to intentionally name and form an internal culture—an alternative way to live—and to be more vocal with families about how and why we do this.

ROADBLOCK #3: *When the Way the Church Does Ministry Unintentionally Divides Generations in the Family*

Over the past several decades, the church has convinced parents that the professionals can do a better job of forming their kids into Christians than they can, although research shows the role of parents is much more important.[10] Presently, it seems we are hard-pressed to reverse this belief.

Growing out of all the changes taking place mid-twentieth century, the church found itself in a more reactive mode as it lost its place as the primary influencer of the culture. In short, the church found itself in a position of either competing with the changing cultural values or, more often, accommodating those changes in order to hold onto the hearts and minds of all ages, particularly its youth. The church therefore took on a consumerist or marketing mode. This stands to reason, given the swift changes in cultural influencers taking place in mid-to late twentieth century. This caused the church to move toward a siloed model of ministry, focusing on developmentally appropriate age groupings. For example, starting soon after World War II, many churches moved toward a segmented, programmatic approach to ministry. In little more than two decades, this segmented-programmatic model became—at least in most people's perceptions—seen as "traditional."[11]

Beginning in the last couple of decades of the twentieth century, visionary church leaders began addressing the dangers of such approaches. Several ministry leaders at that time, used the phrase "octopus model" or

---

10. There are numerous studies that come to the conclusion that the primary influences on children's spiritual and emotional formation are their parents or other significant adults in their lives. For example, Lisa Miller, *The Spiritual Child: The New Science on Parenting for Health and Lifelong Thriving* (New York: Picador, 2015).

11. Timothy Paul Jones and Bryan Nelson, "The Problem and Promise of Family Ministry," *The Journal of Family Ministry* 1, no. 1 (2010): 36–43.

"octopus without a brain" to describe what was happening.[12] Instead of one unified ministry, the church had, in effect, separated the congregation into age and stage groupings that coexisted in the church with little impact across generations and interests.[13]

ROADBLOCK #4: *When Parents and Other Adults Are Not Confident in Their Own Faith Knowledge*

The final roadblock we address in this chapter[14] is the lack of basic biblical knowledge and spiritual practices among parents and other adults. There are various reasons why the church finds itself facing this crisis today; however, one primary cause relates closely to the previous three roadblocks. When the church began to accommodate the surrounding culture, a large part of that accommodation was the convenience of a one-hour commitment on Sunday mornings.[15] Instead of all ages engaging for two hours—education and worship—the church began to ask less. As Kang and Parrett point out, whatever the gains of a one-hour Sunday commitment, "this [movement] typically results in two significant losses: children [no longer] worshiping with their parents, and parents not being as well instructed as their children."[16]

To replace the regular offering of biblical education (e.g., Sunday school) for many adults, churches began to offer small groups. Kang and Parrett also note, "In some cases, this has resulted in a new teaching venue that is effective and is reaching a significant number of congregants. In many cases, however, the small group turns out to be a good setting for fostering fellowship and accountability, but not necessarily for substantive teaching of the essentials of the [Christian] faith, devolving into rather

---

12. For more on this model of ministry, see Chap Clark, *The Youth Worker's Handbook to Family Ministry* (Grand Rapids, MI: Zondervan, 1997), 24–25 and Timothy Paul Jones, *Perspectives on Family Ministry: 3 Views* (Nashville, TN: B&H Academic, 2009), 11.

13. Jones and Nelson, "The Problem and Promise of Family Ministry," 36–43.

14. In addition to the four discussed in this chapter, there may very well be other roadblocks standing in your way as your congregation seeks to equip and empower spiritual formation with families. Therefore, this last roadblock should not end your ministry evaluation on how best to equip and empower families in the spiritual formation of children.

15. For more on this late 20th/early 21st century phenomenon, see, for example: Andrew Root, *Faith Formation in a Secular Age* (Grand Rapids, MI: Baker, 2017).

16. Gary A. Parrett and S. Steve Kang, *Teaching the Faith, Forming the Faithful* (Downers Grove, IL: IVP 2012), 142.

uninformed and highly subjective 'sharing' about the Bible: 'So, what does this text mean to *you*?'"[17]

The existence of an undereducated set of adults matters for many reasons. For the purpose of this chapter, it matters because, when parents are considered to be the primary faith models and faith educators for their children yet those parents are ill-equipped in biblical knowledge, we are setting up families for failure.

BUILDING UP FAMILIES FOR EFFECTIVE SPIRITUAL FORMATION WITH CHILDREN

Let's now turn our attention to a few examples of spiritual practices for engaging, equipping, and empowering families in the home to live faithfully with children. None of these is a quick fix or program for the church to offer; instead, they are simply part of the process of moving our churches and families toward a more effective role in children's spiritual formation. Many families clearly need assistance to do the important task of spiritual formation. Those of us in ministry have a unique opportunity to support them, and here are some specific things we can do.

FAITH-FORMING PRACTICE #1:
Remembering the Stories to Which We Belong

A powerful way to live within the tension of the changing face of the Western family is to practice remembering and telling the story to which we belong. Andrew Peterson is often quoted as saying, "If you want someone to hear the truth, you should tell them the truth. But if you want someone to LOVE the truth, you should tell them a story.[18] The act of sharing our stories has the potential to shape the worldview, identity, and belonging within a particular community. Warren Cole Smith points out that "stories shape our imaginations—stories teach us what is true. If you

---

17. Ibid.
18. Warren Cole Smith, "C.S. Lewis, Madeleine L'Engle, and the Power of Storytelling," *The Rabbit Room* Podcast, November 29, 2018, https://rabbitroom.com/2018/11/c-s-lewis-madeline-lengle-and-the-power-of-storytelling/.

can control the stories a people see, hear, and tell each other, you can ultimately control what they think and even how they think."[19]

By telling the Bible as God's story, we are engaged in the realization that we belong to something bigger and deeper and older than the here and now. Our ancestors in faith have much to teach us about trusting God, and most of them did not belong to a traditional family by twentieth century standards. Michael Novelli reminds us that "all human communities live out some story that provides a context for understanding the meaning of history and gives shape and direction to their lives. If we allow the Bible to become fragmented, [our family] is in danger of being absorbed into whatever other story is shaping our culture, and the Scripture and heritage will thus cease to shape our lives as it should."[20]

When we read, for example, the Genesis account of God's covenant with Abraham and Sarah, we can remind our children that they are part of that covenant promise, a part of God's great family that is as numerous as stars in the night sky. What might this mean for the choices we make in life? What might this mean for our responsibility to one another and to God's created world? These are the sorts of questions that create space for our children to imagine who they are and to find their place in the story of God. Books such as Sally Lloyd-Jones' *Jesus Storybook Bible*[21] or Walter Wangerin's *Book of God*[22] give us these Bible stories written in ways that inspire us and invite us into God's story.

Along with our biblical story, sharing our own family stories also creates a way of belonging in family. Jerome Berryman, creator of Godly Play, shows the importance of this when he tells of his work as part of an interdisciplinary team caring for suicidal children and families.

What these families had in common was that they did not tell stories. They did not tell stories about vacations, funny things that happened, sad things, grandparents, births, deaths, pets, hopes, trips, dreams,

---

19. Ibid.

20. Michael Novelli, *Shaped by the Story: Helping Students Encounter God in a New Way* (Grand Rapids, MI: Zondervan, 2008).

21. Sally Lloyd-Jones, *The Jesus Storybook Bible: Every Story Whispers His Name* (Grand Rapids, MI: Zondervan, 2007).

22. Walter Wangerin, *The Book of God: The Bible as a Novel* (Grand Rapids, MI: Zondervan, 1996).

or any other tales I took for granted, since I had come from a storytelling family. Their communication was reduced to commands,
demands, exclamations, brief explanations, and questions requiring
short, factual answers. The family members were like neighboring
islands without any bridges. There was no narrative to connect them.
What was the treatment? We set up ways to encourage them to tell
stories face-to-face.[23]

It is a powerful thing to know that we belong to a story. Parents who
feel inadequate to share their faith testimony with their children often
find that reading or telling stories is more comfortable. When parents
are encouraged to follow up stories with imagining[24] and "wondering"
questions[25] (open-ended questions that promote conversation), much of the
task of being primary faith educators in the lives of their children is done!

FAITH-FORMING PRACTICE #2:
Creating Strong Internal Family Culture
When our internal culture becomes the forming center of our worldview, we are all better equipped to exist under the influence of values
espoused by the external culture. As we begin to see ourselves as multiple
generations of unique people in God's story who are enriched by regularly
practicing disciplines that connect and form us into the people God desires
us to be, we are better able to act as witnesses of an alternative way to live.

Our practices of corporate faith rituals, traditions, and rites of passage,[26]
as well as rituals and traditions practiced in our homes, have the potential
to invite us and our children into experiences of mystery and wonder.

---

23. Jerome Berryman, *Stories of God at Home* (New York: Church Publishing, 2018), 22.

24. For an example of using imagination in storytelling see: Jared Patrick Boyd, *Imaginative
Prayer: A Yearlong Guide for Your Child's Spiritual Formation* (Downers Grove, IL: IVP, 2017).

25. For an example of using wondering questions in storytelling, see: Trevecca Okholm, "An
Invitation to Worship & Wonder: An Overview of Contemplative Models of Spiritual Formation,"
in *Story, Formation, and Culture: From Theory to Practice in Ministry with Children*, eds. Benjamin D.
Espinoza, et. al. (Eugene, OR: Wipf & Stock, 2018), 65-75.

26. A *ritual* is an action or series of actions that express a belief (for example: the ritual of lighting
Advent Candles or kneeling to say our prayers or even where we sit around the table or in worship).
A *tradition* is the collective experience upon which a belief is based (for example, the experience of
celebrating Christ's birth on December 25, or following the liturgical seasons of the church year
calendar). A *rite of passage* marks a unique one-time experience of life such as being confirmed in
one's faith or receiving our third grade Bible in worship.

James K. A. Smith reminds us that "our ultimate love/desire is shaped by practices, not ideas that are merely communicated to us."[27] Practicing rituals together in community creates meaning in our lives together. It may be that through these intentional practices, adult Christians begin to engage deeper biblical and theological truths as they understand more about the importance of these rituals and, perhaps, learn why Christians do them. This way, parents will be better equipped to answer children's questions about these rituals.

Sometimes it is more a matter of learning to recognize and name those rituals and traditions in our everyday lives. Anglican priest and young mother Tish Harrison Warren, author of *Liturgy of the Ordinary*, takes the everyday, ordinary life of raising kids and shows how even the daily ritual of something as ordinary as brushing teeth can lead us to reflect together and recognize the rituals in daily life, as well as in our corporate rhythm of worship.[28] Every Christian family should be able to know, name, and articulate the habits and rituals that create a sense of awe, wonder, and reverence in them. We are people formed by rituals and traditions. If the church and the family fail to fill children's lives with "named" rituals, then the culture will readily step in to form them.[29]

FAITH-FORMING PRACTICE #3:
Practicing Reverence, Paying Attention, and Taking Detours

In *Reverence*, philosopher Paul Woodruff writes that reverence "is an ancient virtue that survives among us in half-forgotten patterns of civility, in moments of inarticulate awe, and in nostalgia for the lost ways of traditional cultures. We have the word 'reverence' in our language, but we scarcely know how to use it."[30] There are many possibilities for rekindling a sense of this lost virtue with our children. After all, reverence is a virtue,

---

27. James K. A. Smith, *Desiring the Kingdom: Worship, Worldview, and Cultural Formation* (Grand Rapids, MI: Baker Academic, 2009), 27.

28. Tish Warren Harrison, *Liturgy of the Ordinary: Sacred Practices in Everyday Life* (Downers Grove, IL: IVP, 2016).

29. To read about examples of rituals and traditions that form and strengthen our internal family culture, read (especially chapters 5 and 7) Trevecca Okholm, *Kingdom Family: Re-Envisioning God's Plan for Marriage and Family* (Eugene, OR: Cascade, 2012). See also: James K. A. Smith, "Redeeming Rituals: Penance Takes Practice," The Table: Biola CCT, July 4, 2014, www.youtube.com/watch?v=M5R2m221wMw.

30. Paul Woodruff, *Reverence: Renewing a Forgotten Virtue* (New York: Oxford University Press, 2014), 1.

and by their very nature, virtues grow in us through being used—through practice. Reverence develops when we make familiar habits out of our rituals and traditions. It can take place, for example, in our worshiping community when generations come together in awe of the majesty of a God who is treated not as our good friend who is there to bail us out, but rather as a God who is recognized as holy. Both our practices of corporate faith rituals, as well as intentional rituals and traditions practiced in our homes, have the potential to invite us and our children into the experience of reverence. While these practices are crucial, articulating to our children and ourselves what we are doing and why is an important step in helping these ideas to stay with us. Treating the space as special is important, and talking about doing it makes it clearer. Treating God as holy is vital. Making that clear to our children is, too. Harrison's book has helped me discover that reverence may be recognized and practiced in our daily lives if we are willing to pay attention to what treasures may be hiding in plain sight.

One summer day, after I retold the parable of the treasure hidden in the field to our four-year-old granddaughter, and the story was folded neatly back into our gold parable box,[31] she suggested it would be fun to go outside and dig for hidden treasure in our backyard. Thinking quickly, I responded, "Of course, but how about we dig with our eyes and hands and not with a shovel?" Off we went into our very tiny backyard in search of treasure. And what did we find? Tiny flowers hidden among the blades of grass and tiny insects that gave us lots to discuss about God's amazingly diverse creation. We found spiderwebs and lovely flat stones. We looked at butterflies and birds, which caused us to sit quietly for a while by the fountain and watch to see if any hummingbirds might come and bathe there. It turned out that it was not exactly the time of day for hummingbirds to bathe, so I suggested she wake me early in the morning and we would go out to watch for hummingbirds.

Around 6:00 a.m. the next day, I awoke to see two little eyes peering into my face at close range. Ah! Yes, now I remembered. So quietly I poured my necessary-for-treasure-hunting cup of coffee and we sat oh-so-quietly

---

31. For explanation of a gold parable box see Sonja Stewart and Jerome Berryman, *Young Children and Worship* (Louisville KY: Westminster John Knox, 1989). For parable of the treasure see Sally Lloyd-Jones, *The Jesus Storybook Bible: Every Story Whispers His Name* (Grand Rapids, MI: Zondervan, 2007), 250–255. See also: Matthew 13:44–46.

and waited. It was a magical moment—probably more so for me than for her—to sit reverently beside the fountain in the early summer morning while everyone else in the house was still asleep, watching and waiting for one of God's kingdom treasures, a tiny hummingbird, to appear. We were not disappointed. Several showed up, and we pondered anew the treasures of the kingdom hidden in a field—or, in this case, a suburban backyard.

Our lives together can easily become blurry when our focus is distracted. We really want to be the ideal family, but life and too many choices demand our attention. Too many good options and too many directions pull families apart. In a culture that puts value on consumerism, entertainment, and the proliferation of choice, distraction is inevitable, keeping us focused on the mundane of life and keeping our eyes off the extraordinary.

Seeking treasures and experiencing reverence does not just happen unless we are being intentional about paying attention and willing to take detours in our busy lives. In her book, *An Altar in the World*,[32] Barbara Brown Taylor gives the example of Moses and the burning bush. Moses was busy tending his father-in-law's sheep. As he was guiding the sheep down the trail, a flash of light caught his eye. He could have thought, "That's interesting. I should come back and check that out when I'm not so busy." Or he might have been so focused on his job that he walked by without even noticing. But the Scripture says Moses stopped, left his flock, and walked toward the burning bush where he encountered God (Ex. 3:1–17).

How many burning bushes have you and your children missed in your hurry to get from point A to point B? How many encounters with the living God? How many tiny flowers in the grass or hummingbirds bathing in the fountain? There are times when my granddaughters and I intentionally take detours and sometimes get lost. (I confess, I am more intentional with grandchildren than I was when my children were growing up. I guess grandchildren are a sort of do-over, a chance to recapture all the things we wish we'd done when our children were young.)

Paying attention and taking detours provides those family stories that so richly connect us to one another, providing us with "remember when . . ." opportunities for years to come. They are lessons in truth: the true worth of relationships, the true value of being intentionally unhurried. The demands

---

32. Barbara Brown Taylor, *An Altar in the World: A Geography of Faith* (New York: HarperOne, 2009), 24-25.

of daily life will always be there, piling on more and more, but moments of reverence and moments of getting lost and discovering treasures may easily remain undiscovered if we don't watch out for them.

As we read biblical stories together, we are often reminded of the gifts of taking detours and paying attention. As another example, the prophet Elijah took a long detour (see 1 Kings 19) when he trekked all the way south to Mt. Horeb and hung out in a cave having a pity party and waiting for the almighty God to show up. And God did show up, but not in the wind, nor the earthquake, nor the fire. God showed up in a still, small whisper. If Elijah had not been paying attention, he might have missed that whisper.

Stephen Covey, in his pivotal work, *The Seven Habits of Highly Effective People*, reminds us that as human beings, we have the ability to be proactive rather than always reacting to what life throws our way. He created a time management matrix,[33] divided into four quadrants, for situations that are: (1) urgent and also important (e.g., deadlines or emergencies); (2) urgent but not important (e.g., some meetings or some emails or TV shows); (3) important but not urgent (e.g., reading, exercise, relationship building, sharing faith with our children); and (4) not urgent and not important (e.g., social media posts when they become "escape" activities). Too often the quadrant that is most neglected is #3—opportunities that are important but not urgent. This is the quadrant in which taking detours usually falls.

For church communities, paying attention, taking detours, and experiencing reverence with our children and youth just might mean restructuring worship to include all generations in meaningful engagement and value-shaping rituals together. It might mean becoming more aware and intentional in encouraging or providing service and mission opportunities for families together. It might even mean being still and quiet and reflective together in community. You never know when you might encounter a burning bush, a hummingbird, or a still, small voice that makes all the difference.

---

33. Stephen Covey, *The Seven Habits of Highly Effective People* (New York: Simon & Schuster, 2013), 151.

CHAPTER 7

THE ROLE OF FAITH OR SPIRITUALITY IN A CHILD'S RESPONSE TO GRIEF AND LOSS

SHELLY MELIA

It was the phone call no one wants to get.

It was the last day of Vacation Bible School (and I was the children's minister at our church at the time) when I received word that my husband had been in an automobile accident. Just a few hours later, I became a young widow completely responsible for helping our six-, four-, and two-year-olds navigate through the pain of losing their father. During the twenty-minute drive home from the hospital, I prepared myself to tell my children their father had died. While I knew I needed to focus on the task at hand, my thoughts were consumed with how this tragic event would impact their young lives. Since I was also a licensed professional counselor, I knew all the statistics about children who grow up in fatherless homes. I knew they were going to face challenges I had never planned or imagined for their lives. While I had the book knowledge of how to talk to my children about death, no amount of education could have adequately prepared me for that moment. My prior learning and study *about* children and grief gave me a good theoretical foundation. The experience of going through grief *with* my children required me to translate theory into practice.

Shortly after my husband's death, I began journaling my experience of walking with my children through loss. One of my first journal entries expressed the worries I had about my children's view of God. I considered these two possible outcomes:

1. They will think God is unfair and does not care about their pain.
2. They will experience the love and comfort of God in such a powerful way that it makes them want to spend the rest of their lives following him.

While those two options were simplistic, polar opposites, and emotionally charged, I believed my children would be faced with a choice to either run to God or run away from God with their pain. In my role as a counselor, I had seen teenagers and adults struggle to reconcile a loving God with undeserved suffering. My fear was that they might grow to mistrust or even hate God as a result of this tragedy in their lives. My hope and earnest prayer was that my children's faith would help them be resilient in spite of this undeserved loss. While the concept of resilience was familiar to me, this life event pushed me to explore it in more depth and with great passion. Thus, I began the journey of trying to understand the relationship between the faith or spirituality of my children and how that might impact their capacity for resilience in their response to the death of their father.

DEFINING IMPORTANT THEORETICAL CONCEPTS

The purpose of this book is to bridge the gap between theory and practice. To build this bridge, careful attention must be paid to key theoretical concepts. I will outline a basic understanding of resilience, protective factors, and spirituality in children in order to set the stage for understanding how a child's spirituality impacts his or her response to grief and loss.

Resilience can be defined as the ability to bounce back from hardships and difficulties in life. In children, this means they are able to continue to reach developmental milestones even in the face of significant adversity and stress.[1] While resilience is a psychological construct, it also has significant theological foundations. Resilience speaks to the hope and assurance found in Romans 8:28: "And we know that in all things God works for the good of those who love him, who have been called according to his purpose." Wayne Grudem puts it this way: "God uses all things to fulfill His purpose and even uses evil for His glory and our good."[2]

The Bible is full of references and stories indicating Christians will have trials, pain, and suffering. Job 5:7 says, "Yet man is born to trouble as surely as sparks fly upward." Nahum 1:7 asserts, "The LORD is good, a refuge in times of trouble." In the New Testament, Jesus speaks this truth to his disciples in John 16:33: "I have told you these things, so that in me you may have peace. In this world you will have trouble. But take heart! I have overcome the world." The apostle Paul, in his second letter to the Corinthians, illustrates further that a relationship with God does not exempt a person from suffering, struggle, or pain. In fact, Paul uses the thorn in his flesh to illustrate the sufficiency of God's grace in any situation: "That is why, for Christ's sake, I delight in weaknesses, in insults, in hardships, in persecutions, in difficulties. For when I am weak, then I am strong" (2 Cor. 12:10).

Once the normalcy and expectation of suffering has been established, important questions surface. Why are some children resilient while others are not? What can be learned from children who are resilient? The research is still in its infancy. However, there is agreement about the importance of protective factors in the lives of children. A protective factor is something that serves as a buffer or resource for the child while working through hardships and difficulties. One way to flesh out this concept is to think of protective factors as the panes of an umbrella. An umbrella provides protection from the rain. In the same way, the presence of protective factors in a child's life may provide protection from the effects of a stressful event or traumatic event.

In labeling the protective factors as the panes of an umbrella, these five categories emerge:

---

1. Jack A. Naglieri and Paul A. LeBuffee, *Measuring Resilience in Children: From Theory to Practice* (New York: Springer, 2006), 108.
2. Wayne Grudem, *Systematic Theology: An Introduction to Biblical Doctrine* (Grand Rapids, MI: Zondervan, 1994), 327.

1. INTERNAL ASSETS: Temperament, intelligence, ability to problem solve, and self-regulation all contribute to capacity for resilience.
2. EXTERNAL RESOURCES: Resources that exist outside of the child such as schools, communities, and neighborhoods often provide a caring and supportive structure that promotes resilience.
3. FAMILY DYNAMICS: The way a family functions impacts a child's ability to produce resilience. Consistent care and support during infancy and childhood helps support an appropriate level of cohesion that enables children to view life as manageable and meaningful.[3]
4. RELATIONSHIPS AND CONNECTIONS: Relationships provide a sense of belonging and attachment that can serve as a buffer against difficulty. Resilience is impacted by how well children are connected and how well they relate to others.
5. FAITH OR SPIRITUALITY: The beliefs, behaviors, and relationships that exist within the context of faith or spirituality serve as an important protective factor in the lives of children.

The protective factor of faith or spirituality is the least understood and most understudied of the five factors. Both religious and non-religious researchers agree that faith or spirituality is an important part of the umbrella; they just do not know how to define it or measure it.

---

3. Abraham P. Greeff and Berquin Human, "Resilience in Families in which a Parent Has Died," *The American Journal of Family Therapy* 32, (2004): 29.

A simple definition of spirituality is "God's ways of being with children and children's ways of being with God."[4] Annette Jerome defines it this way: "Spirituality is the inner expression of an individual's most fundamental belief system."[5] For the purposes of this chapter, spirituality will be defined cohesively as a broad array of beliefs, behaviors, and relationships that exist as a result of an emphasis on relating with and to God. In this sense, faith or spirituality is not based solely upon conversion or spiritual regeneration. Rather, it also includes the rituals and relationships that occur as a result of valuing and desiring a relationship with God. In this definition, there is an intentional acknowledgement of the benefit children receive from the faith communities they are a part of, regardless of their age or level of spiritual formation. My children were very young in their faith development and had not yet made individual professions of faith when their father died, yet the faith community played a critical role in their ability to work through his death. They *experienced* God through the comforting rituals and loving relationships with people who chose to be the hands and feet of Christ to our family.

Unfortunately, not all children experience the benefit of their faith or spirituality as an effective protective factor. Erik Erikson recognized both the potential for good and for harm when he noted, "[T]rust born of care is, in fact, the touchstone of the actuality of a given religion."[6] Conversely, he states, "there are many who profess faith, yet in practice breathe mistrust both of life and man."[7] Froma Walsh further emphasizes that there must be congruence between beliefs and behaviors in order for spirituality to positively contribute to resilience.[8]

PRACTICAL APPLICATION

How can parents, ministers, counselors, and teachers help children utilize their faith or spirituality as a protective factor during grief and loss? Let's relate this back to the umbrella illustration: in order for an umbrella

---

4. Rebecca Nye, *Children's Spirituality: What it is and Why it Matters* (London: Church House Publishing, 2009), 5.

5. Annette Jerome, "Comforting Children and Families who Grieve: Incorporating Spiritual Support," *School Psychology International* 32, no. 2 (2011): 32.

6. Erik H. Erikson, *Childhood and Society* (New York: W.W. Norton & Company, 1963), 250.

7. Ibid., 251.

8. Froma Walsh, *Strengthening Family Resilience*, 2nd ed. (New York: The Guilford Press, 2006), 72.

to provide protection in a storm, it must be used appropriately. A big, beautiful umbrella is of no use unless it is taken out and opened. In the same way, children may have strengths in several protective factors (internal assets, external resources, family dynamics, relationships and connections, and faith or spirituality) and still be unable to demonstrate resilience when faced with grief and loss. In effect, children must learn to use what they have in order to navigate through grief and loss. While some children may instinctually know how to use their umbrella of protection, most need the guidance and support of loving adults.

BELIEFS, BEHAVIORS, AND RELATIONSHIPS

The faith or spirituality of a child centers around three important elements: beliefs, behaviors, and relationships. Each one of these has the potential to play an important role in providing comfort, strength, and support for a child experiencing grief and loss. The focus of this chapter will now shift to expounding upon each of the elements in greater detail. Special consideration will be given to how child development impacts the experience.

BELIEFS

Beliefs are the most difficult to describe and delineate. Since children are in a constant state of holistic development, their beliefs are often difficult to articulate and measure. Most adults struggle to remember what it is like to think like a child. It is important to remember that children process information according to their cognitive development. In 1 Corinthians 13:11, the apostle Paul confirms this concept: "When I was a child, I talked like a child, I thought like a child, I reasoned like a child." Another verse often quoted to support the holistic development of children relates to a description of the boy Jesus, found in Luke 2:52: "And Jesus grew in wisdom and stature, and in favor with God and man."

Both development and experience impact the beliefs of each child. Jean Piaget's work provides the framework for determining where each child is in his or her cognitive development. He emphasized the way children take in new information and build upon previously understood concepts. In this sense, development drives how each new experience is woven into previous and current mental structures.[9] This process is complicated by the fact that young children often do not have prior experiences with death.

Like adults, the beliefs of children generally center on two recurring themes: hope and meaning. Children often express hope through their belief that God is trustworthy, loving, and in control. Also like adults, children want and need to make meaning of their loss. However, the difference between adults and children lies in *how* and *when* they are able to make meaning of their loss.[10]

For children, making meaning of loss becomes a lifelong journey. The reason for this is based on the understanding that children grieve in bits and pieces. This is why children may have moments of sadness but also continue to laugh and play with other children who may be present during the first few days and weeks after the loss. As a result, children often provide much needed levity and perspective during times when adults are most focused on their own grief. Children may not immediately and intensely grieve the effect of the loss because they are unable to understand the full impact of the finality of death. At each age and stage, children will understand their loss in new and deeper ways. Likewise, they will make or revise meaning based on what they come to understand at each developmental milestone.

My daughter was four years old when her father died. Our church had a father-daughter Valentine banquet each year. For nine years after his death, a good friend took her to the Valentine banquet and treated her like his own daughter. She always looked forward to going and never indicated it was difficult for her emotionally. However, when she turned thirteen, things changed. She began to understand the loss at a much deeper level as a typically developmental adolescent.

She came home from the banquet and burst into tears. She was heartbroken as she explained that the speaker at the banquet had focused on the importance of the father in a little girl's life. He had emphasized statistics about girls who grow up without a father and challenged the fathers in the room to step up and love their daughters so that their daughters would make good choices and not turn out like the statistics he had quoted. In between

---

9. Kim Pond, "A Study of Childhood Grief and the Church's Response," *Christian Education Journal* 9, no. 1 (2012): 35.

10. Catherine R. Andrews and Sylvia A. Marotta, "Spirituality and Coping among Grieving Children: A Preliminary Study," *Counseling and Values* 50, (October, 2005): 38.

sobs she said, "I don't have a dad to do all those things . . . and I am not going to be OK." She grieved harder that night than she had during any other time during the journey of losing her father. She understood the loss and pain at a new level because the words of the speaker revealed a potential deficit in her life that she had never considered. Her beliefs about God were challenged, and she had to make new meaning about the loss in her life.

This revision in her beliefs and meaning did not happen overnight. She needed space to grieve and freedom to revisit the loss. When children experience grief and loss at an early age, they may have triggers or significant life events that bring their grief back to the forefront for a period of time. Children and teens should not be discouraged from exploring and grieving the loss at each new age and stage. Adults often fail to understand the importance and value of the process of grief by describing individuals as "lacking" faith or being "stuck" in their grief when they revisit the loss. After many emotional conversations, my daughter found comfort and meaning in Psalm 68:5: "A father to the fatherless, a defender of widows, is God in his holy dwelling." She reconciled her crisis of belief about her future with the assurance that God would be the One to fill in those gaps. Three years later, she chose, on her own, to have the reference "Psalm 68:5" made into a patch to be worn on her letter jacket. The patch represented the new meaning she made of her loss. As a result of her painful experience at the Valentine banquet, her beliefs about God were revised to include a new understanding of God as her father.

BEHAVIORS

The second element of a child's faith or spirituality involves behaviors. Fortunately, behaviors tend to be more concrete and easier to measure than beliefs. Behaviors related to a child's faith or spirituality include prayer, church attendance, Bible study, and participation in religious rituals such as worship and church ordinances. It is important to understand that behaviors linked to spirituality have the potential for both comfort and distress. The role of a caring adult is to help children recognize and reconcile the distress they may experience while also encouraging and supporting those behaviors that bring comfort.

Grief often disorients spiritually mature adults in their belief systems. For example, songs that were sung during worship prior to the loss may have just been words on a screen that were sung easily and freely. After the loss, a new sensitivity may make the words painful and confusing. For example, an individual may wonder, *If God is really a "good, good father"* (as the popular Chris Tomlin worship song states) *then why did he let this happen to me?* As a result, it may be harder to worship. If adults experience this and have difficulty articulating and managing the distress, children have an even greater challenge.

For children, the struggle might involve anger and confusion toward themselves, which makes relating to a God who let something sad happen in their lives extremely difficult. Most notably, children are egocentric, with a tendency to make everything about them. Similarly to children whose parents divorce, they may come to the conclusion that if they had behaved a certain way, they could have prevented the loss. They may place undue blame and shame on themselves. They may also think God is mad at them or that they did something to cause the person they love to die. As a result, participation in anything related to their spirituality may be extremely difficult and emotionally overwhelming. A wise and caring adult will watch for signs of distress and help the child recognize why things that were not painful before are now hard to manage.

Researchers have noted the positive effects of behaviors related to a child's faith or spirituality. In particular, prayer has been shown to be an important expression of a child's spirituality during times of crisis. Gunnestad and Thwala, in their study of orphans in South Africa, found that most of the children in their study reported that prayer is an important coping mechanism during times of grief.[11] Prayer offers children the opportunity to connect with God and express their need for comfort and protection.

Church attendance can also have a positive impact on children experiencing grief and loss. The rituals and routines can provide comfort and stability during a time when everything else in their lives is chaotic and unpredictable. Children should be integrated into the important rituals of their faith community. They need to see adults modeling the use of faith or spirituality in order to learn how to make meaning of their loss. This is one of the reasons many experts in children's ministry are concerned about the increased amount of age segregation in modern church life. Children need more than just their peers at church in order to get through hard

---

11. Arve Gunnestad and S'lungile Thwala, "Resilience and Religion in Children and Youth in Southern Africa," *International Journal of Children's Spirituality* 16, no. 2 (2011): 176.

times. They need to hear stories of people who have gone before them so that they can begin to develop their own theology of suffering.

Finally, and perhaps most importantly, Bible study provides children with the potential for using faith or spirituality as an important protective factor. The Bible is full of stories about suffering, grief, and loss. The most noted example is Job. Job goes through undeserved suffering and comes out on the other side a resilient and blessed man. The process to get through his suffering is messy, painful, confusing, and emotional. However, in the end, God gives Job his presence and blessing. This gift of presence sustains and propels Job to find meaning and grace in the midst of his grief and loss. Children need to hear stories from the Bible about suffering. They also need to memorize verses that will provide comfort during hard times. Churches that prepare children for suffering will produce children who can use their faith or spirituality to move towards resilience.

RELATIONSHIPS

Relationships have an important impact on children's ability to use their faith or spirituality in response to grief and loss. The most fundamental relationship that faith or spirituality offers is a relationship with God. This ultimate attachment relationship with God is described in the scriptures where: God says, "Never will I leave you: never will I forsake you" (Deut. 31:6); and when the Psalmist cries out, "The Lord is with me; I will not be afraid. What can mere mortals do to me?" (Ps. 118:6). For the purposes of this chapter, it is important to remember that the spiritual formation of children is difficult to pinpoint in terms of their personal relationship with God. Thus, the benefit of faith or spirituality extends beyond just those children who have made a personal profession of faith.

In addition to a relationship with God, faith or spirituality often provides children access to significant relationships within their faith community. In early childhood, children experience the benefits of faith or spirituality primarily through its effects on their parents and families. For example, during times of grief and loss, relationships with people in the faith community can be a source of support through meals, visits, prayer, financial assistance, and childcare.[12] In effect, faith communities provide

---

12. Gunnestad and Thwala, "Resilience and Religion in Children and Youth in Southern Africa," 178.

a powerful network of relationships that children and families can access during times of difficulty and distress. These relationships provide a unique form of support that can serve as a tangible expression and reminder of God's presence and comfort.

The relationship component of faith or spirituality continues to be the anchoring memory for my children when they describe the experience of losing their father. They remember very little about the words I used to explain the death of their father, nor do they remember what other people did or did not say to them. When asked about their most vivid memory related to the death of their father, they all three say the same thing: they remember how many people from our church helped us. They remember the experience of being loved and comforted in countless tangible ways.

How did that become their most vivid memory and the anchoring point for their experience? The answer is a reflection of the fact that children are concrete, literal thinkers who rely on experiences to shape their understanding of abstract concepts related to faith and spirituality. Scripture provides the model for this. The children of Israel were instructed to place stones of remembrance for generations who would follow so they would know that, just as God had protected and provided for them, he would do the same for future generations.

How can we create or provide experiences for children who are facing grief and loss that will serve to bolster their faith or spirituality? There are likely many ways to do this, and this simple example is not meant to limit your thinking about the endless ways it could occur. However, perhaps it will be helpful in illustrating the value of relationships in the faith community.

I had been on staff at my church for nine years when my husband died. Our roots there were deep, and the church had celebrated with us through the births of our three children and numerous other major life events. When my husband died, we were overwhelmed by the acts of kindness we experienced. People brought us meals for over a year, paid for the funeral, mowed our lawn for several months, paid for someone to clean our house for the first year, made repairs around the house, started an education fund for my children, washed and detailed my car—the list could go on and on. One of my prayers from my journal was that my children would experience the love and comfort of God in such a powerful way that they would want to run *to* God rather than run *away* from God with their pain. One way to influence their response to the pain was to be intentional in teaching them to look for God's presence in the practical ways he was helping our family. I tried to do this by connecting what people did for us with God's presence and provision. Every time someone did something kind for us, I would ask them the same question: "Do you know why they did that?" At first, they did not know the answer. I would then tell them, "The reason they did that for us was because they love God and they love us, and that is what you do when people are hurting." Over and over and over again, this scenario played out. In time, they were able to answer my question with a response that indicated they understood God was using people (relationships) to help us.

Understanding the role of faith or spirituality in a child's response to grief and loss is vitally important in ministering to children in our care. While this is just one of the panes of the umbrella, it can make a huge difference in a child's capacity for resilience. Consider the following practical suggestions for supporting children who are experiencing grief and loss.

WAYS TO SUPPORT AND NURTURE THE BELIEFS, BEHAVIORS, AND RELATIONSHIPS OF GRIEVING CHILDREN

- Respond to questions honestly and age-appropriately.
- Ask open-ended questions in order to more fully understand their experience. Assure them nothing they did caused the death.
- Talk about characters in the Bible who experienced God's comfort during difficult times.
- Recall and retell stories of God's comfort and healing in the past.
- Answer each question every time it is asked as if it is the first time it has been asked. Children often become repetitive in their questions about grief and loss. They are trying to make sense of information they do not yet fully understand. Repetition is necessary in order to understand and master abstract concepts.
- Expect, encourage, and embrace revisions in beliefs and meaning. This allows the depth of understanding of God to change as the

child develops and experiences the loss in increasingly profound and complex ways.

- Normalize suffering and struggle. Throughout their lifetimes, children will have many opportunities to utilize their beliefs in response to difficulties. Help them to know they are never alone in their struggle.
- Include children in the rituals of your faith community. Pass on the faith by creating ministries that rely on intergenerational relationships.
- Mobilize the people with whom they have relationships to minister to them in tangible ways after the loss. Include children in ministering to their peers in age-appropriate ways.
- Teach children to look for God in times of grief and loss. Emphasize how God uses people to minister to us when we are hurting.

CHAPTER 8

RESILIENCE, TRAUMA, AND CHILDREN'S SPIRITUALITY

HOLLY CATTERTON ALLEN
WITH KAYLEE FRANK AND MEGAN LARRY

—————|||—————

Carlos[1] is one of the children who survived the Sandy Hook Elementary School shooting in 2012. The shooter, Adam Lanza, entered Carlos's classroom, looked around, then shot the teacher and a six-year-old girl. While Lanza was reloading, Carlos and other children ran out of the classroom, past the bodies of their principal and others in the hall. Carlos heard many of the 156 shots fired by Lanza. Since that time, Carlos has had recurring nightmares; he asks about his friends who were killed, and he asks why this happened.[2]

When Chloe was ten, she was diagnosed with a brain tumor. For the next two years, her life and her family's life centered on her medical care and recovery. Chloe had multiple surgeries (some of which were life-or-death situations) and was in the hospital fifteen times. Chloe has been in and out of school; her head was shaved for two of the surgeries, and the medications have caused her to gain weight. These medical situations have yielded some name-calling and bullying from schoolmates. Chloe has asked her mom why God would allow this.

---

1. Carlos is a pseudonym.
2. "Parents reveal the terrible nightmares of Sandy Hook survivors," *Daily Mail*, September 29, 2013, http://www.dailymail.co.uk/news/article-2437438/CHILDREN-survived-Sandy-Hook -massacre-LIVE-IN-TERROR-endure-frequent-nightmares.html.

Eshal is nine years old and is one of five children in her family. Three years ago, her family was forced to flee from their home country, the Democratic Republic of Congo, and relocate. Since settling in Nashville, Eshal has been grieving the grandparents her family left behind in her home country; she misses them every day. Eshal has also had to learn English, which has caused her to struggle academically and socially at school. Like many refugee children, Eshal has exhibited signs of emotional fragility, fearfulness, and aggression.

Children around the world experience situations similar to those Carlos, Chloe, and Eshal have faced. In recent memory, children have survived population-wide traumas such as the southeast Asia tsunami of 2004, Hurricane Katrina in 2005, and the earthquake in Haiti in 2010. Children and their parents who live in war zones such as Aleppo, Syria, have suffered the terror of bombs and gunfire along with waning food supplies, scarce medical care, and the injury and death of relatives. Children in Syria and other conflicted areas have become refugees surviving in short-or long-term refugee camps, again enduring food shortages, lack of medical care, poor shelter, and the distress of an unknown future. Other children have survived long-term personal or family traumas such as living with physical or sexual abuse, with parental addictions or mental illness, or in chronically violent neighborhoods.

While some children come through such traumatic circumstances, overcoming even severe adversity remarkably well, other children remain fragile into adulthood. Current research is examining factors that can encourage resilience in children who have faced long-term adversity in their lives, ranging from homelessness and generational poverty to the ravages of war, terrorism, and disaster. A current book, Ann Masten's *Ordinary Magic: Resilience in Development*,[3] summarizes and synthesizes key research on resilience in children and adolescents.

In her decades of research, Masten has constructed a list of ten "protective" factors associated with resilience in young people, along with associated adaptive systems that can foster these resilience factors[4]:

---

3. Ann S. Masten, *Ordinary Magic: Resilience in Development* (New York: Guilford Press, 2015).

4. Masten, *Ordinary Magic: Resilience in Development*, 148; Emily Crawford, Margaret O'Dougherty Wright, and Anne S. Masten, "Resilience and Spirituality in Youth," in *The Handbook of Spiritual*

Ten protective factors:	Basic human adaptive systems:
• capable parenting • close relationships • intelligence; problem-solving skills • self-control • motivation to succeed • self-confidence, self-efficacy • faith, hope, and belief that life has meaning • effective schools • effective neighborhoods • effective cultural practices	• attachment relationships; family systems • attachment; social networks • a functioning central nervous system • neurocognitive control systems • mastery motivation and reward systems • religion and spirituality • education systems • functioning community systems • thriving culture

Shelly Melia, a licensed professional counselor specializing in grief and trauma, has recently telescoped the protective factors discussed by Masten and other resiliency experts into five categories.[5] You can read some of Melia's work in another chapter in this book. Most relevant to this chapter's focus is the protective factor Masten describes as *faith, hope, and the belief that life has meaning* with spiritual and religious belief systems as the adaptive systems that promote faith, hope, and belief (emphasis ours).[6] Melia's term is faith/spirituality.

Much research supports the idea that this basic construct—including faith, hope, and religious belief systems—promotes resilience in children encountering hardship. For example, in their study with one at-risk population, Nesmith and Ruhland connect *religiosity* to resilience, noting that church and faith were important to many of the children in their study: "church offered an immediate support group while their faith helped them feel that their struggles had a deeper meaning."[7] Prayer played a role as well: "I pray," said one interviewee. "I have to talk sometimes and I say a prayer

Development in Childhood and Adolescence, ed. Eugene. C. Roehlkepartain, et al. (Thousand Oaks, CA: Sage, 2006), 356–357.

    5. Shelly Melia, "The Role of Spirituality in Resilience," paper presentation at Children's Spirituality Summit, Nashville TN, June 26, 2018.

    6. Crawford, et al., "Resilience and Spirituality in Youth."

    7. Andrea Nesmith and Ebony Ruhland, "Children of Incarcerated Parents: Challenges and Resiliency, in Their Own Words," *Children and Youth Services Review* 30, no. 10 (2008): 1127. doi:10.1016/j.childyouth.2008.02.006.

and it just goes away. . . ."[8] And the authors of the chapter "Resilience and Spirituality in Youth" indicate that multiple studies of resilience report faith and *spiritual support* as protective factors in children and youth who face overwhelming adversity.[9]

Resilience research connects religiosity, faith, hope, belief, church attendance, prayer, and spiritual support to resilience in children recovering from trauma. Therefore, organizations or individuals who work with these children will recognize that not only must the physical and psychological needs of these children be met, but their spiritual needs should be addressed as well. Nurturing their relationships with themselves, others, the world, and God (as the child understands God) can be a profound part of the healing for these traumatized children. This chapter will offer specific ways to address the spiritual needs and fears of this fragile population.

DEFINITIONS

RESILIENCE

In her recent comprehensive summary of resilience theory and research, Masten explains that for a person or family to be described as exhibiting resilience, two things must be present:

- "challenges (risks, stressors, or adversities) confronting the child or family [that pose] a significant threat to their well-being or function, and
- positive adaptation typically judged by indicators of good function or competence."[10]

In this chapter, we will use Masten's well-considered definition of resilience: "positive patterns of adaptation or development manifested by individuals who have experienced a heavy burden of risky or adverse conditions."[11] In other words, if persons who have suffered significant

---

8. Ibid.

9. Crawford, et al., "Resilience and Spirituality in Youth."

10. Ann Masten, "Resilience Theory and Research on Children and Families: Past, Present, and Promise," *Journal of Family Theory & Review* 10, (March 2018): 12–31. doi:10.1111/jftr.12255.v

11. Crawford et al., "Resilience and Spirituality in Youth," 356.

adversity are later said to be managing *well enough* the developmental tasks that are typical for their age in their context, they are said to be resilient. Typical developmental tasks for children would be doing well in school, getting along with other children, and following the behavioral rules of their society in general.[12] Conversely, problematic development could be reflected in poor performance in school, aggressive behaviors toward other children, social withdrawal patterns, mental disorders such as depression, and violent or other antisocial behavior in general.

SPIRITUALITY AND RELIGION

Both spirituality and religion can play a central role in the lives of children. In this chapter, children's spirituality will be defined as a quality present in every child from birth, out of which children seek to establish relationships with the self, others, the world, and God (as they understand God).[13]

Religion is generally understood to be a cultural system of beliefs, attitudes, and practices that interconnects humankind with the supernatural or transcendent. Though religion and spirituality are often used interchangeably, they are not synonymous, nor are they mutually exclusive. Religion is often infused with spirituality, though it can exist without it. Conversely, many persons view themselves as spiritual but have no specific religious affiliation. Frequently, spirituality and religion intersect and overlap.

We focus primarily on connections between spirituality (rather than religion) and resilience. However, in the literature, religion and spirituality are sometimes conflated. Thus, some of the resilience findings are related to both religious practices and spirituality. This chapter explores what is known about spiritually supporting children who have experienced sustained traumas such as those described in the introduction. Common behaviors of children who have experienced sustained trauma can be oversensitivity, manipulation, aggression, bullying, disobedience, self-comforting, indiscriminate friendliness, lack of attachment, and over-compliance.[14]

---

12. Ibid.
13. This is a definition my students and I have constructed over the past decade built primarily around David Hay and Rebecca Nye's definition in *Spirit of the Child* (London: Jessica Kingsley, 2006) and Barbara Kimes Myers definition in *Young Children and Spirituality* (New York: Routledge, 1997).
14. Thema Bryant-Davis, Monica U. Ellis, Elizabeth Burke-Maynard, Nathan Moon, Pamela

These children experience grief, fear, confusion, shame, anxiety, anger, depression, sadness, and self-blame.[15] They need safety, hope, security, structure, boundaries, compassion, and respect.[16] They also often need assistance in making meaning of their experiences, in revisiting and possibly adjusting their understanding of God, and in dealing with forgiveness.[17]

HOW SPIRITUALITY CAN BE
A PROTECTIVE FACTOR

In the 1980s, early resilience researchers noted a connection between religion, faith, or spirituality and good outcomes in those who had experienced negative life circumstances. More recent research is attempting to establish how and why religious or spiritual resources may contribute to resilience in those who have suffered trauma.[18]

Crawford, Wright, and Masten offer a rich discussion on the ways religion or spirituality might operate in resilience in their chapter on resilience and spirituality in the internationally recognized 2006 text, *The Handbook of Spirituality Development in Childhood and Adolescence*.[19] They describe twenty-seven different processes, some of which are explicitly religious. For example, when a family loses a child, the family's religious community usually offers much social support in the form of prayers for the family, visits, counseling, bringing food, and death and burial rituals. Other processes could be considered more specifically *spiritual* (though not exclusively so), such as possessing a relationship with a benevolent, loving

A. Counts, and Gera Anderson, "Religiosity, Spirituality, and Trauma Recovery in the Lives of Children and Adolescents," *Professional Psychology: Research and Practice* 43, no. 4 (2012): 306–314; Crawford et al., "Resilience and Spirituality in Youth"; Nathan Chiroma, "Providing Mentoring for Orphans and Vulnerable Children in Internally Displaced Person Camps: The Case of Northern Nigeria," *HTS Teologiese Studies/ Theological Studies* 72 (October, 2016): doi.org/10.4102/hts.v72i1.3544; James Garbarino and Claire Bedard, "Spiritual Challenges to Children Facing Violent Trauma," *Childhood* 3, no. 4 (1996): 467–478; Francis Grossman, Lynn Sorsoli, and Maryam Kia-Kealing, "A Gale Force Wind: Meaning Making by Male Survivors of Childhood Sexual Abuse," *American Journal of Orthopsychiatry* 76 (2006): 434–443. Masten, *Ordinary Magic: Resilience in Development*.

15. Ibid.
16. Ibid.
17. Grossman et al., "A Gale Force Wind: Meaning Making by Male Survivors of Childhood Sexual Abuse."
18. Crawford et al., "Resilience and Spirituality in Youth."
19. Ibid.

spiritual being; practicing such virtues as forgiveness, hope, and persever-ance; and making meaning of loss and trauma. Let's look at these in turn.

POSSESSING A RELATIONSHIP WITH A BENEVOLENT, LOVING SPIRITUAL BEING

Having a relationship with God can help children thrive in ordinary as well as difficult circumstances. It can also reduce stress and promote positive coping strategies in children.[20]

When questioned about how he copes, one child whose dad is in prison said, "I pray. It helps me calm down."[21] Research shows that believing in a benevolent, loving higher power can be a source of strength to children (and adults) as they face adversity. A belief that this higher power can effect change in one's circumstances, and can uphold and sustain one can "provide a profound sense of security and well-being."[22]

PRACTICING SUCH VIRTUES AS FORGIVENESS, HOPE, AND PERSEVERANCE

Children who have been trafficked or who have been used as child soldiers—among the most traumatic situations possible—face a difficult recovery, one aspect of which is forgiveness. As one former child soldier said, "Papa God, please forgive me. I did not want to do it. They made me do it."[23] These children desperately need to know that God forgives them before they can begin the process of forgiving themselves and the subsequent process of forgiving those who have used and abused them.

Self-blame is common in children from many difficult circumstances,[24] for example, in children who have been sexually abused and children whose families have been killed. These children can be taught that they are not

---

20. Mark D. Holder, Ben Coleman, and Judi M. Wallace, "Spirituality, Religiousness, and Happiness in Children Aged 8–12 Years," *Journal of Happiness Studies* 11 (2010): 131–150; Nesmith and Ruhland, "Children of Incarcerated Parents."

21. Nesmith and Ruhland, "Children of Incarcerated Parents: Challenges and Resiliency, in Their Own Words,"1127.

22. Crawford et al., "Resilience and Spirituality in Youth," 357.

23. Stephanie Goins, "The Place of Forgiveness in the Reintegration of Child Soldiers in Sierra Leone," in *Nurturing Children's Spirituality: Christian Perspectives and Best Practices* ed. Holly C. Allen (Eugene, OR: Cascade, 2008) 297.

24. Grossman et al., "A Gale Force Wind: Meaning Making by Male Survivors of Childhood Sexual Abuse."

to blame, though indeed it may take years for them to *feel* that they did not cause the losses they have endured.

Sometimes children have misunderstandings about forgiveness. For example, they may think that forgiving the offender means pretending what happened didn't matter or that it was actually helpful. Sometimes they think they must forgive so the offender feels better. And sometimes they believe they are required to *immediately* forgive those who wounded them or their families.[25]

Those who support children who have been hurt by others can teach about forgiveness, helping the child see that forgiving the offender will help the child begin to heal. They can help the child see that forgiveness is a process—not an immediate requirement for going forward; they can help them see that a little progress is good, and that fuller forgiveness may eventually come.[26] One way children can know they are beginning to forgive is when they realize they no longer want revenge.

MAKING MEANING OF LOSS AND TRAUMA

Trauma is a tremendous challenge to anyone's understanding of the meaning and purpose of life, but especially to children.[27] Well-known children's spirituality researcher Robert Coles says, "children try to understand not only *what* is happening to them but *why*; and in doing that, they call upon the religious life they have experienced, the spiritual values they have received, as well as other sources of potential explanation."[28] When children believe in an all-benevolent higher power who exists to protect them, experiencing a personal, family, or population-wide trauma can cause cognitive, or perhaps we should say *spiritual*, dissonance.[29] The cognitive skills adults use to make sense of the world are less developed in children, and they have limited experience making meaning of the world at all. Children are typically more likely than adults to develop PTSD following a traumatic event.[30]

---

25. Bryant-Davis et al., "Religiosity, Spirituality, and Trauma Recovery in the Lives of Children and Adolescents."

26. Ibid.

27. Garbarino and Bedard, "Spiritual Challenges to Children Facing Violent Trauma," 470.

28. Robert Coles, *The Spiritual Life of Children* (Boston, MA: Houghton Mifflin, 1990), 100.

29. Ibid., 470–471.

30. Jonathan Davidson and Rebecca Smith, "Traumatic Experiences in Psychiatric Outpatients," *Journal of Traumatic Stress Studies* 3, (1990): 459–475.

USEFUL PRACTICES FOR FOSTERING SPIRITUALITY IN CHILDREN WHO HAVE EXPERIENCED GRIEF, LOSS, OR TRAUMA

Many children recovering from harrowing experiences will need one-on-one trauma counseling or trauma-focused cognitive behavioral therapy. Beyond individual counseling, children will need strong social and parental support as they rebuild their lives. Parents can be the most important agents in this rebuilding process, though if the parents themselves were also affected by the event, they may not be able to provide the support their children need.

Some children are part of a church that can help them; others attend after-school programs, live in readjustment or rehabilitation centers, or participate in recovery support groups. Of course, every child who has suffered deep trauma needs individual or group counseling; however, the literature frequently says many counselors are unwilling or feel unqualified to discuss spiritual issues with clients. Sometimes ordinary caregivers will be the only people the children have who are willing to enter the spiritual realm.

As part of a course on children's spirituality at Lipscomb University in Nashville, Tennessee, students worked in an after-school program for refugee children, utilizing practices built on principles gleaned from the sources cited earlier. These are practices that can be used by parents, teachers, and caregivers as well as psychologists and counselors. We designed these activities to generate opportunities for children to tap into some of the twenty-seven processes that nurture the spirituality that can promote resilience; we have used them in the last few years with children whose parents are incarcerated, children who are living in generational poverty, and most recently with refugee children.

Kaylee Frank and Megan Larry, coauthors of this chapter, were among eleven students who participated in the children's spirituality course; below, they share some of their experiences with refugee children in the after-school program utilizing the practices we have designed.

READING CHILDREN'S BOOKS

Traumatic experience often yields such spiritual challenges as feeling unworthy of God's intervention or feeling tested by God. Children may blame God for their suffering or wonder how God could allow such abuse to happen.[31] Providing safe places for children to raise these questions, express their anger or confusion, and simply talk about their experiences is part of the process of engaging the trauma spiritually. Reading children's books open the possibilities for such discussions to emerge. Kaylee shared:

> *I read A Chair for My Mother[32] to Eshal, a book that discussed family and community relationships, and living in a lower socioeconomic position from the perspective of an eight-year-old girl. After reading, I asked Eshal, "Who are you in this book?" She replied, "Well, I guess I'm the little girl, but not really." After some prompting, Eshal answered, "The girl in the book loves her mom, and I love my mom. But she has a grandma who lives in her house with her, and my grandma still lives in my country." Eshal shared that her grandparents were not able to migrate to the United States like the rest of her family, and her family experienced deep sadness and loss because of it.*

Olivia (another Lipscomb student in the spirituality course) shared that her greatest breakthrough, while mentoring twelve-year-old refugee, Nahla,[33] happened when they read a book together. The book, *Nana Upstairs & Downstairs*,[34] is about a little boy who loves and eventually loses his grandmother and great-grandmother. Nahla said she connected with the book because, when she was six, her twin sister was hit by a car and killed in front of her. Nahla further stated that she didn't think God heard her prayers because, when her sister was dying, she pleaded with God not to let her die. This conversation changed the relationship between Olivia and Nahla; Olivia recognized that her role was to listen while Nahla shared about this hard event in her life and the spiritual dissonance she felt in the ensuing years. Sharing a rich and textured children's book created a space where Olivia, through listening and empathizing, became a safe person Nahla could trust, someone with whom she could share her doubts.

---

31. Bryant-Davis et al., "Religiosity, Spirituality, and Trauma Recovery in the Lives of Children and Adolescents," 310.

32. Vera B. Williams, *A Chair for My Mother*, reprint ed. (New York: Greenwillow Books, 2007).

33. The children's names in this chapter are pseudonyms.

34. Tomie dePaola, *Nana Upstairs & Nana Downstairs* (New York: Puffin Press, 2000).

CREATING A NARRATIVE

Several sources recommend that children write, draw, or tell their stories.[35] These stories can depict the events leading up to the traumatic situation, the trauma event itself, and the rescue or resolution. The technique can provide further ways for children to ask questions they may have—about God, about hope, death, or guilt. Eventually, constructing a written or visual narrative can help children with the crucial process of making meaning that is so integrally connected with resilience.[36]

The Lipscomb students were cautioned to avoid initiating conversations about the children's refugee experiences, but they were encouraged to allow the children to talk about their experiences if the children themselves initiated the conversations. The following two stories illustrate how these refugee children are making meaning of their lives and the losses they are enduring:

I (Kaylee) asked Eshal [age eight] to draw a picture of her family for me. Eshal drew all seven members of her family, including herself, which included both of her parents, her sisters, and her two younger brothers. She then told me that she did not draw her grandparents because they are still in Africa. This opened up the opportunity for Eshal to talk further about her feelings in relation to missing her grandparents and how their absence impacts the rest of her family. Eshal shared feelings of sadness and confusion, saying she didn't understand why her grandparents couldn't come with them to the United States. In this conversation, I saw my role as simply to listen and let Eshal verbally process some of the emotions that have been stirring in her mind and heart since she left her grandparents behind.

I [Megan] sat with Zehra [age eight] and asked her to draw God. Her drawing was of a field, some clouds, and a floating angel. I asked her about the drawing and what it meant. Zehra told me that God's home is "in the sky, with the angels and his son Jesus and the people who have already died." Over the ten weeks that we met together, I began to realize this conversation had allowed Zehra to process her thoughts about where the people she has lost have gone.

---

35. Donald F. Walker, Jennifer B. Reese, John P. Hughes, and Melissa J. Troskie, "Addressing Religious and Spiritual Issues in Trauma-Focused Cognitive Behavior Therapy for Children and Adolescents," *Professional Psychology: Research and Practice* 41 (2010): 178. doi:10.1037/a0017782.

36. Masten, *Ordinary Magic: Resilience in Development*.

Writing a Letter to God

When questions about God arise such as "Where was God?" or "Why did God let this happen?," a good response is to ask children if they would like to write (or dictate) a letter to God. They may wish to accompany their letter with a drawing. Again, this process offers an opportunity for the child to engage the meaning-making process and re-visit the child–God relationship.

Kaylee stated:

> *I told Eshal we were going to write a special letter, a letter to God. When I first said this, she stared at me in confusion, not understanding what I meant. I explained that just like we can pray to God or talk and sing to God, we can write to God whenever we want. She wrote for about five minutes, as did I, and then we read our letters aloud to each other. In her letter, Eshal wrote that she knows that God made her and loves her and that he also made her family. She thanked God for "making me good at reading and writing." At first glance, I thought that this was a fairly surface-level letter, until I realized that in this statement, Eshal recognizes that God is with her in the midst of her current challenges and struggles as she is learning to read and write English in this new place; she was thanking God for giving her perseverance and the ability to be "a good reader."*

Processing the Trauma with Other Children Who Experienced It

One of the most interesting children's books that derives from a population-wide trauma is *Story of a Storm: A Book about Hurricane Katrina*.[37] This book was written and illustrated by thirty fifth-grade children and their teacher, Reola Visser, who live on the Mississippi Gulf Coast and survived the hurricane. They wrote about and drew their experiences before, during ("Katrina's winds were terrible, and blew things to pieces"), and after the hurricane while living in FEMA housing ("Our new home was not the same, but it was a home"). These children processed their

---

37. Reona Visser, *Story of a Storm: A Book about Hurricane Katrina* (Brandon, MS: Quail Ridge Press, 2006).

experiences, their losses, their adjustments, their survival together—all of which can be seen as spiritual processes that are connected to resilience.

As part of her research for her senior project on children's spirituality, Kaylee spent time with Abby Mosby, the director of Nations Ministry, an after-school program for refugee children. The director told Kaylee that one of the greatest strengths of an after-school program specifically for refugee children is that the children can form bonds with others who have been through similar traumas. She explained that many of the children exhibit emotional instability and experience frequent breakdowns; they are living in a low-income neighborhood, adjusting to a language barrier, and struggling in academic and social situations. Ms. Mosby concluded this train of thought by saying, "Instead of being judged for these behaviors or struggles, the refugee children have an opportunity to connect with children who are enduring similar challenges. This can be healing for refugee children, and can help them establish a strong sense of belonging that they may have difficulty finding elsewhere in their country of refuge."[38]

SPIRITUAL PRACTICES IN CHRISTIAN SETTINGS

Some settings where children receive care are explicitly Christian.[39] In those settings, biblical stories and prayer can be healing opportunities. Specifically, engaging children with stories about young people in Scripture who suffered through difficult situations can be comforting for children.[40] In fact, many children in Scripture faced tremendously adverse circumstances; for example, Joseph's kidnapping by his brothers and eventual sale into slavery, the slave girl who was taken from Israel by Naaman, Miriam's role in watching her brother in the Nile, the epileptic boy healed by Jesus, Eutychus's fall and healing, and all the Israelite children who left Egypt and wandered in the wilderness with their families. Orphans, population-wide trauma survivors, chronically ill children, and refugees can relate in deep ways to the children of Scripture who endured, listened to stories about God, and told their own children about God's provision.

---

38. Abby Mosby, conversation with Director of Nation's Ministry, February, 2018.

39. Though there were children from both Muslim and Christian families in the after-school refugee program, the director of the program chose children from Christian families for the mentoring partnerships for the spirituality class.

40. Walker et al., "Addressing Religious and Spiritual Issues in Trauma-Focused Cognitive Behavior Therapy for Children and Adolescents," 178.

Other stories from Scripture can also yield opportunities for insight and discussion. Kaylee shared this experience with Eshal:

When we began telling the story of the Good Samaritan, Eshal easily entered into the story, but became very concerned when she found out that the traveler in the story had been left for dead. Eshal was relieved when the Samaritan man finally came to help, but she didn't understand why someone would pass by a person who was hurting. She kept asking, "Did their mom and dad tell the other men not to help him?" As we discussed the robbers, the Levite, the priest, and the Good Samaritan, the story opened up a conversation about looking for hope and goodness in the world around us.

Prayer can also be a powerful source of comfort to children. Psychologists have begun to consider the potential role that personal religious and spiritual faith might have in recovery from trauma. Donald Walker and his team of researchers reviewed and analyzed thirty-four studies of child abuse as they relate to spirituality and religiosity.[41] In some of the studies, counselors who practice trauma-focused cognitive behavior therapy were seeking ways to incorporate clients' healthy beliefs about God into their recovery.[42] An example of this approach appears in one of Walker's own studies. The article recounts the story of Isabel, a strong Christian believer, who had been raped. Counselors encouraged her to repeat the Jesus prayer with which she had been familiar, "Lord Jesus, have mercy on me," when she became anxious in thinking about the rape. "She reported that praying in this way helped her to focus on Jesus, and to feel more peaceful and relaxed."[43]

Megan shared the following:

One week at the after-school program, Zehra and I walked a small labyrinth together. We walked slowly to the center of the labyrinth in silence. There we sat down and took time for quiet reflection and prayer. As we sat there,

---

41. Donald F. Walker, Henri Webb Reid, Tiffany O'Neill, and Lindsay Brown, "Changes in Personal Religion/Spirituality during and after Childhood Abuse: A Review and Synthesis," *Psychological Trauma: Theory, Research, Practice, and Policy* 1, (2009): 130–145.

42. Walker et al., "Changes in Personal Religion/Spirituality during and after Childhood Abuse: A Review and Synthesis."

43. Walker et al., "Addressing Religious and Spiritual Issues in Trauma-Focused Cognitive Behavior Therapy for Children and Adolescents," 177.

I could tell she was focused and praying intently to God. After a few minutes, I asked Zehra if there was another time she felt God's presence closely, and she told me, "when we were in Africa and came to the United States." This peaceful, dedicated time of prayer helped Zehra to reflect on the difficult transition she experienced as a refugee and how God had been present in that story. I affirmed with her that God is by her side, even in situations she cannot control.

Zehra, Eshal, Awilo (see story below), Nahla, and the other refugee children in the after-school program at Nations Ministry who were mentored by Lipscomb students were given many opportunities to draw on and lean into their spiritual and religious lives. The Walker review of dozens of studies of spirituality and childhood abuse suggests that personal religious and spiritual faith can moderate the degree to which some participants experience PTSD and other distressing symptoms associated with childhood trauma.[44] In some of the studies, the clients' religious beliefs and practices, such as prayer, became part of the healing process.

For the rest of their lives, Zehra, Eshal, Awilo, Nahla, and the other children will continue to process the circumstances surrounding their refugee experience, the flight from their homes, memories of those they left behind, the refugee camps they lived in, their journey to a new country, and their introduction to a new school, a new neighborhood, and a new language. Their experiences with their Lipscomb mentors modeled for them how to bring their religious beliefs and their emerging relationship with God into a lifelong process of healing and making meaning of their life-changing experiences.

CONCLUSION

Bryant-Davis and colleagues conclude their article on spirituality and trauma recovery for children saying that much research[45] supports religious

---

44. Walker et al., "Changes in Personal Religion/Spirituality during and after Childhood Abuse: A Review and Synthesis."
45. Bryant-Davis et al., "Religiosity, Spirituality, and Trauma Recovery in the Lives of Children and Adolescents." 306.

and spiritual forms of coping, such as meaning-making, a sense of hope, and a sense of belonging, and the belief that these spiritual coping mechanisms "contribute to decreased depressive symptoms, greater self-esteem, and overall greater life satisfaction."[46] We found this to be true. The most important thing we learned in our time with the children of Nations Ministry was the significance of constructing a bridge from the children's already-existing spirituality to the actual experiences of their lives, believing as we do (and as research supports) that this connection yields resilience in these children in ineffable ways.

During our ten weeks at Nations Ministry, Awilo, a seven-year-old refugee from the Democratic Republic of Congo, exhibited unremitting disobedience and aggression toward his peers and authority figures. After four difficult weeks of trying to connect with him, his mentor, Erika, invited him to walk through a labyrinth. Up until this point, all efforts to welcome Awilo into conversation or structured activity had failed. Intrigued by the maze-looking structure, Awilo listened attentively to the explanation regarding the journey of a labyrinth, then willingly participated. In the center of the labyrinth, Erika explained that we can talk to God, God can hear our prayers, and we can listen for God's voice. Awilo was fascinated by Erika's explanation and began asking questions about prayer and hearing God's voice. As they sat down in the center, Erika gently suggested that Awilo take a time of silence to pray in his own heart and listen for God to speak. To Erika's surprise (and delight), Awilo did exactly as she suggested. When the moment was over, Erika asked Awilo if he wanted to share. Awilo looked at Erika with shining eyes, and said, "God said he loves me."

Erika described the labyrinth as a turning point in her relationship with Awilo, stating that afterwards, he displayed a level of trust and cooperation he had not exhibited before. Walking the labyrinth provided an opportunity for Awilo to be curious, to ask questions, to pray, and to listen to God. The experience also yielded a new, warm connection with Erika, which allowed her to more easily address his needs for safety, hope, structure, boundaries, compassion, and respect, and to more effectively nurture his relationships with himself, others, and God. It took time, but these intentional spiritual

46. Ibid.

practices helped the children we mentored bring their growing relationships with God, themselves, and others to the meaning-making task of processing their experiences as refugees and immigrants.

We believe these practices will foster spirituality in other children who have experienced grief, loss, or trauma, children such as Carlos and Chloe from the opening vignettes of this chapter. As current research is finding and as we experienced, a flourishing spirituality can contribute to the resilience these children need to heal, to survive, and ultimately, to thrive.

The Importance of
STORY IN A CHILD'S
SPIRITUALITY

CHAPTER 9

THE BIBLICAL BASIS FOR USING STORY IN A CHILD'S FORMATION

MARVA HOOPES

———— |++| ————

Since the use of story is wildly popular in Christian education circles today, it may be helpful for Christian leaders to identify biblical foundations for its continual use with children. What kind of guidance can we receive from Scripture to help parents and leaders analyze our approach to teaching children and nurture their spiritual growth? Stanley Hauerwas claims that through the biblical story, children must move from simply knowing facts *about* God, to actually *knowing* God.[1] So we must ask: What is the biblical basis for using story in the spiritual formation of children? In examining Scripture itself, we will see that: (1) Scripture is explicit in its call for adults to teach God's Word to children, (2) God uses story to get to the heart of his creation—the form of Scripture is story, and (3) the content of Scripture's story includes children.

SCRIPTURE IS EXPLICIT IN THE CALL FOR ADULTS TO TEACH GOD'S WORD TO CHILDREN

Scripture clearly instructs parents and leaders of the faith community to actively teach God's Word to children. The family of origin and the faith

---

1. Stanley Hauerwas, "The Gesture of a Truthful Story," *Theology Today* 42, no. 2 (1985): 181–89.

community are both instrumental in grounding spirituality and faith. If children were incapable of spiritual understanding, there would be no need for the older generation to teach children the truths of God; the passing on of the faith could wait until they were adults. Children, however, need the help and guidance of invested adults to nurture them. This point is illustrated in the following passages.

DEUTERONOMY 4

After years of wandering in the desert, the people of God stand at the brink of entering the Promised Land. Moses delivers a series of speeches to the people challenging them to remember and learn from God's mighty acts (Deut. 1:6–4:43) and reviews the law (Deut. 4:44–28:68). In Deuteronomy 4, Moses asserts that obedience to God is of utmost importance.

> Only be careful, and watch yourselves closely so that you do not forget the things your eyes have seen or let them fade from your heart as long as you live. Teach them to your children and to their children after them. (Deut. 4:9)

They were to faithfully obey the law and make sure the next generations would have a respect and reverence for it as well.

DEUTERONOMY 6

In this essential message, Moses reiterates that in the promised land, the people should be faithful to observe God's commands. Furthermore, they are to teach them to their children and to all future generations. Israel is reminded that "the LORD is one," and that they are to love the Lord "with all your heart and with all your soul and with all your strength" (Deut. 6:4–5). This confession of faith, known as the *Shema*, has been affirmed in synagogues around the world for many centuries. Moses directs the people to instruct their children in God's ways: "Impress them on your children. Talk about them when you sit at home and when you walk along the road, when you lie down and when you get up" (Deut. 6:7). These vital lessons were to happen naturally as life unfolded in teachable moments at home, on the road, at bedtime, and in preparing for the day ahead. Parents were to share God's Word with their children responsibly, intentionally, and diligently.

DEUTERONOMY 31

As Moses will not accompany the people into the promised land, he gives his final words and instructions in Deuteronomy 31. Again, he admonishes the leaders to teach the people God's ways. Few people could actually read, so religious instruction took place orally during special times. The Feast of Tabernacles, described more fully in Deuteronomy 16, was a joyous occasion for everyone that included feasting and celebration. Every seven years, men, women, children, and foreigners alike were to gather for the public reading and teaching of the Law. By gathering all generations together in a regular renewal of commitment to God, children could observe the faith of their parents and other significant adults in the faith community.[2]

JOSHUA 3–4

As the Israelites prepared to finally enter the promised land, they came to the banks of the Jordan River. How could they cross? God provided a mighty miracle that day. He stopped the flow of the river so that all the people could cross over the Jordan on dry ground, just as they had crossed the Red Sea years earlier. God commanded Joshua to send twelve men, representing the twelve tribes, to collect twelve stones from the dry riverbed, to build a memorial at Gilgal, where they would camp that night. They also built a mound of stones in the middle of the riverbed at the place where the priests carrying the ark of the covenant were standing.

The mound of stones commemorating Israel's crossing into the promised land would evoke curiosity in children, prompting parents to tell the story of how their powerful God delivered them safely into the promised land.[3] When the waters of the Jordan flowed again, the heap of stones in the middle of the riverbed was submerged, no longer visible. Perhaps when children asked about the stones at Gilgal, parents would describe the miracle and could have responded as Warren Wiersbe suggests:

---

2. Lawrence O. Richards, *The Bible Reader's Companion*, electronic ed. (Wheaton, IL: Victor Books, 1991).

3. Donald K. Campbell, "Joshua," in The Bible Knowledge Commentary: An Exposition of the Scriptures, ed. John F. Walvoord, et al. (Wheaton, IL: Victor Books, 1985), 325–372.

"But there's another monument in the middle of the river where the priests stood with the ark. You can't see it, but it's there. It reminds us that our old life has been buried, and we must live a new life in obedience to the Lord." The children would have to accept this fact by faith; and if they did, it could make a great difference in the way they related to God and to his will for their lives.[4]

The function of the stones was unmistakably pedagogical. Children who asked about the stones were not sent to the priests for answers; fathers were to tell them the story.[5] In fact, these stones represented the broader purpose "that all the peoples of the earth might know that the hand of the LORD is powerful" (Josh. 4:24).

PSALM 78

Psalm 78 presents lessons from Israel's history. The psalmist, identified as Asaph, reminds the people that God not only gave the Law to their ancestors, but commanded each generation to teach the next generation, so that "they in turn would tell their children" (Ps. 78:6). The story is of Israel's experiences in Egypt, in the wilderness, and of the men of Ephraim, who "did not keep God's covenant and refused to live by his law. They forgot what he had done" (Ps. 78:10–11). This story of Israel's faithlessness and God's faithfulness is passed from each generation to the next to inspire trust in God, remembrance of his deeds, and obedience to his commands.

PSALM 145

Psalm 145, denoted as a psalm of David, is titled, "A psalm of praise." In the original Hebrew, the psalm is an acrostic. Each verse begins with a letter of the Hebrew alphabet, in regular order, minus one letter. The psalmist speaks on behalf of Israel, offering praise to God for his greatness, goodness, glory, and grace. Particularly relevant is verse 4, which declares, "One generation commends your works to another; they tell of your mighty acts." As the older generation passes on God's great story to the next generation, praise is the natural result.

---

4. Warren W. Wiersbe, *Be Strong* (Wheaton, IL: Victor Books, 1993), 53.
5. Campbell, "Joshua."

These examples from Deuteronomy, Joshua, and Psalms demonstrate the mandate that children are to be taught God's ways and God's laws. God desires parents and leaders to actively and intentionally teach children the truths of God's Word, so that the faith may be passed on to the next generation.

SCRIPTURE IS STORY

God's Word comes to us as story. The Bible itself is more story than theological proposition. Narrative sections comprise "some 65–75 percent of the text, depending on the definition."[6] There are sections of Scripture that consist of laws, lists, propositions, and sermons, but the dominant literary form is narrative, or story.

God, rather than the human characters, is the hero of the story and should be the main focus of the biblical narrative. Stories in Scripture do not exist merely to entertain or to record history. As Fee and Stuart point out, "Their purpose is to show God at work in his creation and among his people. The narratives glorify him, help us to understand and appreciate him, and give us a picture of his providence and protection."[7] The story of the Bible offers the story of creation, the entrance of sin into the world, redemption, and restoration. Some theologians call the grand story of Scripture *Heilsgeschichte*, or, translated from the German, "salvation history." This refers to the way God provides us redemption.

THE FIRST FIVE BOOKS: *Story with Embedded Legal Codex*

The first five books of the Bible—Genesis, Exodus, Leviticus, Numbers, and Deuteronomy—are known in the Hebrew tradition as the Torah, derived from the Hebrew *tôrâ*, meaning "instruction." The Pentateuch is a continuous chronological narrative that combines prose, law, drama, story, song, and poetry. The long story in the Pentateuch contains six main divisions:

---

6. Tom A. Steffen, *Reconnecting God's Story to Ministry: Cross-cultural Storytelling at Home and Abroad* (Downers Grove, IL: InterVarsity Press, 2005), 34.

7. Gordon D. Fee and Douglas Stuart, *How to Read the Bible for All Its Worth: A Guide to Understanding the Bible* (Grand Rapids, MI: Zondervan, 1993), 79.

A. the story of creation, the fall of humans, the first families, the flood, the tower of Babel,

B. the story of the patriarchs—Abraham, Isaac, Jacob, and Joseph,

C. Moses and the exodus from Egypt,

D. the giving of the Law, building of the tabernacle, establishment of the levitical system,

E. the wilderness wanderings,

F. the final speeches of Moses in preparation to enter the promised land.[8]

It is true that the books of the Law, as the Pentateuch is sometimes called, contain the legal codex for God's people; however, "narrative, not 'law,' is the dominant genre of the Pentateuch."[9]

JESUS USES STORIES TO EXPLAIN TRUTH AND TEACH THEOLOGY

The New Testament begins with the four Gospels: Matthew, Mark, Luke, and John. All four tell the story of Jesus, the culmination of God's redemption of humankind. McIlwain shows how all of scripture is about Jesus when he writes:

> The whole Bible is God's message about His Son, the Savior. God's chief purpose in writing His Book was to reveal Christ. The Old Testament is the preparation for Christ. The New Testament is the manifestation of Christ. The Scriptures reveal Christ from Genesis to Revelation.[10]

Jesus uses stories to explain truth and teach theology. The use of stories is not accidental, nor is it a mere convention to reach a first-century audience. Rather, Jesus repeated the method of God delivering his Word to us throughout the entire canon. The Creator knows story is the best way to get to the heart of his creation. Jesus as God in flesh uses story for the same reason.

---

8. David A. Hubbard, "Pentateuch," in *New Bible Dictionary*, eds. D. R. W. Wood and I. Howard Marshall (Downers Grove, IL: InterVarsity Press, 1996), 893.

9. Daniel I. Block, "Pentateuch," in *Holman Illustrated Bible Dictionary*, eds. Chad Brand, et. al. (Nashville, TN: Holman Reference, 2003), 1268.

10. Trevor McIlwain, *Building on Firm Foundations – Volume 1: Guidelines for Evangelism and Teaching Believers*, Revised ed. (Sanford, FL: New Tribes Mission, 2005), 42.

Jesus often uses the method of a parable, "a metaphor or simile often extended to a short narrative; in biblical contexts almost always formulated to reveal and illustrate the kingdom of God."[11] A significant example lies in the three stories in Luke 15: the lost sheep, the lost coin, and the lost son. These parables illustrate the truth that God graciously and joyfully receives repentant sinners, and that we should also rejoice when the lost come to God.[12] Through the powerful story of the lost son (Luke 15:11–32), Jesus addresses ungodly attitudes, evokes emotion, and uses familiar settings and problems to gain understanding and identification with the characters. He uses vivid imagery that sparks imagination; the surprises and plot twists gain attention and provoke thought. It is a story simple enough for children to understand, deep enough for scholars to analyze, yet profound enough to evoke transformation in the lives of those who have "ears to hear" (Luke 14:35).

NEW TESTAMENT PREACHING INCLUDES HISTORY-OF-SALVATION AS A KEY PART IN THE STORY OF GOD'S WORK.

In the book of Acts, various apostles deliver pivotal sermons that feature the redemptive story of salvation. These sermons use story in powerful ways to bring repentance and transformation as the message is spread across the Roman world. It is accomplished as these preachers, empowered by the Holy Spirit, interpret Jesus' life and ministry to their audiences. This powerful use of story can be seen in the following three examples:

Acts 2: Peter's sermon

During his last days on earth, Jesus gave his disciples the command to stay in Jerusalem and wait for the gift of the Holy Spirit (Acts 1:4–5). Acts 2 describes this amazing event at Pentecost. The Holy Spirit suddenly descends on the gathered disciples with a sound like a violent, blowing wind, with tongues of fire, and enables them to speak in other tongues. A curious crowd gathers, amazed at what they see and hear. Some, however, scoff, prompting Peter to stand up and address the crowd. Beginning with

---

11. Craig L. Blomberg, "Parables," in *The International Standard Bible Encyclopedia*, Revised ed., ed. Geoffrey W. Bromiley (Grand Rapids, MI: W. B. Eerdmans, 2002), 655.
12. Frank E. Gaebelein, J.D. Douglas, and Dick Polcyn, The Expositor's Bible Commentary: Volume 8 (Matthew, Mark, Luke) (Grand Rapids, MI: Zondervan, 1984).

the writings of the prophet Joel, Peter explains how the outpouring of the Spirit was foretold. He then tells the story of Jesus' life, death, resurrection, and how this all fulfilled Davidic prophecy about Jesus, the Messiah God had sent—and they had crucified him! "When the people heard this, they were cut to the heart and said to Peter and the other apostles, 'Brothers, what shall we do?'" (Acts 2:37). This powerful use of story in a sermon prompts repentance in about three thousand people as it resonates in their hearts, resulting in saving faith.

Acts 7: Stephen's witness

Stephen, "a man full of God's grace and power" (Acts 6:8), is one of seven chosen to be responsible for the fair distribution of food. Stephen's opponents accuse him of blasphemy and haul him before the Sanhedrin. Stephen's defense is an eloquent story. He traces the history of Israel and concludes with the charge that, like their forefathers who persistently rejected God's chosen leaders, they continue to do so by resisting the Holy Spirit, denying prophecy, and rejecting Jesus, whom they betrayed and murdered. The infuriated council drags Stephen out of the city, where he is stoned to death. Stephen's witness is delivered powerfully through story, and his point is clearly understood.

Acts 22; 26: Paul's testimony

The story of Paul's conversion is first described in Acts 9. Later, in Acts 21, Paul comes to Jerusalem and is accused by an angry mob of bringing a gentile into the temple. Through the intervention of a Roman commander, Paul speaks to the crowd and simply tells his story. He describes his background, the astonishing story of his conversion, and finally, his mission to the gentiles. When the crowd, who had been listening intently and respectfully, hears that hated word, *gentiles*, their anger is again inflamed. Paul is taken into custody, transferred to Caesarea, put on trial by Governor Felix, and jailed for two years.

In Acts 26, Paul has further opportunity to tell his story to the new governor, Festus, and King Agrippa. Paul acknowledges Agrippa's acquaintance with Jewish customs and shares his story from that perspective. Paul affirms that he is not saying anything "beyond what the prophets and Moses said would happen—that the Messiah would suffer and, as the first to rise from the dead, would bring the message of light to his own people and to the Gentiles" (Acts 26:22–23). Festus blurts out that Paul must be crazy, but Paul continues logically and calmly making his case. He directs a pointed question to King Agrippa, who brushes it aside. But Paul's story impacts his audience, and it continues to do so with readers even today. His personal story is used to share the message of the gospel.

THE CONTENT OF SCRIPTURE'S STORY INCLUDES CHILDREN

The content of the story of Scripture is not limited to adults. God draws children to himself, gaining their attention by using stories featuring children. When material contains characters with whom children can identify, their interest increases. They can hear stories about those who, like themselves, are also brothers, sisters, babies, older children, and friends. In these stories, some children face difficult situations and suffer illnesses; some love and follow God, while others are rebellious. These stories open children's (and even adults') eyes to significant points regarding God's character, what he values and expects of us, our response to him, and how children are included in the family of faith.

Some Scripture stories including children in the Old Testament:

ISAAC (GENESIS 21–22)

The story of Isaac is memorable for showing God's faithfulness. Children are the means by which God is going to bless the world, of which Isaac is preeminent. Walvoord notes that his miraculous birth brought great joy.

> The name Isaac ("he laughs") is cleverly explained in this passage. Sarah said that God gave her laughter, that is joy. Her laughter of unbelief was now changed to rejoicing through the provision of her son. Everyone who would hear about this would laugh, that is rejoice, with her.[13]

---

13. Allen P. Ross, "Genesis 21: 1–7," in The Bible Knowledge Commentary: An Exposition of the Scriptures, ed. John F. Walvoord, et al. (Wheaton, IL: Victor Books, 1985), 62.

When Isaac is twelve years old, God tests Abraham (Gen. 22:1). Because Isaac is willing to submit himself to the larger plan, it raises the tension in the narrative as to whether God's promise will be thwarted by the sacrifice of Isaac. But God provides in an unexpected way. God gave Isaac to Abraham. Abraham was able to give his son back to God, and God then gave Isaac back to Abraham. Although Isaac's role in these accounts is passive, he is portrayed as treasured. The narrative of this child in Scripture uses the picture of the love between father and son to illustrate the sacrifice made by the heavenly Father in giving his treasured Son, showing us God's love for humankind.

SAMUEL (1 SAMUEL 1–3)

Wiersbe points out that the story of God speaking to young Samuel in the night helps us understand that "God speaks to children and young people, and adults should make it easy for them to hear God's voice and respond in faith."[14] Eli, the priest who has charge of Samuel, has sons who do not follow God. Spiritual leadership from one generation to the next is never to be taken for granted. It hinges upon every young person to respond to God's call authentically and faithfully. Sadly, later in the story, we see that Samuel's sons also do not follow in his way. We are reminded of the vital necessity of intentional teaching and making sure that each generation is equipped to follow faithfully in the Lord's ways.

JEREMIAH (JEREMIAH 1:4–8)

The calling of the prophet Jeremiah demonstrates how God sets apart, calls, and employs people of any age to accomplish his purposes. God sets apart Jeremiah while he is still in his mother's womb. When God calls Jeremiah to service, he protests, saying, "I do not know how to speak; I am too young" (Jer. 1:6). Chisholm explains "When Jeremiah objected that he was too young and inarticulate for the task, the Lord assured him of his protective presence. The prophet's divinely appointed words would determine the destiny of nations."[15]

---

14. Warren W. Wiersbe, "1 Samuel 3," in Wiersbe's Expository Outlines on the Old Testament (Wheaton, IL: Victor Books, 1993), 257-258.

15. Robert B. Chisholm, "The Major Prophets," in *Holman Concise Bible Commentary*, ed. D. S. Dockery (Nashville, TN: B&H Publishing Group, 1998), 294.

OTHER STORIES IN THE OLD TESTAMENT THAT FEATURE CHILDREN INCLUDE:

- Naaman's servant girl points him to the prophet Elisha and the God of Israel for healing from leprosy (2 Kings 5).
- Miriam and young Moses are used by God for his grand plan to save his people (Ex. 2).
- The firstborn of the Egyptians are slain, and the Israelite children are saved in the Passover (Ex. 12).
- Young Josiah becomes king at age eight and later makes significant reforms to bring people back to worship Yahweh (2 Chron. 34).
- Jephthah's daughter's life is tragically ended through a foolish vow, even though she is committed to her father and her God (Judges 11).
- David defeats the giant and declares that the whole world will know there is a God in Israel (1 Sam. 16–17).
- The son of the widow of Zarephath is raised from the dead by Elijah (1 Kings 17).
- The Shunammite's son is raised from the dead by Elisha (2 Kings 4).
- The account of the insolent children is a sobering, negative example of delinquent boys who jeer at the prophet Elisha (2 Kings 2:23–25).
- Despite being the uncherished and rejected child, God provides for Ishmael (Gen.16; 21), even though he is not the son of promise.
- Young Daniel and his friends remain loyal and obedient to God, refusing the king's food (Dan. 1).
- Shadrach, Meshach, and Abednego remain faithful to God in spite of persecution and danger (Dan. 3).

Some Scripture stories including children in the New Testament:

JAIRUS' DAUGHTER IS RAISED FROM THE DEAD (MARK 5; MATTHEW 9; LUKE 8)

Jesus' teaching is interrupted by a desperate father, pleading for his daughter's healing. The fact that Jesus stops what he is doing and goes with Jairus is striking, since in that culture children were loved but still considered less important than adults. Jesus makes room in his schedule for a child. After a brief interruption for another healing, Jesus continues on to Jairus' house, where the girl has died and noisy mourners have gathered. Dispensing with them, Jesus privately raises the girl from the dead, requesting that she be given something to eat. Jesus is sensitive and considerate to many kinds of needs—even those of a twelve-year-old girl and her family!

JESUS WELCOMES THE CHILDREN
(MARK 10:13–16; MATTHEW 19:13–15; LUKE 18:15–17)

The familiar, brief story of Jesus blessing the children clearly demonstrates his love and concern for them. Jesus' response to the disciples, who are rebuking the parents for bringing their children, lets us know how wrong he feels this is. Children are not to be hindered in coming to him! Mark records that Jesus hugged the children: "And he took the children in his arms, placed his hands on them and blessed them" (Mark 10:16). What a reassuring story for children!

Jesus' comment in verse 15 seems harsh: "Anyone who will not receive the kingdom of God like a little child will never enter it." But the narrative immediately following this is of the rich young man who is unwilling to let go of his riches in order to follow Jesus. Jesus says, "How hard it is for the rich to enter the kingdom of God" (Mark 10:23). Both of these statements may seem a little harsh; after all, we have known adults and rich people who have come to Christ. As Eubanks states, "Just as wealth erects a formidable barrier to salvation for many people, perhaps Jesus is saying that age is a difficult barrier also."[16] This concept gives a particular urgency to the importance of training in the faith for our children. Jesus does not leave adults without hope, however. The disciples ask, "Who then can be saved?" and Jesus proclaims, "With man this is impossible, but not with God; all things are possible with God" (Mark 10:26–27).

THE CHILDREN PRAISE JESUS IN THE TEMPLE
(MATTHEW 21:12–17)

During the final week of Jesus' life, as Jesus heals the blind and lame in the temple, little children come skipping in, singing his praises, using the words they had heard earlier: "Hosanna to the Son of David!" (Matthew 21:15). The seething religious leaders challenge Jesus' acceptance

---

16. Larry L. Eubanks, "Mark 10:13–16," *Review and Expositor* 91, no. 3 (August 1994): 401–405.

of this messianic praise, but he supports the children in verse 16, quoting Psalm 8:2: "Have you never read, 'From the lips of children and infants you, Lord, have called forth your praise'?" The contrast between the unbelieving, sullen adults and the joyful, exuberant children is striking. Jesus accepts the children's praise then, and he accepts it now, as well.

OTHER NEW TESTAMENT STORIES DESERVING RECOGNITION THAT INCLUDE CHILDREN:

• A nobleman's son is healed (John 4).
• A boy possessed by demons receives deliverance (Matt. 17; Mark 9; Luke 9).
• The daughter of the woman from Syrian Phoenicia is healed (Matt. 15; Mark 7).
• A boy gives his lunch for a miracle feeding of five thousand (John 6).
• Jesus brings a child into the people's midst to teach a spiritual lesson (Matt. 18; Mark 9; Luke 9).
• Paul's nephew plays a strategic role in saving his life (Acts 23).
• Timothy's childhood is mentioned as being highly important (2 Tim. 3).

It is significant that the content of God's grand story is not limited to adults, but includes children. These stories open our eyes to salient points regarding God's character (he is faithful and generous to young and old alike), what he values (children!), what our response to him should be (authentic with faithful praise), and that children are included in the family of faith.

SUMMARY OF BIBLICAL FOUNDATIONS

What does Scripture have to say to parents and leaders in the faith community about teaching children? First, Scripture is explicit in its call for adults to intentionally teach God's Word to children. Parents and spiritual leaders are to take an active role in teaching children the truths of God, ensuring that the faith will be passed on to future generations. Also, God uses story to get to the heart of his creation—the form of Scripture is story. The Pentateuch is the story of God's plan and action with his people. Jesus effectively uses story to teach truth. New Testament preaching with story shows the power of salvation history as part of God's revealing work on earth. And finally, the content of Scripture's story includes children. It is significant that in form and content, the Bible uses story to capture the attention of children and to instruct them in God's ways. It is important to note the many instances that children are included in biblical stories as this reveals God's acceptance of and care for children. As children engage with God's story, they come to know him in a way that produces faithful following and adherence to his Word.

Affirming the value of story in the faith development of children, John Westerhoff in his book *Will Our Children Have Faith?* declares, "At the heart of our Christian faith is story. And at the heart of Christian education must be this same story . . . Unless the story is known, understood, owned, and lived, we and our children will not have Christian faith."[17] There is great power in story to transform lives in a way that cognitive, rational proclamation cannot. The power of story is available to all people, regardless of social or economic status, educational level or intelligence, age or experience. Let us use story with intentionality, measuring the influence it will have, covering it with prayer, with the leading and power of the Holy Spirit, in the name of Jesus Christ, for the glory of the Father, to lead children into God's family of faith.

---

17. John H. Westerhoff III, *Will Our Children Have Faith?* Revised ed. (New York: Morehouse, 2000), 32.

CHAPTER 10

SHARING HARD STORIES WITH CHILDREN

ROBERT J. KEELEY

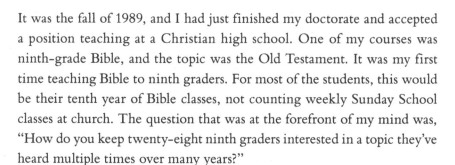

It was the fall of 1989, and I had just finished my doctorate and accepted a position teaching at a Christian high school. One of my courses was ninth-grade Bible, and the topic was the Old Testament. It was my first time teaching Bible to ninth graders. For most of the students, this would be their tenth year of Bible classes, not counting weekly Sunday School classes at church. The question that was at the forefront of my mind was, "How do you keep twenty-eight ninth graders interested in a topic they've heard multiple times over many years?"

It was a challenge. I started the year just trying to be as engaging as possible, but what I noticed, as the course went on, was that the interest level of the students was higher when I hit stories they had not been told before. I soon learned there were many stories in the Bible that these students—who had been taught the Bible most of their lives—had never heard. These were the stories that might feature elements of sex or violence. Several were more theologically challenging as well.

Consider, for example, the story of David and Bathsheba in 2 Samuel 11 and 12. After you tell or read the story, what do you say to explain the story and its meaning? Clearly, David was being called out for his sin, and he is punished through the death of his son, who was conceived during the illicit affair between the king and the wife of one of his soldiers. Surely, David and Bathsheba grieved for their child, but note that it was the child who died, not the parents! Then, to further complicate things, David and Bathsheba's second child, Solomon, becomes king and part of the line of Christ. His name, Solomon, is similar in Hebrew to the word for "peace." We're told that the Lord loved this child and gave him an additional name, Jedidiah, which means "the LORD loved him" (2 Sam. 12:25).

Stories like this one are not easy to explain.

Some passages are troubling on first reading, like the story of the Levite and his concubine in Judges 19–21. Others are more difficult as you dive more deeply into the details, like the David and Bathsheba story. All Scripture is important and worthy of study. All Scripture should be taught. But some stories are particularly troubling.

That semester marked the beginning of a lifelong fascination with those types of stories and with how we should present them to children and teens. Noah's ark, for example, is really a gruesome tale wherein God wipes out almost every human being on the planet. But we often present it to children with pictures of cheery animals coexisting on an ark that is more like a cruise ship than a lifeboat. We gloss over the more difficult parts of the story and rarely talk about Noah's drunken nakedness (Gen. 9:20–27).

Many years ago, I saw an advertisement for Bible action figures. The person who developed these toys wanted children to have biblical alternatives to the action figures his own children played with. But his choice of action figures had the unfortunate effect of endorsing these characters as role models, as people to admire. One of the figures was Samson, who is a notoriously bad example of how men should behave towards women. But because God used Samson in a powerful way (despite his personal failings), we have elevated Samson to hero status, turning a blind eye to his many and obvious flaws.

My ninth-grade students enjoyed learning things that challenged this "good guys" of the Bible mentality. As we studied the less familiar Bible passages, or even looked more closely at some of the familiar stories, unearthing the uncomfortable details we usually leave out, these students found that the Bible is a much more nuanced book than they had initially been led to believe. This gave us an opportunity to have deeper conversations about the nature of people and of our relationships with God. Granted, wisdom is needed when we share details from stories so that we do so mindfully and in age-appropriate ways, but there is also a problem we need to address here. If our children get to high school and have never studied the difficult elements of the Bible, we are not doing our job. We must commit to teaching all of Scripture, even the parts that are hard to hear and difficult to understand. In my personal study of these "strange" stories that we hesitate to tell, I've found they can lead to a deeper grasp of the most profound truths found in Scripture. These passages don't have good theology in them *despite* their difficulty for modern ears; they have good theology in them *because* of their difficulty.

AN EXAMPLE

Let's look closely at one example. The last 13 chapters of Genesis follow the story of Joseph, and we get an amazing amount of detail in this story. Curiously, in Genesis 38, after we read about Joseph's brothers selling him into slavery, the story leaves Joseph and focuses on his brother, Judah. Judah was the brother who held out his brother's bloody coat of many colors to show his father and said, "Examine it to see whether it is your son's robe" (Gen. 37:32).

We learn that Judah leaves his father's family and heads out to a town called Adullam. While there, he meets and marries a Canaanite woman named Shua. We need to remember that Abraham, Judah's great-grandfather, made a point of sending his servant to find a wife among Abraham's relatives for his son Isaac, specifically saying to his servant, "I want you to swear . . . that you will not get a wife for my son from the daughters of the Canaanites" (Gen. 24:3). And Judah's father, Jacob, also married women who were the daughters of his mother's brother, Laban. But Judah is the first in his line to marry a Canaanite woman, departing from the command to Abraham. This is a signal that Judah is not careful in his obedience to the laws or to his God.

Judah and his Canaanite wife, Shua, have three sons; Er, Onan, and Shelah. Judah finds a wife for his oldest son, Er, named Tamar. This was a time of arranged marriages, which is a cultural detail that may need explanation for some children and youth. The arrangement itself is not all that unusual, but we do learn that Er is quite wicked, and God puts him to death for his wickedness. That's all we know about Er: "Er, Judah's

firstborn, was wicked in the LORD's sight; so the LORD put him to death"
(Gen. 38:7).

In those days, women had little power or social status. They could not
own property, and their role was restricted to bearing children and taking
care of the home. This is one reason why God repeatedly speaks of the
need to care for widows and orphans.[1] The cultural systems provided for
and protected women through dependence on the husband and father, and
if you have neither of those, you're alone.[2] It is because of this that Judah
says to son number two—Onan—"Sleep with your brother's wife and
fulfill your duty to her as a brother-in-law to raise up offspring for your
brother" (Gen. 38:8). This practice was known as "levirate marriage," and
it referred to a brother-in-law's duty to care for the widow of his brother.[3]
These children would be counted as Er's children, not Onan's, so there
was no benefit to Onan in helping his dead brother's wife. Any children
conceived with Tamar would not legally be his children, so Onan did not
cooperate. Again, God saw his actions as wicked, and we are told that
Onan also died for his sin.

At this point, Judah has lost two of his sons in some connection to
Tamar, and he doesn't want to lose his third son, Shelah. So Judah says to
Tamar, "Shelah is too young to be married, so go live as a widow in your
father's house until Shelah gets older." A careful reader will see that this
is just a ruse, that Judah has no intention of ever providing for Tamar by
giving her to Shelah. Tamar is stuck. She is pledged to Shelah, and she has
no option other than to wait for her father-in-law to do something to help
her. Several years pass, and Tamar is still wearing widow's clothes.

We are told that Shua, Judah's wife, dies after "a long time," an indi-
cation that Tamar, too, has been waiting quite a while for something to
happen (Gen. 38:12). After Judah has mourned his wife, he travels to
Timnah, where his sheep are being sheared. Tamar hears of this, and she
decides it is time to act. She takes off her widow's clothes, puts on a veil,

---

1. There are at least six verses in the book of Deuteronomy alone that refer to orphans. Widows
are mentioned even more frequently.

2. Jan Verbruggen, "Social Justice in Ancient Israel," *Transformed: Living the Gospel in an Everyday
World*, Western Theological Seminary, November 18, 2013, transformedblog.westernseminary.
edu/2013/11/18/social-justice-in-ancient-israel/.

3. Tikva Frymer-Kensky, "Tamar: Bible," *Jewish Women: A Comprehensive Historical Encyclopedia*,
The Jewish Women's Archive, March 20, 2009, jwa.org/encyclopedia/article/tamar-bible.

and dresses like a prostitute. She goes to hang out by the city gate to wait for Judah. When she sees him, he approaches her for sex, thinking that she is a prostitute. Judah doesn't recognize his daughter-in-law because she's wearing a veil—her disguise works well! They agree on the price of a young goat for her services. Judah does not have a goat on hand, so he says to her, "I don't have a goat with me, but I'll send my man with one to you tomorrow." Tamar requests his signet ring and staff as a promise of future payment, as collateral, a guarantee that she will be paid. Judah agrees to the terms of the business arrangement, and the two of them go off to complete the transaction. Tamar is still veiled, so Judah does not recognize her as his widowed daughter-in-law. After Judah leaves, Tamar removes her veil and puts her widow's clothes back on.

The next day, Judah sends one of his friends with a goat to the city gate to retrieve his collateral. The man looks everywhere, but cannot find her. He soon learns that there is no prostitute who frequents that location. When he reports back to Judah, Judah resigns himself to the loss of his ring and staff.

Months pass, and we learn that Tamar is pregnant. When her pregnancy is discovered, she is condemned as a prostitute, and when Judah is told of her pregnancy, he is indignant, ordering Tamar to be burned to death. But Tamar sends a message to Judah, along with the ring and staff. She says to him, "This is the man whose baby I am carrying. Do you recognize these?"

This question provides a helpful link between this story and the story of Joseph that has been interrupted. The Hebrew language uses the same word, *nakar* ("to recognize"), in both this story and the previous narrative of Joseph.[4] In the Tamar story, Judah is being asked if he recognizes his own ring and staff—evidence of what he has done with Tamar. This is an intentional allusion to the previous story, wherein Judah is the one holding his brother Joseph's bloody coat, asking if his father recognizes whose it is. The connection is clear: Judah is on the receiving end of his own deception this time.

Judah acknowledges the items presented to him by Tamar, and says, "She is more righteous than I, since I wouldn't give her to my son Shelah"

---

4. The meaning and biblical usage of this Hebrew word, as well as its use in the two passages referenced can be seen at https://www.blueletterbible.org/lang/lexicon/lexicon.cfm?Strongs=H5234&t=KJV.

(Gen. 38:26). Judah accepts Tamar back into his household, and we learn she gives birth to twins, naming them Perez and Zerah. Amazingly, Tamar and one of her twin sons are included in the bloodline of Jesus Christ.

This is a story filled with difficult cultural elements. It requires nuance to tell the story in a way that is instructive and helpful. Can you imagine a congregation hearing, "This is the word of the Lord" after this story? "Thanks be to God," is the right thing to say, but frankly, most listeners are more likely to respond with stunned silence.

First, we need to admit that to our modern ears, this is a strange story. We need to be sure we aren't guilty of assuming that the Bible and its meaning must fit our own cultural biases and assumptions. What sounds strange to us may be perfectly normal in other cultures and times. But we also need to be aware that things that seem strange to us can also be a signal that all was not right with the people in the story. Judah, for example, should not have sent Tamar back to her father after Onan died, but should have immediately given her in marriage to Shelah.

But a story like this is also helpful in another way. I often use this story to illustrate to my students the danger of trying to find a moral lesson with every Bible story. There is no one who acts honorably in this story; not Judah, nor his three sons, nor even Tamar. If we're looking for someone to emulate, a role model to hold up to others, we're out of luck. And even the idea that wickedness results in punishment is not clearly illustrated. While God punished Er and Onan for their sin, Shelah, Judah, and Tamar are not put to death, and the Bible never says why.

WHY TELL THIS STORY?

Yet there is much we can learn from this story. Jack, a friend and colleague, lost his young daughter a number of years ago.[5] As Jack and I were talking about the story of Judah and Tamar and what it might mean, he said to me, "If I could go back in time and change what happened to my daughter, would I? In a heartbeat. But that experience changed me and gave me insights that have shaped who I am today. I'd be a different person without that experience."

Jack's comment, and others like it, have been helpful in reminding

---

5. The name Jack is a pseudonym.

me that when we look at a story or an experience, we need to see it not only in the immediate details, but also from a broader perspective. And we find something similar in the story of Tamar. After the story of Joseph reaches its conclusion in Genesis, and his father Jacob has died, we are told that Joseph's brothers—including Judah—were afraid that Joseph would turn against them. But Joseph assured them that this was not the case. He says, "You intended to harm me, but God intended it for good" (Gen. 50:20).

As my friend Jack made clear, we do not celebrate death or loss. We acknowledge the pain and grieve. And we do not suggest that God has orchestrated a bad situation. In the stories of Joseph and Tamar, God is not to be blamed for Joseph being thrown in a pit, nor is God at fault for Tamar being treated badly by her father-in-law. Yet God allows human sin and suffering. Bad things happen, even if God does not directly cause them—a subtle, but important difference. And while there is evil in the world, as we see in the stories of Joseph and Tamar, we also see God entering those situations and bringing grace into the brokenness so that his light can shine through. The story of Tamar is, among other things, a story of a God who is present in a bad situation, bringing grace to those in need. That's what God did in the story of Joseph. That's what he does in numerous other stories throughout the Bible. And that's what God still does today.

THE IMPORTANCE OF KNOWING DIFFICULT STORIES

One of the essential keys to making some sense of the difficult or tricky stories of the Bible is to ask, *What is God doing in this story?* Too often we focus our attention on the people in the story, looking to them as moral examples. We ask whether what they did was right or wrong. We look for a lesson from their lives that we can emulate or avoid in our own life. But this approach takes the focus off God and puts it on human beings, who may or may not be worth emulating. Ultimately, it places the focus on you or on me and an immediate application for our lives today. But this is not always—or even often—the goal of the stories of the Bible. The focus of the Bible is on what we can learn about God, about the human condition, and about our relationship to God. If we keep this perspective in mind, we can begin to learn from these stories rather than just shaking our heads in puzzlement and confusion.

In 2004, a team of researchers from the University of California, Davis and South China Normal University conducted a study[6] on problem-solving, sometimes referred to as critical thinking. They gave a series of problems to students from the US and from China to see how they did solving these problems. One problem was called the *cave problem*, and it "described a scenario in which a treasure hunter needed to travel into a cave and then find his way out again, without the benefit of a map or compass."[7] The solution involved leaving a trail of sand or stones so that you could get in and out of the cave. The results were very interesting. Seventy-five percent of the US students in the sample solved the problem. Yet only 25 percent of the Chinese students were able to solve it.

Perhaps when I was describing the cave problem, you thought of the story of Hansel and Gretel. Here is a brief synopsis of the story:

> A woodsman and his wife were very poor and could not afford to feed themselves and their two small children, Hansel and Gretel. As a solution, the wife suggested that they lead the children out into the deep forest and leave them there. So the next day, they took them out to the forest to chop wood. Hansel, with his pockets full of pebbles, dropped one at regular intervals to mark a path back home. Later, while the children napped, the parents returned home without them. That night, the children followed the trail of pebbles that Hansel had left behind all the way home. When they arrived home, the parents acted happy at their return but immediately planned to take them back into the forest again the next day. Hansel, aware of the plan, wanted to go outside that night to get more pebbles. However, the wife locked both of the children in their room before he could do so. The next morning, she gave both children a piece of bread for lunch.

---

6. Zhe Chen, et al., "Having the Memory of an Elephant: Long-Term Retrieval and the Use of Analogues in Problem Solving," *Journal of Experimental Psychology: General* 133, no. 3 (September 2004): 415–33.

7. Ibid., 418.

Instead of saving the bread to eat, Hansel tore pieces off and left them on the trail to mark the way home. . . . [8]

In that story, Hansel marks a trail so that he and his sister can find their way back home. Lots of US children know that story, but many Chinese children do not.

Before we assume that something is wrong with Chinese education or Chinese culture, let's consider a second question asked in the study—the *statue problem:*

"The statue problem described a scenario in which a chief of a village by a river needed to use the weight of a stone statue to approximate the amount of gold coins that he must collect in taxes from a neighboring village. Because a conventional balance scale was not available, the chief faced a problem of matching the weights of the statue and the gold coins."[9]

The results of this problem were almost the opposite. Sixty-nine percent of the Chinese students solved that one, compared to just 8 percent of the US students.

Some of you, when you hear the statue problem, may think of the story of "Weighing the Elephant," a story well known by many Chinese children but not by many US children. Here is a brief summary of that story:

Long ago in China, there lived a powerful emperor. Every year, the rulers of the surrounding countries had to give him jewelry, gold, cloth materials, and animals as presents. One day, a ruler of a southern country presented him with an elephant as a gift. The emperor was delighted to see the elephant and asked the ruler what the weight of the elephant was. The ruler was embarrassed because even the biggest scale he owned was too small to weigh the huge elephant. The emperor's youngest son, named Chao Chong, came up with an idea: "You could find a boat, put the elephant in it, and mark the new

---

8. This story synopsis is used in the paper by Chen et. al., "Having the Memory of an Elephant: Long-Term Retrieval and the Use of Analogues in Problem Solving," 432.

9. Ibid., 418.

water level on the boat. Then, you could take the elephant out of the boat and put smaller stones into the boat until the water level reaches the same mark. Then, you could weigh those stones separately with a small scale. When you add up all the weights, you would know how heavy the elephant is." Everyone was surprised and impressed by the boy's solution.[10]

The results of this study—illustrated by the differing responses to the two problems—teach us that what we think of as problem-solving or critical thinking is specific to the things we already know. If we know a situation in which we can solve a problem, we naturally transfer that solution to analogous situations. If we do not have an analogous situation, we have a much harder time solving the problem.

This research can impact the way we think about faith formation and shows that students need specific, analogous knowledge to solve problems. As children and teens face situations in their lives which require critical faith thinking, they will need a rich and holistic biblical knowledge base if we want them to solve "faith problems."

I found I could make better sense of the story of my friend Jack's loss because I had seen how God had brought grace into the brokenness of Tamar's life. Because I have thought about the story of David and Bathsheba, I can better see how God will listen to my plea for forgiveness. I can more easily believe that God will not forsake me if I know the stories of Judges and Hosea. The Bible is, among other things, a testament to God's faithfulness, and these stories give us additional ways of receiving that message.

HOW TO TELL DIFFICULT STORIES

I am not advocating just gathering a bunch of preschoolers together and telling them all the stories they have not heard before. That is neither helpful nor educationally sound. But we can share these difficult stories and do it well if we remember several important things.

---

10. Ibid., 432.

GOD IS THE HERO OF THE STORY

It is incumbent on us, as church educators and as parents, to present these stories as stories of what God has done and what God does, instead of messages about how we should behave. If we try to turn the story of Judah and Tamar into a lesson about sexual morality, we will twist ourselves into knots trying to teach that sex outside of marriage is wrong while admitting that Tamar was rewarded for acting like a prostitute. When we read the story of Cain and Abel or of the Israelites and the golden calf, students know that God was not pleased with the sin of his people. We can talk about God's punishment and make it clear that God wants us to live holy lives.

But we should also teach the more difficult stories of Scripture. These stories require more nuance and explanation, but they often teach us that God brings grace to our brokenness. These are not moral tales, like Aesop's Fables. The hero is never Judah or Joseph or Samson or David. The hero is God, and the way we tell these stories needs to show that Scripture is, above all, a story of God and his faithfulness to his people. These stories point to the gospel of salvation, showing us that through Jesus' victory over death, the stain of our sins is washed away. They draw our attention to the larger story of the gospel of grace.

TELL STORIES IN AGE-APPROPRIATE WAYS

Before you rush out to tell the story of Judah and Tamar, or the Levite and his concubine (Judges 19) to ten-year-olds, make sure you are prepared to share them in age-appropriate ways. There is a time to add some of these stories to the list of passages we share with children and a time to wait until they are a little older. Yet sadly, most of the teens in our formation programs have never heard these stories at all. Even working in a Christian university, I find that many students don't realize these stories are in the Bible. And that's a disservice to them.

One rule of thumb in telling these stories is that one should never tell something that is not true about a story. Telling an untruth is different than leaving things out. For example, telling the story of Noah without mentioning the drunken episode at the end of the story (Genesis 9) makes sense for young children. Leaving it out is not being untruthful or giving them a false impression of the story, as long as we don't paint Noah as the hero.

YOU DON'T HAVE TO KNOW EVERYTHING

Much of the Bible is mysterious. Why did God choose Samson to be a judge (Judges 13–16)? Why did he give us the story of the Levite and his concubine (Judges 19–20)? Why did Jesus only take a few of his disciples with him to the garden of Gethsemane (Matt. 26)? I don't know the answers to any of these questions. I have some guesses and some ideas about how to start thinking about these things, but I have no answers. It is good to let children know that. Mystery is an important part of our faith. A God we can fully grasp is a God who is too small. These difficult stories are part of what makes our relationship with God full of mystery.

We should be authentic. It is fine to say that we don't know something. But then explore that together with children. Wonder together about what things might be behind wanting this story in our Bible. Children will learn more about how a person of faith addresses tough sections of the Bible in that exploration than they will if you try to give them a pat answer.

CONCLUSION

While it is important to highlight God as the hero of the Bible's grand story, the church also needs to prepare kids and teens for a life that includes hard questions and hard stories. We need to teach the Bible in a way that readies our students to face the hardship of seeing grandma's deterioration in the nursing home or a young classmate who receives a diagnosis of leukemia. They will quickly learn that people who lie and cheat may get ahead, while others who try to live with integrity face one setback after another. If we never present the hard stories of Scripture, our students won't have these stories in their hearts and minds when they face the hardships of real life. They will not see how God is present in their own suffering and sin.

We need to come alongside children, ask them what they need, listen to their responses, and walk with them. This isn't a radical new idea or program—this is simply giving kids and teens the story of who God is and what he does. The "big story" is found in the little stories we know well, as well as the little stories that we don't. Our students will be better prepared for life if they know more of the story. And it's a great story—the best story! Let's make sure we give them all of it.

CHAPTER 11

LITTLE THEOLOGIANS

Learning with and from Children as
We Live in the Story Together

DANA KENNAMER

———————|||———————

Something significant happens when we enter the biblical story with children open to what we will find together and trusting that children are capable of discovering and revealing truth. God's presence is evident as we engage in a posture of wonder, providing a space for mutual theological meaning-making. This requires courageous comfort with the mystery of God's story and the questions we have—adults and children alike.

I have been teaching children's Bible classes for forty-six years, beginning at age thirteen in my small hometown church. But my way of being with children in the Bible changed dramatically while I was completing my dissertation.[1] The question that guided my inquiry was, "How do children perceive God?" Because I was doing "research" and not "teaching," I was limited to asking questions and listening rather than telling and explaining. This listening posture changed everything!

My five-and six-year-old participants graciously shared their insights about God, heaven, the Bible, Jesus, joy, sorrow, life, and death. I learned not to dismiss their ideas as reflections of immaturity and began to "listen

---

1. For an expanded description of my dissertation, see Dana Hood, "Six Children Seeking God," in *Children's Spirituality: Christian Perspectives, Research and Applications*, ed. Donald Radcliff (Eugene, OR: Cascade Books, 2004), 233–248.

with anticipation that children have something meaningful and personal to share."[2] I discovered that the child's relationship to God is indeed "a source for theology in the truest sense of the word."[3]

This listening process was the beginning of my journey to transform the way I am with children in the sacred story. It challenges me to reconsider what I believe about the Bible; what it means to "learn about" or "know" God; and the role of the teacher—the adult who joins children on this journey of faith.

THE BIBLE ON ITS OWN TERMS

I grew up in a conservative, cognitive tradition that valued knowing the Bible. This is a blessing of my heritage that I treasure. However, I internalized that "knowing" was about facts and being right. I still value knowing details about wilderness wanderings, prophets and kings, the life of Jesus, and Paul's missionary journeys. But the focus on details and explanations kept truths to be found in the mystery of God's story hidden from me.

When I gather with my kindergarten and first-grade friends on Sundays, we often talk about mystery as we dwell in the story together. They describe a mystery as something that you have to look at again and again. You have to watch for clues, to pay attention. A mystery can be hard to figure out. When I ask if the mystery of Jesus is easy or hard, they affirm that it is a hard mystery, one we will always be trying to figure out. The children are comfortable with this mystery, though—with the knowing and the not knowing.

To share this sacred text with integrity, we must remember what the Bible is and what the Bible is not. It is not a book of rules or a history textbook. Despite common approaches to curriculum, the Bible is, as Csinos says, "not a storehouse of propositional truth about God or even a legal constitution that lays out the rules for proper living."[4] It is primarily a book

2. Ibid., 246.
3. Sofia Cavalletti, *The Religious Potential of the Child: 6–12 Years Old* (Chicago: Catechesis of the Good Shepherd Publications, 2002), 132.
4. David M. Csinos, *Children's Ministry in the Way of Jesus* (Downers Grove, IL: Intervarsity Press, 2013), 83.

of stories written over hundreds of years. These stories tell us how "God works through, for, and often, in spite of God's people."[5]

Peter Enns reminds us that this sacred book of stories is not going to "behave"—nor should we seek to make it do so. We must take the Bible on its own terms. It will inspire us, challenge us, and transform us as God draws us into the story with all its complexities and unanswered questions. "As all good stories do, the Bible shapes and molds us by drawing us into a world and inviting us to connect on many different levels, wherever we are in our journey, and to see ourselves better by its light by stirring our imagination to walk closer with God."[6]

COMPELLED TO WONDER

The Bible leaves a lot to the imagination. Eugene Peterson addresses this when he writes, "One of the characteristic marks of biblical storytellers is a certain reticence . . . They leave a lot of blanks in the narration, an implicit invitation to enter the story, just as we are, and to discover for ourselves how we fit into it."[7] The text compels us to wonder.

One Sunday, the children and I explored one of these "blanks." Our story was Jesus in the temple at twelve. Before we began, I said, "Boys and girls, in our story today, Jesus is twelve years old. A lot of time has passed since shepherds and wise men, but the Bible doesn't tell us about Jesus as a child. I wonder what Jesus was like as a little boy."

The children debated whether Jesus ever got in trouble. If he was really a little boy, he must have misbehaved. But if he was God, he wouldn't do anything bad. Some wondered if other kids liked Jesus. Was Jesus always nice so other children liked him, or was he too different to be their friend? They wondered when Jesus knew he was the son of God.

A first-grade friend exclaimed, "Teacher Dana, this is hard!" I said, "You're right. It's hard. Wise people have tried to figure this out for hundreds

5. Dana K. Pemberton, "Respect the Text and Respect the Children: Reconsidering Our Approaches to Bible School," in *Along the Way: Conversations about Children and Faith*, eds. Ron Bruner and Dana Kennamer Pemberton (Abilene, TX: Abilene Christian University Press, 2015), 186.

6. Peter Enns, *The Bible Tells Me So* (New York: HarperCollins, 2014), 136.

7. Eugene H. Peterson, *Eat this Book: A Conversation in the Art of Spiritual Reading* (Grand Rapids, MI: Eerdmans, 2006), 42.

of years. I still wonder, too." These little theologians grappled with the implications of the incarnation. What does it mean to have a God who put on skin, was a child, and grew up like us? This is serious stuff!

Sofia Cavalletti reminds us that wondering is not a superficial process: "Wonder is a very serious thing that, rather than leading us away from reality, can arise only from an attentive observation of reality."[8] Children can join and even lead us in serious, attentive wondering as we engage together in imaginative interpretation of the text. They are, as we know, particularly gifted with imagination.

MOVING INTO WONDER

As I shared at the beginning of this chapter, I am from a conservative cognitive tradition. But my journey to trusting the spiritual capacity of children has been shaped by those who have developed contemplative models of children's ministry, such as Catechesis of the Good Shepherd[9] and Godly Play.[10] I have read books and articles and attended conferences. I have visited churches implementing these deeply intentional models. Still, I do not claim to be trained in Godly Play or the Catechesis of the Good Shepherd, nor do I claim that I am "teaching" these models. My context makes full application difficult as these models require very specific training, materials, space, and time.

Despite these challenges, in partnership with my dear friend and children's pastor, Suzzetta Nutt,[11] our practices have been transformed by applying principles of these models in our own unique context. The first change we made was the use of wondering questions. Berryman cautions that these questions must be authentic: "If you think you already know the 'answer' to a wondering question, you are not wondering."[12] This seemingly small change was more transformative than we anticipated.

---

8. Sofia Cavalletti, *The Religious Potential of the Child: Experiencing Scripture and Liturgy with Young Children* (Chicago: Liturgy Training Publications, 1992), 139.

9. Catechesis of the Good Shepherd was developed by Sofia Cavalletti.

10. Godly Play was developed by Jerome Berryman.

11. My journey toward joining children in theological meaning making cannot be told without including Suzetta Nutt. To read about Suzetta's journey to integrate contemplative practices in her context, see Suzetta Nutt, "Practicing Spiritual Disciplines with Children," in *Along the Way: Conversations about Children and Faith*, eds. Ron Bruner and Dana Kennamer Pemberton (Abilene, TX: Abilene Christian University Press, 2015), 191–206.

12. Jerome W. Berryman, *Teaching Godly Play: How to Mentor the Spiritual Development of Children* (Denver: CO: Morehouse Education Resources, 2009), 53.

As you begin this process, start with a bit of wondering yourself. Allow yourself to live in the mystery and embrace your own questions. Trust that God will meet you there. While answers may not be clearly revealed, God's presence is made known in that space of open listening. The meaning of the story expands, inviting you to enter. God welcomes our questions, and through our wonderings, he reveals truth.

One Sunday morning, my kindergarten and first-grade friends and I lived in the story of Jesus being presented in the temple at eight days old. We talked about Mary and Joseph and the offering of two pigeons. We read the surprising words of Simeon and Anna, and we wondered about waiting for promises and women prophets.

As the story ended I said, "I wonder what Mary was thinking when she heard Simeon's words." There were several responses you might expect: "She was surprised." "She was confused." "She was glad because it meant that Jesus really was who the angel said he would be." And then a first-grader said, "I think she was happy, sad, and maybe mad, too. She could be happy that Jesus really was the one God promised. But he said people would reject Jesus, so that made her sad. And then I wonder if she was mad, like, 'What does he know? He shouldn't say things about my heart being broken!'"

Children are drawn into the story if we make space for wonder. Their interpretations and insights demonstrate a depth of engagement with the story that is surprising. I am reminded again and again to trust the children, trust the Spirit, trust the power of God's story, and be cautious about providing my own explanations. Scottie May wrote that "Meaning is embedded in the story itself . . . listeners hear and interpret story as it connects with their own understanding, experience and need. For this reason, explaining what the story means may short-circuit its impact for the learners."[13]

WONDER AS HOSPITALITY

On Wednesday evenings, we gather in a multi-age context with 60–70 children, kindergarten through fifth grade. Suzetta and her volunteers welcome a diverse group of children each week. Some have been part of the faith community all their lives, along with their families. Others come on their own from the surrounding neighborhood, where they live with

---

13. Scottie May, et al., *Children Matter: Celebrating Their Place in the Church, Family and Community* (Grand Rapids, MI: Eerdmans, 2005), 189.

a high level of poverty. There are children identified as gifted and those with disabilities. Their stories include foster families, single-parent families, traditional families, parents in prison, and children raised by grandparents. Our wonderings have opened a space of hospitality for all children, no matter the age, life situation, or previous experience with the story.

One evening, Suzetta shared the story of Rahab and the spies. She closed the story and began transitioning to response time when a first grader said, "Miss Suzetta, I have a wonder question. How did people in Jericho know about what God had done for the Israelites? They didn't have TV or anything." Some of the children offered the idea that as people traveled, they shared stories. The miracles God had done were big news. Word would have spread.

After this discussion, Suzetta again began the transition to reflection and response time when a fourth grader said, "I have a wonder question, too. I know they told stories and then they got written down. But how did those stories end up in our Bible today? How did they decide which stories to include?" She was wondering how the biblical canon was created! One of our retired pastors was a volunteer and engaged the children in conversation about how those choices were made—including that many Christians use Bibles that include books our Bibles do not.

Finally, everyone seemed ready to go to response time when a kindergartner interjected, "I have a wonder question, too. It's really important!" With furrowed brow, he said, "I think we need to think about it and not answer right away." We all waited. "Here is my question." We waited again. "How did the spies get to the roof?"

You might expect that laughter followed, but that was not the case. An older child talked about illustrations he had seen of houses in biblical times. Others said that in biblical times, people used their roofs like another room.

In that sacred context of wonder and hospitality, the children had learned to respectfully receive the questions of everyone else in the room. Wonder communicates that there are, as Nye writes, "differences in the ways people react and respond to each Bible story, and the children learn to respect the variety of ways people make meaning. The interactive process allows for the individuality of spiritual life to be honored; there is no herding into a common consensus."[14]

---

14. Rebecca Nye, *Children's Spirituality: What It Is and Why It Matters* (London: Church House Publishing, 2011), 67.

Hospitality also requires us to remember that words spoken do not fully represent a child's understandings, nor does silence communicate a lack of meaningful reflection. A child's age, personality, culture, and even events on a particular day play a part in what we see. And what we see is a small part of what the child knows of God. Stonehouse and May noted this when they wrote,"We must be careful not to judge children negatively based on our limited knowledge of what God may be revealing to them."[15]

Then there are times when nothing of significance seems to happen. The children do not appear to engage, and all I can say about the time we spent together is that they heard the words "God" and "Jesus" and went home still breathing! But as I reflect on the "less than successful" days, I realize it is not up to me to work in the heart of a child. I remind myself to trust that God lives and breathes in the speaking of the Word. Yes, they went home breathing.

METHODS MATTER

If we want to create space for wonder and hospitable listening, the way we tell the stories matters. Our methods say as much as the words we use. We share the stories for varied purposes in varied contexts with varied methods. Still, when we sanitize it, jazz it up, oversimplify it, or offer a predetermined "point," we are communicating that children are not capable of encountering the text in a meaningful way or that the Spirit cannot reveal truth through the story. We disregard the gift of the child's capacity to imagine and to wonder.

When we believe that children have genuine interpretive capacities, we make space for their imaginations. We trust that, as Stonehouse and May write, "God's presence will be real and the Spirit will be the teacher revealing to each child what he or she most needs to hear from God."[16] Rather than "talking *about* scripture," Berryman suggests we join children by "being *in* scripture."[17] Sofia Cavaletti tells us that the literal meaning of the Italian word for teaching is "to point." Rather than dictating or interpreting the message for children, we "point" to the reality the story

15. Catherine Stonehouse and Scottie May, *Listening to Children on the Spiritual Journey: Guidance for Those Who Teach and Nurture* (Grand Rapids, MI: Baker Academic, 2010), 6.

16. Ibid, 7.

17. Jerome W. Berryman, *Godly Play: An Imaginative Approach to Religious Education* (Minneapolis, MN: Augsburg, 1991), 69.

holds and move into the story with them, and, "Reality itself will then engage them in a profound educational process."[18]

THE TEXT AND SPIRIT WILL GUIDE

This "pointing" and "joining" is only possible if the teacher is living in the story as well. Our preparation is less about making materials and designing activities. It is dwelling in the text ourselves without predetermined goals. When I do this, I am almost always surprised. I discover details of the story I had forgotten or never noticed before. New questions emerge. Connections are revealed between my life and the life of a biblical character. I discover again that the Word truly is "alive and active" (Heb. 4:12).

Early in my own journey towards changing how I enter the story with children, I was at our church in the middle of the day, in our children's ministry resource room. A fellow volunteer happened to be there at the same time. She said, "Oh Dana, I am so glad you are here. I am getting ready for my class on Sunday and need some ideas." She told me she was teaching Balaam and just didn't know what to do with the story because it was so confusing and "they are only four. They really can't understand it. I thought maybe there was an activity in a book or something."

I avoided pointing out that I don't really understand the story of Balaam and instead asked her what she was thinking. She said, "I thought we would just talk about saying nice words to our friends." I asked, "Is that what the story is about?" Again, she emphasized that they were too young to understand the story and she just needed an idea. And then, I said it before I could stop myself: "Go home. Read the text. Pray. See what God reveals to you in the story."

Her face said it all. I was crazy and of no help! "Well," she said, "I just thought you might tell me a book that had something in it." I gently repeated, "Go home. Read the text. Pray. See what God reveals to you in the story." I confess that as she left (still quite bewildered), I looked heavenward and said, "God, if you can back me up on this one, it would be great."

I saw her after class that Sunday and asked how it went. She told me, "When I read the story over and over, I kept seeing that God wants to bless his people. We acted out the story and then we talked about blessing.

---

18. Cavalletti, *The Religious Potential of the Child: 6–12 Years Old*, 39.

It worked. They are only four, but they amazed me!" While this may or may not have been a significant event for my friend (I don't even know if she remembers it now), it was affirmation to me that I was on the right track. Read the text. Pray. See what God reveals. And allow the children to do the same.

THE STORY AT THE CENTER

I continued to reflect on this idea, and wondered, "How am I getting in the way of God's revelation as I share the story?" I noticed distractions in what I previously saw as "effective and engaging storytelling." I believed the story was effective if the children could recite the point of the lesson, which occurred if the point was repeated and simple enough for the children to understand and remember. I believed the story was engaging if the kids had fun or participated in hands-on activities. *But I was the distraction*—pointing children away from the mystery of the story.

Changing required an act of trust. Did I really believe God would be revealed if I moved out of the way? It was time to learn storytelling methods that pointed children to the story and not to me. My most important guide in this journey was Jerome Berryman, the developer of Godly Play. If you have not had the privilege of observing a Godly Play storyteller, find a church using the model and go! If that isn't possible, you can find Godly Play Foundation videos online to get a small taste of the simple, profound ways the storyteller invites children to enter into God's story.

In Godly Play, the story is placed in the center of the circle. The story is told using simple objects, slowly, with spaces of silence. The storyteller's gaze is often on the story itself, not on the children. Placing the story in the center communicates that the story belongs to us all and, as Berryman writes, "shows that we are all the same distance from ultimate truth and that it is no one's exclusive possession—not even the teacher's. God is far beyond all of us, yet as near as the center of the circle or within our own skins."[19]

Again, I am not trained in Godly Play, but the practice of slow, simple, and shared storytelling transformed the way I enter the story with children. At times I tell the story in ways modeled by Godly Play. We gather in a circle. As I tell the story, I place simple items or even shapes cut from

---

19. Berryman, *Teaching Godly Play: How to Mentor the Spiritual Development of Children*, 38.

paper on a cloth I've laid out with quiet, reverent anticipation. I point the children to the story by focusing my gaze there as well. We don't rush but leave spaces of quiet—an invitation for God to enter the story with us.

When I began using these methods, I was quite nervous. *What if it doesn't work? What if the kids won't pay attention?* My fears were unfounded. Children sense the importance of the story. When we begin, their focus changes. The children show me again and again that they are capable of entering the story—and that they want to hear from God.

DRAWING THE STORY

There are other ways to tell the story using simple and shared practices. One of my favorites is to draw the story together. Sometimes I place a large piece of paper on the wall. Then, as we read and talk about the story, I stop occasionally and ask the children what I should draw to help us remember and think about what we have heard.

Don't panic. This requires no artistic ability. The children and I establish that these drawings are to help us enter the story. We don't worry about how pretty it is, and we don't make time for details. We draw to reflect and remember. I warn you that the children will let you know when your horse looks like a dog and are willing to provide advice for how you might fix that, but they do not require stylistically impressive images. I also believe that my willingness to draw like this gives them permission to draw as well with no expectations of perfection.

At times the children draw the story. I provide them with clipboards, markers, and a paper divided into sections: three, four, or six—whatever works best for the story. Before we begin, I tell the children to listen as we tell the story and think about what they hear and what they wonder. During the story, we stop occasionally for the children to reflect and record their thoughts using words and pictures. We share our wonderings with each other as we go.

This listening, reflecting, writing, and drawing process is powerful. I have used this strategy with kindergarten through fifth grade. Children with varying levels of artistic ability and literacy skills can participate meaningfully in reflecting on and representing the story. In addition, this is a way of being in the text that they can take with them into adulthood. Try it yourself. Read the text, markers and paper in hand. What do you hear and what do you wonder? Prepare to be surprised.

THE MOST IMPORTANT THING

The concerning thing about the traditional "takeaway" is the danger of communicating that there is only one important thing to learn from a story. When you learn that, you move on. No need to return to that story again! But stories have layers. We bring our own stories to the text that shape how we hear and read. What is most important changes as we change.

At times I use simple, premade illustrations to support the telling of the story. Again, I lay these out in the center as the story unfolds. I am picky about the images I use. I want them to accurately represent the ethnicity of people in the biblical world. I avoid images that are overly comical or cute. One source I often use is Lamp Bible Pictures. This online source provides drawings with appropriate skin tones that are simple but do not trivialize the story.

After the story is finished, we look at the images laid out before us. I say, "I wonder, what do you think is the most important part of the story?" There are always multiple viewpoints and varying reasons for choices. Once, as we finished the story of the man who was let down through the roof to Jesus, I asked the "most important part" question. The children responded, "When Jesus told the man he was forgiven. That told people that Jesus was the son of God," and "When the man got up and walked. That was a miracle. It showed Jesus' power."

Then one of my kindergarten friends pointed to the friends carrying the stretcher up to the roof, and said, "I think that is the most important part. They were desperate to get their friend to Jesus. They didn't let crowds stop them. They knew they had to get him to Jesus. That is how we need to be. We need to be desperate to get people to Jesus, too." Well, that will preach!

THE STORY CONTINUES

Telling the story with open spaces communicates to the children that God's story is never finished and provides a path to enter the story in new ways as they grow. They discover that this is not just a story of long ago; it is their story as well.

When children realize that they are a part of this story, that God's story is also their story, that God's story connects with their own expanding self-narratives, they become responsible for ensuring that the episodes in which they make appearances are faithful to the overall script that God has laid out and that they help move the story forward to the concluding eschatological scene.[20]

One Wednesday night before Easter, the children and I gathered around a fabric cross laid out on the floor. About seventy children, ages five to eleven, read together the words that Jesus spoke on the cross from large notecards and then placed the cards on the cross. We wondered about the soldiers, the thief, the darkness, and what Jesus was feeling and thinking.

Through tears, I told the children that Jesus' words to Mary and John were words my heart needed. As a mommy, Jesus' care for his mother touches me. I asked the children which words Jesus spoke were words for them. They shared, "They don't know what they are doing. I do things I shouldn't, and I don't always know why. But Jesus forgives," and "Because he said it was finished, we know he did everything he came to do. We can trust that. He did it even though it was so hard," and "When he told the thief he would be with him in paradise. I mean, Jesus didn't do anything, but that thief did. And still, Jesus loved him."

When it was time to close the story, I said, "Boys and girls, we know the end of the story. We know that Easter is coming on Sunday. But tonight, we are going to leave Jesus on the cross—in the dark part. This is hard, but it is important to remember the darkness. We will finish the story next week." And then one of my little third-grade theologians spoke words of truth for us all: "Teacher Dana, the story doesn't end next week. The story never ends. The story goes on in all of us."

Once again, one of the children I am "teaching" instead taught me. The story goes on. We can always learn something new. God's mystery will always surprise us if we are willing to experience imagination and wonder. And sometimes we need a little theologian to point us to reality.

---

20. David M. Csinos and Ivy Beckwith, *Children's Ministry in the Way of Jesus* (Downers Grove, IL: IVP Press, 2013), 89.

Nurturing Children's Spirituality

THROUGH DIFFERENT
METHODS

CHAPTER 12

DOES THE CHURCH CARE IF CHILDREN CAN THINK?

MIMI L. LARSON

As the lone Christian educator in a doctoral philosophy of education class, I was often challenged by my colleagues, who would ask me if the church really cared about educating children. They believed the church didn't have any interest in whether children could really think. The church, they accused, just wanted to indoctrinate children in what they should believe and wasn't concerned if children could think and believe for themselves.

Their question haunted me as I wondered whether there was an element of truth in it. While I believe Christian educators desire children to embrace a biblical worldview, I wondered, do we encourage children to learn how to think about things biblically, or do we tell them what they should believe? Do we allow room for children to question? Do we provide space for children to explore and evaluate different ideas? Do we give children authority to propose a new solution to a problem and provide them agency to see if it might work?

I believe the church desires children to learn and be spiritually formed as a result of instruction, but are we engaging in methods that will actually increase their learning and formation? There is great concern that, when they are grown, children will leave the church and the faith behind. Is it possible that how we engage them in the learning process might hinder their ownership of faith? While current curriculum may encourage factual biblical knowledge, it doesn't mean that children are able to understand or apply these concepts in a personalized way.[1] Since many ministries rely heavily on published curriculum to guide their instruction, does the curriculum we use encourage children to engage in thinking, or are we actually doing what my colleagues accused us of—indoctrinating children with just "right" answers? Does our curriculum push past the foundational understandings and engage children in higher levels of thinking? Are we telling children *what* to think biblically, or are we teaching children *how* to think biblically?

THE DIFFERENT WAYS OF THINKING

To understand the difference between *what* to think and *how* to think, let's take a look at an example based on Mark 12:30–31. Mark's Gospel tells us that a teacher of the Law came to Jesus and asked him which is the most important commandment. Jesus answered:

> "Love the Lord your God with all your heart and with all your soul and with all your mind and with all your strength." The second is this: "Love your neighbor as yourself." There is no commandment greater than these. (Mark 12:30–31)

Based on this biblical passage, let's propose four different activities for elementary-age children.

ACTIVITY #1: Memorize and recite Mark 12:30–31.
ACTIVITY #2: Name different ways we can love our neighbors.
ACTIVITY #3: Examine Acts 2:42–47 and identify the different ways the early church demonstrates love. Which do you think is the best way to love your neighbor? Why is this the best way? (Defend your answer.)
ACTIVITY #4: Who is our neighbor? What do you suggest we can do to best demonstrate love to this neighbor?

Can you see any difference between these activities? The first activity involves specific knowledge—reciting Mark 12:30–31 from memory.

---

1. Larry D. Burton, Eliane E. Paroschi, Donna J. Habenicht, and Candice C. Hollingsead, "Curriculum Design and Children's Learning at Church," *Religious Education* 101, no. 1 (2006): 4–20.

There is only one correct answer. The second activity uses the acquired or prior knowledge and applies it to a new situation. The third activity begins to get a little more complicated. We have to compare and contrast two different things—the passages in Acts and in Mark—to determine how they relate to one another. But then it adds in a judgment call: which do *you* think is the best way? There isn't just one right answer to that question. Each student might have a different thought on why his or her idea is best. And the last activity becomes even more complicated since it involves a variety of steps: (1) identify who our neighbor is; (2) name ways to love our neighbors; (3) evaluate which is the best way; and (4) propose (and hopefully implement) a new idea based on this thinking.

BLOOM'S TAXONOMY

In 1956, Benjamin Bloom created a six-tiered model that classified cognitive thinking.[2] The three lower levels of thinking included Knowledge, Comprehension, and Application. The three higher levels of thinking included Analysis, Evaluation, and Synthesis. In 2001, educators revised the taxonomy, renaming the categories and interchanging levels 5 and 6. Bloom's original taxonomy listed Synthesis (Create) as the fifth level and Evaluation as the sixth. The revised taxonomy (see figure 1) now has Evaluate as the fifth level and Create (Synthesis) as the highest level of cognitive thinking.

FIGURE 1

Level 6: Create

Level 5: Evaluate

Level 4: Analyze

Level 3: Apply

Level 2: Understand

Level 1: Remember

---

2. Benjamin S. Bloom and Max D. Engelhart, *The Classification of Educational Goals: Handbook 1—Cognitive Domain* (New York: David McKay Company, Inc., 1956).

The first level, Remember, focuses on knowing and engages the act of remembering or recalling previously learned information. It is where relevant information is retrieved from long-term memory and is done usually through memorization, recognition, or recall of information. While foundational, it is the lowest level of thinking because it does not assume that the learner understands the information, just that he or she is able to recall it. Reciting a memory verse or listing all the kings of the northern or southern kingdoms are forms of level 1 thinking. Biblical information is retrieved and recited.

Level 2, Understand, expects the learner to demonstrate comprehension and understanding of information. Here is where learners begin to construct meaning from instructional messages. As learners make sense of the material being studied, this information can be utilized in the future. While this type of learning goes beyond basic recall and recognition, it is still categorized as a low level of comprehension.[3] An activity wherein learners "name different ways we can love our neighbors" engages in this type of thinking. Learners are asked to demonstrate their understanding by giving descriptions of the different ways we can love our neighbors.

The third level, Apply, is where knowledge is utilized in a given situation through problem-solving. A person takes the knowledge they have retrieved and comprehended and now applies it to a new situation. As David Sousa discusses in his book *How the Brain Learns,* "It includes the application of such things as rules, concepts, methods, and theories to solve problems. The learner activates procedural memory and uses convergent thinking to select, transfer, and apply data to complete a new task."[4] Practice is essential at this level to master the new task, but the goal is to apply the understandings they have gained in a particular situation. An example of this would be giving children a situation wherein they could role-play and apply different ways they could express love to their neighbors in a particular situation.

Level 4, Analyze, starts moving the learner into a higher level of thinking. In analysis, information is broken down into smaller or simpler parts, and learners must determine how these parts relate to one another and to an overall purpose. Thinking is more complex at this level because

3. David A. Sousa, *How the Brain Learns, 3rd ed.* (Thousand Oaks, CA: Corwin Press, 2006), 250.
4. Ibid., 251.

the learner is aware of the content and structure of material, as well as metacognition and the thought processes involved.[5] When children are asked to compare and contrast the passages in Mark and Acts, they engage in an analysis of relationships between two different biblical stories, and they have to determine how these ideas relate to one another. In this higher level of thinking, children are moving from acquiring biblical information to developing a biblical worldview. By engaging in higher levels of thinking such as analysis, learners begin to integrate ideas into an individual's life and potentially shape and change behavior.[6]

Level 5, Evaluate, is where learners make and defend judgments based on certain criteria or standards. As they present ideas, learners must defend their opinion based on these standards. These standards or criteria can be created by or given to the learner. Most activities at this level will have multiple solutions or answers. This is a higher level of thinking because in order to evaluate, a learner must draw on the other levels of thought and then make a conscious choice or judgment. When done well, learners often become open to others and their opinions. The second half of Activity #3 is an evaluation activity. After completing an analysis of Acts and Mark, children are asked to make a judgment call on which they believe is the best way to love your neighbor. The criteria have already been established with Jesus' words, and children have to defend their decision with a reason. This type of thinking means that there might be multiple answers to a question. Each child might choose a different way of loving as the "best" way.

Level 6, Create, is where learners create something new. They form a new pattern or structure, utilizing learned elements from the other levels of thinking. This level stresses creativity and encourages learners to engage in an original idea, proposing something new or an alternative solution. By asking children "Who is our neighbor?" they must recall, understand, and apply knowledge. Then by going further and asking them to create a new way to demonstrate love to this neighbor, children move into higher levels of thinking and synthesize all the different levels of cognitive knowledge to create a new idea. This is more than just application of an idea. It is the action of creating, along with the goal of implementing, something new.

    5. Ibid., 252.
    6. Leona M. English, "The Subversive Curriculum: What Religious Educators Are Learning Informally and Incidentally," *Religious Education* 95, no. 2 (2000): 167–180.

While some scholars critique the taxonomy as placing too much importance on higher-level thinking skills and not on the underlying lower-level
knowledge on which higher order thinking is founded,[7] Bloom believed
that the idea of mastering learning "can develop a lifelong interest in
learning."[8] If this is true for secular education, can it also be true for faith
development? Is higher-level thinking a key to encouraging lifelong faith?

CURRICULUM AND THE LEVELS OF THINKING

The goal for curriculum and instruction is for learners to gain mastery of
a subject. Curriculum, in the form of published ministry materials, provides intentional activities wherein children are provided a foundation for
biblical learning. The implicit understanding of curriculum is that when
we cognitively teach biblical truths to children, they are able to internalize
biblical truth, and their hearts are turned towards God and his creation. In
the revision of the taxonomy, Bloom and his colleagues identify that "One
of the most important goals of education is to provide learners the abilities
and affective dispositions which will permit them to adapt to a wide variety
of situations."[9] In Christian education, we desire children to gain biblical
knowledge and understanding so that they are able to develop a biblical
worldview, utilizing this worldview as they engage in a wide variety of life
situations. How do we do this? By engaging in higher levels of thinking where
learners can "analyze situations, make and defend decisions, solve problems."[10]
These skills are all gained at the higher levels of Bloom's Taxonomy.

In Christian education, we strive to not only provide cognitive understanding, but also to impact beliefs and behavior. Can we achieve this impact
just by presenting knowledge and pressing children to understand and apply it?
The goal of Christian educators is internalization, where information grows
into a belief, and this belief impacts behavior. Remembering, understanding,

---

7. Mark Seaman, "Bloom's Taxonomy: Its Evaluation, Revision, and Use in the Field of
Education," *Curriculum & Teaching Dialogue* 13, no. 1/2 (2011): 29–43.

8. Bloom, *The Classification of Educational Goals: Handbook 1—Cognitive Domain*, 174.

9. Lorin W. Anderson, David R. Krathwohl, and Benjamin S. Bloom, *A Taxonomy for Learning,
Teaching, and Assessing: A Revision of Bloom's Taxonomy of Educational Objectives* (New York: Longman,
2001), 127.

10. Ibid.

and applying knowledge are all important. But as some experts assert, "knowledge possessed does not automatically mean knowledge deployed."[11] It is through the higher levels of thinking, the questions of analysis and evaluation, along with the ability to create a new solution, that children are given the opportunity to work out their understandings and develop their thinking. As they start deploying the knowledge they have been given and the understandings they have created, learners can begin to attach meaning through analysis and evaluation. Thus, it is essential that Christian education curriculum contains these higher-level questions and activities,[12] and provides the opportunity for children to move from simply knowing and understanding materials to a place of internalization of beliefs and biblical truth.

HOW DOES CURRICULUM MEASURE UP?

Does the curriculum churches use push past foundational understandings and encourage children to attain higher levels of thinking? To answer this question, I had to look at actual curriculum to see how it measured up. This research project examined five popular, evangelical, mostly non-denominational children's curricula. The thirty-nine randomly selected elementary-age lessons contained several variables, including age range (kindergarten through sixth grade); a variety of different categories of curricula, including large group/small group and traditional classroom structures; and a wide range of biblical lessons, including both Old and New Testament. Activities within these lessons were analyzed and categorized based on design and educational intent into the categories established in Bloom's levels of thinking. Just because an activity utilized language and verbs for a certain level did not mean that was the educational intent or purpose for that activity. For example, one curriculum included a craft activity, which could have been interpreted as a Level 6—Create activity. Children were to take clay and create a new structure from it. But the intent of the activity was not to create a new idea, nor was it an activity that put

---

11. Sam Wineburg and Jack Schneider, "Was Bloom's Taxonomy Pointed in the Wrong Direction?" *Phi Delta Kappan* 91, no. 4 (2009): 56–61.
12. Heather A. Lee, "Thinking Levels of Questions in Christian Reading Textbooks," *Journal of Research on Christian Education* 24, no. 2 (2015): 89–100.

elements learned into a new idea. This clay craft activity actually intended to help children remember what they learned and make meaning from it. Thus, it was categorized as a Level 2—Understand activity.

When I looked at the actual activities and questions in published ministry curriculum, what I discovered was more concerning than I had imagined. Over 93 percent of all activities in children's ministry curriculum landed in the lower levels of thinking. (See Figure 2.) While one curriculum strived to utilize verbs associated with Bloom's Taxonomy such as create, evaluate, and analyze, these understandings were very shallow. The object of the activities was not designed to push learners into higher levels of thinking but only to help them understand concepts and construct meaning from them (Level 2—Understand).

FIGURE 2: *How well does children's ministry curriculum engage in the levels of Bloom's Taxonomy?*

Upper Levels of Thinking	**Level 6—Create**	0.5 percent	
	Level 5—Evaluate	1.4 percent	7 percent
	Level 4—Analyze	5 percent	
Lower Levels of Thinking	**Level 3—Apply**	32.3 percent	
	Level 2—Understand	41.8 percent	93 percent
	Level 1—Remember	19 percent	

When a curriculum did utilize a higher level of thinking, these activities were not designed in terms of biblical understanding. For example, one lesson on Noah's Ark included an activity wherein children tested a variety of different items to see if they would sink or float. While this is technically a Level 4—Analyze activity, it did nothing to further understanding of the biblical story. Another activity encouraged children to make a zoo habitat for animals. Again, this is an activity that encourages children to create a new structure, which is technically a higher level of thinking (Level 6—Create), but the biblical story of Noah is much more than a floating zoo. How does creating a zoo habitat help children understand God's judgment and grace?

What was also concerning was *how* children gained their understandings.

Much of Level 1 and Level 2 thinking relied on learner-generated ideas, meaning that the teacher would ask questions, and the children had to think and answer for themselves. The children had to provide the knowledge or demonstrate comprehension. But this ownership changed as we moved up the levels. Most of the Level 3—Apply thinking was done by the teacher and given *to* the learners instead of being generated *by* the children themselves. When a teacher tells children what they are meant to think, the children do not own the thinking. They only receive it. Bloom asserts that thinking must progress from simple awareness and knowledge to a place where "it becomes [a] life outlook."[13] Critical thinking is key for this type of learning, and by engaging in higher levels of thinking, children can begin to own these ideas for themselves.

A CALL FOR BETTER CURRICULUM

Ministries rely heavily on curriculum to direct teaching and activities of learning. This curriculum, then, must hold the tension of strong biblical and theological content with the needs of children and an understanding of how children learn. Karen Estep recognizes this tension and reminds us that failing to do so produces a "curriculum that is irrelevant, and is likewise ineffective for preparing individuals to live a genuine Christian life."[14] The goal of ministry curriculum is to develop disciples. If higher levels of thinking help deepen a child's biblical thinking and develop a deeper internalization of beliefs, there are three key issues that must be addressed.

First, curriculum must be designed and written for children to engage in higher levels of thinking. As one researcher states, current curriculum may encourage factual biblical knowledge, but that doesn't mean children are able to express the messages of biblical story.[15] If children are to engage in the higher levels of thinking in a Christian education setting, they need opportunities to move from simply knowing and understanding materials

---

13. David R. Krathwohl, Benjamin S. Bloom, and Bertram B. Masia, *The Classification of Educational Goals: Handbook II—Affective Domain* (New York: David McKay Company, Inc., 1964), 27.

14. Karen Lynn Estep, "Charting the Course: Curriculum Design," in *Mapping Out Curriculum in Your Church: Cartography for Christian Pilgrims*, eds. James Estep, Roger White, and Karen Estep (Nashville, TN: B&H Publishing Group, 2012), 182.

15. Burton, et al., "Curriculum Design and Children's Learning at Church," 19.

to a place of internalization and expression of beliefs and biblical truth. This internalization and ability to express comes when we intentionally engage in analysis, evaluation, and synthesis.

The most common question I get when talking about Bloom's Taxonomy and children is whether children have the developmental ability to engage in higher levels of thinking. It is suggested that maybe children's ministry curriculum should focus on the lower levels of thinking and allow youth ministry to engage in the higher levels of thinking. I agree that youth ministry should be engaging in the higher levels of thinking. Yet while these discussions and activities can be more complex and dynamic for youth and adults, children are already engaging in the higher levels of thinking. Beyer recognizes, "They make decisions, attack problems, pose hypotheses, evaluate information, and even make inferences."[16] Building on the foundation of the lower levels of thinking, we need to continue to press into the higher levels, calling children to a higher place of learning and expression.

Second, curriculum must engage learners in developing thinking from a biblical perspective. As the research shows, some activities were designed for higher levels of thinking. However, these activities were not utilized to create higher levels of *biblical* thinking. While fun, the activity actually only aided in lower levels of biblical understanding. This is not acceptable when we are desiring to form and nurture children in the faith. The amount of time we have with children is limited. While many activities are fun and enjoyable, we must balance that with purpose and intention.

Ministry curriculum must keep its ultimate purpose at the forefront. Our goal is to develop children's faith and nurture their relationship with God. The activities children engage in must have a purpose to develop biblical understanding and engagement with God. It is essential that the lessons focus on the biblical story and are committed to a theological framework. As researchers explain, "Though the teaching of Scripture should always be presented in age-appropriate ways, a developmental or behavioral grid must not be allowed to interfere with the teaching of the text . . . In Bible-based lessons the purpose of the biblical passage must guide the lesson development process."[17]

---

16. Barry Beyer, "Improving Student Thinking," *Clearing House* 71, no. 5 (May 1998): 262.

17. J. H. Walton, L. D. Bailey, and C. Williford, "Bible-based Curricula and the Crisis of

Finally, curriculum must be designed to encourage the learner to discover for him or herself instead of being told what to think. As the research demonstrates, many ministry curricula rely on the teacher telling the learner what to think instead of the learner discovering ideas on their own. This is exactly what my colleagues accused us of: telling children what to believe instead of encouraging them to think or discover information for themselves. Curriculum must be designed in a way that encourages and nurtures learners to actively construct their own understanding through interactions with the environment and reflections on those actions.

This is a philosophical shift in how we teach and in how we envision learning. Are we encouraging children to just receive and process information that we give them? Or, are we encouraging them to actively engage in biblical understanding and construct their own meaning? As Estep reminds us, "Christian educators need to develop curriculum that values the process of construction by the learner. . . . The learner needs the opportunity to work at solving age-appropriate problems, a process that will enable their cognitive construction of knowledge."[18] By encouraging children to think and discover biblical understandings under the guidance of a skilled teacher and mature believer, the child is learning *how* to think biblically and not just specifically *what* to think.

While telling children what to think might be easier, there is no guarantee that in the telling, children are actually embracing these ideas. It can be uncomfortable to allow children to create meaning, but this is where they internalize learning—where it becomes their own. Critics might say that children are not able to create their own meaning, because our sinfulness and corrupt nature will lead them astray. That is not what I am saying. Children must create their own meaning with the active participation, thoughtful guidance, and intentional scaffolding of a more mature believer. And when they do, this can actually serve the church in a variety of ways. By allowing children to create solutions, it is possible for children to discover something that the church needs to hear. A child discovering a personal understanding in their own context and for their own generation might be able to provide a perspective that we are lacking.

Scriptural Authority," *Christian Education Journal* 13, no. 3 (1993): 86–87.
    18. Estep, et al., *Mapping Out Curriculum in Your Church: Cartography for Christian Pilgrims,* 109.

Revising Curriculum to Engage in Higher Levels of Thinking

It is vitally important that we remember no curriculum is perfect. Each curriculum has strengths and weaknesses. Also, our specific context will influence our choices. When choosing a curriculum, we have to balance our context's particular strengths and weaknesses with what a particular curriculum offers. Often, we choose a curriculum to address one or more of our identified needs. When we do so, it is important that we are aware of how the curriculum aids our teaching as well as how it might hinder learning. What are the deficiencies in a curriculum, and how can we address those flaws? If at all possible, look for a curriculum that is committed to biblical content and is accompanied by strong teaching methods, including engaging children in higher levels of thinking.

But what do you do if you are already committed to a curriculum that doesn't engage learners in the higher levels of thinking? First, look for ways you can enhance activities, expanding them to include higher levels of thinking. What questions can you add that move children into the act of analysis or evaluation? How can you rework an activity to engage both higher levels of thinking and biblical understanding? This will require thought and pre-planning, but if done well, can be exciting and engaging for all involved. Encourage questioning and reward creative thinking. Journey together in the learning process. As Thomas and Thorne write in *How to Increase Higher Order Thinking,* "A teacher should let the student with higher order thinking challenges know that they will work together as partners to achieve increases in the students' skills. With this type of relationship, often the student will bring very practical and effective strategies to the table that the teacher may not have otherwise considered."[19]

If you find that your curriculum is lacking, don't be afraid to add a component by building on the themes that are already established. Create activities and teaching that draws learners into higher levels. If you engage in a large group/small group style of ministry, and a unit focuses on a specific topic, create a module that can be added to the large group time. If you

---

19. A. Thomas and G. Thorne, *How to Increase Higher Level Thinking* (Metarie, LA: Center for Development and Learning, 2009), https://www.cdl.org/articles/how-to-increase-high-order-thinking/.

have a traditional classroom situation, forgo an activity in the curriculum and utilize that time instead to engage in a special focus.

Let's look at an example. For instance, let's say the curriculum you are using focuses on the topic of worship for four weeks. How can you develop a four-week module that takes the theme of worship and engages children in the higher levels of thinking? First, assess how the curriculum is engaging learners. Maybe it already has activities that address various levels of thinking. If not, the first week, you can create an activity that focuses on Level 1—Remember and Level 2—Understand by memorizing a Bible verse that focuses on worship. You can ask children to teach you what it means to worship (an Understand activity). For week 2, you can engage in application (Level 3—Apply) and ask students to demonstrate different ways we can worship. During the third week, you can ask students to list all the different ways we worship and then have them share which they believe the church engages in well and which ones the church doesn't do well. This activity engages both Level 4—Analyze and Level 5—Evaluate. During the final week, you could have kids help design a worship experience for the entire group or even for the church. What would they include? What would they want to focus on? If at all possible, have the children construct and implement the worship service. Actualizing a worship service will help enforce the biblical understandings of worship in a personal and intimate way. Figure 3 is a chart which can serve as a guide for curriculum writers.

CONCLUSION

As ministry leaders, we are concerned that children develop strong biblical knowledge and the ability to think biblically. The challenge is if our curriculum is actually aiding us in this process. While the lower levels of thinking provide the foundation of biblical knowledge, higher levels of thinking aid children in moving from simply knowing and understanding something to a place where beliefs and biblical truth are internalized. Ministry curriculum must embrace higher levels of thinking from a biblical perspective. When children are able to construct biblical understandings for themselves under the guidance of a mature believer, they develop a personal biblical worldview that can serve both themselves and the larger church body.

FIGURE 3: *Bloom's Taxonomy Put into Practice*

Level		Verbs	Sample Activities
6	Create	Construct Design Develop Produce Assemble Create	Design an activity that shows love to your neighbor. Develop and produce a worship service. Write your own psalm of thanksgiving.
5	Evaluate	Judge Assess Appraise Critique Choose Justify	Assess the best way to love your neighbor. Choose which activities are the best way for our group to worship. Critique the older brother's response to his brother's (the prodigal son) return home.
4	Analyze	Compare Contrast Differentiate Examine Subdivide Diagram	Compare two biblical passages and contrast the way they both demonstrate love. Examine how John the Baptist and Jesus are similar and different. Diagram the different books and genres of the Bible.
3	Apply	Practice Implement Use Demonstrate Solve Interpret	Demonstrate or role play how to love your friend at school. Practice praying out loud. Solve story problems that relate to the biblical lesson.
Level		Verbs	Sample Activies
2	Understand	Comprehend Explain Paraphrase Describe Summarize Discuss	Discuss the different ways we can show love. Explain what it means to be kind. Describe how Zechariah lost his voice.
1	Remember	Recognize Name Recite Recall Define List	Recite a memory verse. Define "worship." List the kings of the southern kingdom.

CHAPTER 13

NORMALIZING WHITE SPIRITUALITY IN CHILDREN'S SUNDAY SCHOOL CURRICULA

HENRY ZONIO

———— |+| ————

In a 1952 speech to the Women's Society of Riverside Church in New York, Helen Kenyon declared eleven o'clock on Sunday morning the most segregated hour in America.[1] This statement, popularized by Dr. Martin Luther King Jr., has been reiterated over the years in sermons, books, research, articles, speeches, and more. It succinctly captures racial tensions within the North American church. While there has been marginal growth in the number of multiracial churches in the United States,[2] most attendees at multiracial churches do not differ from those who attend predominantly white churches in their explanations of racial inequalities.[3] While many in the religious, psychological, and sociological worlds have explored the reasoning for the persistence of racialized attitudes within the North American church, there are few studies focused on the role of religious education on children's racial socialization.

---

1. "Worship Hour Found Time of Segregation," *New York Times*, November 4, 1952.
2. Mark Chaves, *American Religion: Contemporary Trends* (Princeton, NJ: Princeton University Press, 2011).
3. Ryon J. Cobb, et al., "United by Faith? Race/Ethnicity, Congregational Diversity, and Explanations of Racial Inequality," *Sociology of Religion* 76, no. 2 (2015): 177–98.

This chapter summarizes how evangelical religious education curricula construct race or, more accurately, normalizes whiteness as the frame for spirituality by way of a subversive invisibility of racial categories and racial meanings.[4] I have focused on these curricula because they are a significant source of material cultural artifacts that children draw from to interpret, transform, and reproduce their understandings of the world.[5]

BACKGROUND

Debra Van Ausdale and Joe Feagin offer one of the most eye-opening studies on how children construct their understanding of race and how they negotiate race as part of their initial peer cultures.[6] Their eleven-month-long ethnographic research within a preschool focusing on how children learn about race when not being surveilled by adults revealed that children as young as three years old have very complex and nuanced understandings of race and use those understandings as inclusive and exclusive strategies amongst their peers.[7] Moreover, Van Ausdale and Feagin found that young children are able to understand the hierarchical nature of race relations, perceiving whiteness as being at the top of racial stratification within the United States.[8]

While Van Ausdale and Feagin focus on children's peer interactions as a means of learning racial rules and meanings, Amanda Lewis examined the hidden racial curriculum in elementary schools taught through written materials and through teachers' interactions with students.[9] One of the main findings in Lewis' research was that teachers and administrators unknowingly participated in practices that downplayed the racialized experiences of children on the playground.[10] Additionally, Lewis notes that many of the behaviors exhibited by middle-and upper-class (mostly

4. Eduardo Bonilla-Silva and David G. Embrick, "'Every Place Has a Ghetto . . .' The Significance of Whites' Social and Residential Segregation," *Symbolic Interaction* 30, no. 3 (2007): 323–45.

5. William A. Corsaro, *The Sociology of Childhood*, 2nd ed. (Thousand Oaks, CA: Pine Forge Press, 2005).

6. Debra Van Ausdale and Joe R. Feagin, *The First R: How Children Learn Race and Racism* (Lanham, MD: Rowman & Littlefield Publishers, Inc., 2001).

7. Ibid., 180.

8. Ibid., 192–193.

9. Amanda E. Lewis, *Race in the Schoolyard: Negotiating the Color Line in Classrooms and Communities* (New Brunswick, NJ: Rutgers University Press, 2003).

10. Ibid., 21.

white) students in the classroom resulted in those children receiving more attention than working-class (mostly non-white) students. Lewis claims that these interactions reproduce racist structures within the United States.

Building on these studies, I examined the hidden racial curriculum within Sunday school materials for preschool and kindergarten children. I used Michael Omi and Howard Winant's concept of racial formation, racial categories, and racial meanings as one frame for analyzing explicit and implicit racial messages in the Sunday school curriculum.[11] I also used Eduardo Bonilla-Silva's concepts of colorblind racism[12] as another framework for understanding the overpowering silence of racial issues in Sunday school curricula.

LOOKING AT CURRICULUM

I examined thirteen sets of religious education curricula, representing seven publishing houses, that provide various religious materials for different Protestant denominations. Six of the publishers were conservative evangelical, and one of them was progressive mainline. In total, I analyzed 169 lessons that were written for use between 2006 and 2016. All the curricula that were used in this study consisted of visuals used for storytelling, some form of worksheets, crafts, or other activities that children worked on and took home, and leaders' guides with detailed lesson plans and scripts. The curricula targeted children between the ages of four and six years old. William Corsaro argues that a majority of children do not begin shaping their primary peer cultures until preschool or kindergarten because, for many children, that is the age when they begin to interact with adults and children outside of their immediate family.[13] Since I am interested in how children construct and negotiate their understanding of race, racial categories, and the meanings attached to those categories, I examined curricula that were targeted for children in preschool and kindergarten.[14]

11. Michael Omi and Howard Winant, *Racial Formation in the United States*, 3rd ed. (New York: Routledge, 2015).

12. Eduardo Bonilla-Silva, *Racism Without Racists: Color-Blind Racism and the Persistence of Racial Inequality in America*, 4th ed. (Lanham, MD: Rowman & Littlefield Publishers, Inc., 2014).

13. William A. Corsaro, *We're Friends, Right?: Inside Kids' Culture* (Washington, D.C.: Joseph Henry Press, 2003) and Corsaro, *The Sociology of Childhood*.

14. I used grounded theory methods (Kathy Charmaz, *Constructing Grounded Theory: A Practical Guide Through Qualitative Analysis* (Thousand Oaks, CA: SAGE Publications, 2006), as a means to

Initially, I focused on racial themes, but I quickly realized that explicit racial themes were left out of the written curriculum. Drawing from the concept of colorblind racism,[15] I turned my attention to colorblind lessons and colorblind identities.

MESSAGES ABOUT RACE ABOUND

Drawing from my experiences growing up in church and working in various capacities with the religious education of children within churches, I was expecting to see very little in Sunday school curricula that specifically dealt with race and/or skin color and issues of inequality and injustice connected to race. What I did find in the curricula was a complex mixture of implicit and explicit messages about race that were problematized by the nature of each curriculum. Messages were explicitly communicated to children verbally as well as implicitly through illustrations and pictures. Moreover, the curricula communicated to the Sunday school teachers through the leaders' guides just as much as they did to the children through the teaching scripts and activities.

A PICTURE IS WORTH A THOUSAND WORDS

A picture is a versatile communication medium that utilizes visual symbols to implicitly and explicitly communicate ideas, feelings, norms, information, and much more. When it comes to passing on stories to children, pictures provide an interpretive bridge by offering visual symbolic representations that feed into a child's understanding of what is considered normal. Analysis of the pictures and illustrations included within the curricula revealed three dominant themes: predominantly white pictorial depictions of Bible stories, overwhelmingly white representations of church, and multiculturalism as diversity.

Predominantly White Bible Characters. Out of the seven publishing companies, all but two of the companies exclusively portrayed the characters

allow analytical themes and categories to arise from the data thus mitigating my biases as a result of my prior involvement as an adult who taught child religious education and as a child who grew up in church.

15. Bonilla-Silva, *Racism Without Racists: Color-Blind Racism and the Persistence of Racial Inequality in America.*

in Bible stories as white people. These pictures were not only passively used as background illustrations that were secondary to the verbal telling of the stories, but many times, these white representations of Bible characters were actively used as part of the storytelling. For example, in a retelling of a story about David and Goliath, pictures of a white David, a white Goliath, and a white Saul were used.

(As you show each [picture], children can finish your sentence by saying what or who is pictured on the card. Show David card 2a) This is David. David likes music; he played a *(show harp card 2b)* harp. One day David was watching his father's *(show sheep card 2c)* sheep. David's' seven brothers were away in the army of *(show King Saul card 2e)* King Saul. David's father asked David to take some *(show lunch card 2d)* cheese and bread to his brothers. (Italics and underlining in curriculum)[16]

In the example above, the white pictures were repeatedly associated with each of the characters in the story, reinforcing white people and whiteness as the normative racial category[17] around the story of David, Goliath, and King Saul. Similar storytelling techniques were repeatedly employed. In another story about David and Jonathan (King Saul's son), paper bag puppets with white representations of the characters were used to tell the story. Furthermore, one of the lessons included children in reenacting a Bible story wherein the children wore paper crowns with white depictions of each character on the crowns.

In curricula from publishers that used people of color to depict Bible story characters, only one exclusively used people of color in their Bible story illustrations. The other publisher included stylized cartoon characters to portray Bible story characters in the material that was sent home with the children, but the more realistic Bible illustrations used for storytelling featured white representations of the Bible story characters. In the end, only one publisher exclusively used people of color to portray Bible characters who were of Jewish descent in the Middle East. Even in those pictures, though, Jesus was usually one of the lightest persons of color in the illustrations.

---

16. Excerpt from one of the lessons on David and Goliath.
17. Bonilla-Silva, "'Every Place Has a Ghetto . . .' The Significance of Whites' Social and Residential Segregation."

In addition to Bible story illustrations, solitary representations of Jesus were predominantly white (except for those from the aforementioned publishing company). One of the curriculum units had a focus on the importance of reading the Bible and going to church. There were two posters meant to hang in the Sunday school classroom to reinforce these points. The poster emphasizing Bible reading featured a white boy reading a Bible with an illustration of a white Jesus on the cover of the boy's Bible. The poster emphasizing the importance of church attendance featured a predominantly white classroom with one Black child and a white female Sunday school teacher holding up an illustration of a white Jesus. Further, a poster stating, "The Bible—A special book that teaches us about God and helps us to know Him" prominently featured a Bible with the same white Jesus on the cover as the Bible in the previous poster.

Repeatedly, children are told to "trust Jesus" and "get to know Jesus." One curriculum take-home sheet told parents, "This quarter your primary child will learn about the greatest Man who ever walked on earth. Jesus is greater than any superhero your child may admire." Above this statement was a picture of a white Jesus. Indeed, each of the curricula I analyzed included a lesson on how much Jesus loves children, using the Bible story of when Jesus publicly acknowledged children despite his followers' objections. In every instance, save one, the pictures were of a white Jesus holding white children. Even in publishers' attempts at diversity in their portrayals of people, Jesus was included as a white character. One take-home sheet illustration depicted an older Black woman teaching a Sunday school class of diverse children. Over her right shoulder was a picture of Jesus hanging on the wall. Jesus was white.

Predominantly White Churches. In contrast to the almost exclusively white characters in Bible story images, the curricula depicted people (who were not characters in the Bible stories) of various pigmentations in activity and take-home pages as well as in most of the leaders' guides. Most of the curricula (four of the seven), still included a larger number of pictures of white people over people of color. Further, in illustrations of churches, most of the leaders were depicted as white. Even in the instances wherein a black person was a leader, like the Sunday school teacher mentioned above, there were indicators, like the picture of the white Jesus behind her, that the church was predominantly made up of white people.

Another example from a different publisher included a take-home sheet with a layout of a church building. The lesson was about the church building and the different areas of the church: foyer, sanctuary, Sunday school classrooms, nursery, kitchen, etc. While there was some racial diversity amongst the people pictured in the church, most of the people attending the church were white. The preacher in the sanctuary was an older white man. Additionally, two of the three Sunday school teachers were white. One detail, which was probably overlooked by the creators of the curriculum, was that the lone person in the church kitchen was a black woman, reinforcing stereotypes like an Aunt Jemima or Mammy caricature.[18] Taken altogether, the visual imagery in this take-home sheet suggested that, while people of color are welcome as congregants and in subservient roles, people of color are a minority and positions of leadership are predominantly held by white people. Out of the 169 lessons in this study, there was only one illustration of a black preacher.

In addition to depictions normalizing white leaders within the church, a vast number of families pictured were white. One glaring example was an advertisement for Christmas magnets depicting baby Jesus, Mary, and Joseph that Christian education directors could purchase for the families at their churches. Not only were the members of the nativity pale white, the family pictured in the ad was also white. The accompanying text stated, "Looking for a fun way to share the Christmas story with your kids?" This ad showed up a couple of times in one of the curricula, and both times the family was white, reinforcing a white hegemony in churches that use this curriculum.

Three of the publishers attempted to equitably include people of color in illustrations and pictures outside of the Bible stories: two of the conservative evangelical publishers and the one progressive mainline publisher. One of the above evangelical curricula included activity pages used in the Sunday school class with illustrations consisting of mostly people of color. However, the sheets that were sent home with students depicted mostly white people. The curriculum for mainline churches utilized activity sheets that depicted an equitable amount of white people and people of color. I took note, though, that there were few pictures that featured mixed-race

---

18. Patricia Hill Collins, *Black Feminist Thought: Knowledge, Consciousness, and the Politics of Empowerment*, 2nd ed. (New York: Routledge, 2000).

groupings. Most of the groups of people were made up of all whites, all non-whites, or individuals. The leaders' guides, on the other hand, did not have many pictures of people in them. If there were illustrations of people, they were abstracted to be gender and race-neutral, and they reminded me of Montessori-style wooden dolls or Russian nested dolls.

Notably, the one publisher that used people of color in the Bible story pictures had three children as the main recurring characters who were used to help tell the Sunday school lessons from week to week. Two of the children were black, and the other child was white. Throughout the rest of this publisher's curriculum, there was an equitable representation of white people versus people of color. However, even though the visual illustrations and pictures in this curriculum were diverse, none of the lessons mentioned racial diversity, whether in the leaders' materials or in the children's activity and take-home sheets.

Multicultural Diversity. One more theme emerged from my analysis of the pictures in the curricula. In several of the visual illustrations and pictures of racially diverse people, the people wore ethno-cultural costuming. For example, Latinos and Latinas wore sombreros, Asians wore silk pants and blouses, Indian girls wore saris, etc. These pictures substituted race with ethnicity and culture, masking racial differences within the United States as a result of structural racism.[19]

WRITTEN AND SPOKEN WORD

The curricula in this study consisted of leaders' guides as well as activity sheets for the children and take-home sheets for the parents. The leaders' guides not only outlined and scripted the Bible stories and activities; they contained inspirational materials for the Sunday school teachers to read and reflect on as they prepared for each week's lesson. As I began to probe for themes about race, racial categories, and racial meanings, I quickly realized there was a dearth of lessons that explicitly referenced race. Of the 169 lessons in this study, there was only one lesson that referenced racial difference, which I will highlight later in this section. Borrowing from Bonilla-Silva's theory of colorblind racism and white habitus,[20] I searched for instances

---

19. Bonilla-Silva, *Racism Without Racists: Color-Blind Racism and the Persistence of Racial Inequality in America.*
20. Ibid.

where race and racial issues could have been addressed but were ignored or glossed over. With this new perspective, I also took notice of the many times various social indicators of identity such as socioeconomic status, ability status, and age were mentioned while racial identity was ignored.

Colorblind lessons. As I began reading through the lessons in this study, I found a scarcity of explicit references to race or racial differences. There were many lessons on kindness, the importance of following God, Christian practices, morals, and many of the Christian narratives. Very rarely did the materials mention race or how race might interact with any of these ideas. In the rare instances race was mentioned, it was mentioned in the materials meant solely for the leaders and not for the children.

One example of this was in the curriculum written for progressive mainline churches. The lesson surrounded a parable Jesus told about a vineyard owner who paid all the day-laborers equally regardless of the time of day they were hired (Matt. 20:1–16). The preparatory materials for the leader brought up issues of implicit racism: "'No fair!' we whine when the immigrant gets elected mayor and the minority student wins the scholarship. When we read today's gospel [sic] we see the workers act like children cheated out of recess. Why are we so uncomfortable with this parable?"[21] The leader's section went on to challenge the traditional American pull-yourself-up-by-your-bootstraps work ethic narrative.

While one could argue that this was not a passage about racism, the authors of the curriculum chose to focus on diversity in their leader notes. Yet the script provided for leaders to use when teaching the same Bible story to children erased all mention of racial conflict and ethnocentrism: "God says, 'I want people. I want old people, boys and girls, babies, grownups and teenagers. I want many, many people.' . . . God says, 'I love all the different people. (Name each child.) I love my people very much!'"[22] The lesson was sanitized and focused on how God loves "all the different people." Implicit racism was replaced by diversity in the shape of gender ["boys and girls"] and age ["old people . . . babies, grownups and teenagers"].

Another lesson in another curriculum did something similar but with the story of the good Samaritan:

---

21. Excerpt of personal reflection about the parable of the vineyard owner found in a leaders' guide.
22. Excerpt of teaching script for lesson about the parable of the vineyard owner found in a leaders' guide.

Because of their mixed race and questionable worship practices, Samaritans were considered unclean and despised by Jews. Yet Jesus chose a Samaritan to be the hero of this parable . . . After the parable, what did Jesus ask? The lawyer answers correctly. Notice, however, that the man did not even say the word Samaritan. He said, "the one who showed mercy." Jesus told the scribe to go and do as the Samaritan had done. How do you think this "righteous" Jew felt when Jesus said to model himself after a despised Samaritan?[23]

This blurb that was included as part of the preparatory materials for the leader addressed the racist attitudes Jewish people had towards Samaritans. But rather than challenging Sunday school teachers to examine their prejudices, the curriculum ended this personal reflection by asking, "How can you show kindness and compassion to others this week?"[24] The assumption seemed to be that those who use this curriculum have no need to evaluate their prejudices. Consequently, children do not need to examine any prejudices they might have, either, as the lesson for the children erases all hints of the racially charged nature of the Bible story and focuses instead on being kind and helping people in need like those with disabilities, the elderly, and those who are hurting.

As mentioned earlier, there was one (out of all 169!) lesson that addressed race in any way. The lesson was from a curriculum that used predominantly white characters in its Bible story illustrations. Part of a unit on God's love for people, the lesson was entitled, "God Loves People of All Colors." Using the story of when one of Jesus' disciples, Philip, tells an Ethiopian about Jesus, the curriculum points out that Philip and the Ethiopian have different-colored skin: "In the desert Philip met a man in a chariot. The man didn't look like Philip. Philip was a Jew. He probably had light brown skin. This man was from Ethiopia. His skin was probably very dark . . . But Philip and the Ethiopian man were alike, too. God loved both of them . . ."[25]

While this lesson did address differences in skin color, it quickly minimized the differences, pointing out that Philip and the Ethiopian "were

---

23. Excerpt of personal reflection about the parable of the good Samaritan found in a leaders' guide.
24. Ibid.
25. Excerpt of teaching script for lesson about the Philip and an Ethiopian found in a leaders' guide.

alike, too." Ironically, even though the curriculum described Philip as "light brown," both the drawings used for telling the Bible story and the drawings in the take-home sheets depicted Philip as white. Furthermore, as the lesson progressed, racial differences were quickly replaced with cultural differences as the pictures and illustrations showed children of different races dressed in ethno-cultural costumes. Another of the publishing companies included the story of Philip and the Ethiopian, but it focused solely on cultural differences and ignored race. This is one of the few instances in the Bible where it is noted that people of different races are interacting, yet activities for this curriculum included learning how Namibians shake hands, eating mangoes like the people of Bangladesh, and saying "G'day" like an Australian, as if racial differences happen primarily between people from different countries rather than within one's own neighborhood or school. More specifically, when multiculturalism is routinely substituted for racial differences, the effect of systemic racial hierarchies on the life experiences of racial minorities is more easily dismissed in favor of interpersonal character flaws between people from two different cultures.

Colorblind identities. As seen in the example above, the curriculum analyzed in this study did not ignore identities. Social indicators such as socioeconomic status, gender, age, and ability were explicitly mentioned in multiple lessons as well as in the leader materials. Most of the curricula devoted extended introductions to helping Sunday school teachers understand how to be aware of and sensitive to children with special needs and differing abilities. Additionally, many lessons encouraged children to notice, appreciate, and help people with limited abilities, those who are hurt, and people who are economically disadvantaged.

Even when story characters were people of color, their racial identity was ignored. For example, one of the take-home sheets featured a story about two black girls, one of whom was living in poverty:

Keisha ran out the door, down the stairs, and out to the playground. As Keisha got closer, she saw that the new girl was wearing clothes that were too old and too big. Her shoes were scuffed. One of them had a hole in it.

That didn't matter to Keisha. She still wanted to be friends with the new girl.

Just then some other kids ran past Keisha. They stopped by the new girl and began to make fun of her clothes.

Suddenly Keisha wasn't sure she wanted to meet the new girl after all.[26]

The focus in the above story was socioeconomic status. It was all right to write about a girl living in poverty, but any mention of the children's race was left out of the narrative. On the surface, it may seem that the racial identity of the two girls is inconsequential because the reason for the differences between them is a result of socioeconomics. However, race *is* important, especially when the examples being used are part of a racial minority group that has historically and systemically been discriminated against in multiple areas of society. By choosing to use black girls in the story and then ignoring the links between race and socioeconomics, the publishers implicitly diminished the links between race and socioeconomics. Further, the church passed up an opportunity to provide young children with the cultural tools to talk about the unfortunate intersections between race and socioeconomics.

CONCLUSION

Throughout my analysis of the curricula in this chapter, I found that multiculturalism and identity were frequently discussed and illustrated throughout all the curricula, regardless of the publishing house. Even on the rare occasions when race and racial themes were brought up, those themes were quickly swept aside to be replaced with multiculturalism and other indicators of identity. According to Omi and Winant, race is a master category within the United States that influences all other identities:[27] "Corporeality continues to determine popular understandings of race and thus to shape both white supremacy and colorblind hegemony in the United States today."[28] By diverting attention away from race and focusing on multiculturalism and other identities (e.g. age, gender, ability status), the curricula in this study masked the hegemonic forces at work to reproduce and reinforce dominant white racial structures and white habitus.

---

26. Excerpt from a story featuring African American girls in a take-home sheet.
27. Omi, *Racial Formation in the United States.*
28. Ibid., 249.

Bonilla-Silva and Embrick state that white habitus "creates and conditions [whites'] views, cognitions, and even sense of beauty and, more importantly, creates a sense of racial solidarity ("we whites")."[29] Furthermore, white habitus is primarily a result of white isolation and segregation from blacks or other minorities. I argue that the Sunday school curricula in this study provide a symbolic isolation of whites from people of color through the predominant use of white characters in Bible stories, construction of images of predominantly white churches, and silence when it comes to race and racial issues in the lessons. As Bonilla-Silva writes, "The social psychology produced by the white habitus leads to the creation of a positive self-view and a negative other-view. The more distant the group in question is from the white 'norm,' other things being equal, the more negative whites will view the group."[30]

My findings, consisting of predominantly white Bible characters and church leaders, coupled with a lack of racial discourse, paint a grim racial picture of evangelical churches, whereby racial structures that privilege white understandings of religion will affect how children in churches construct their categorizations of race and how they co-construct their meanings of those categories. While more research certainly needs to be done, including gathering perspectives and curricula from predominantly black churches and other non-white churches as well as observing how these themes are perpetuated, reinforced, transformed, and potentially challenged in actual Sunday school classrooms, I believe that this research exposes a gap in how religious curricula writers and publishers address issues of racism and racial justice. Further, it addresses the need for church staff and volunteers to critically examine how they adapt curricula to reflect a spirituality that is characterized by diversity, justice, and equity.

SOME PRACTICAL SUGGESTIONS

If the church is to be a catalyst in repairing racial divides and healing hurts brought on by racialized violence (both physical and symbolic), then it must take practical steps to create content, spaces, and experiences that not only expose children to racial diversity but help them see how they

---

29. Bonilla-Silva, "'Every Place Has a Ghetto . . .' The Significance of Whites' Social and Residential Segregation," 340.

30. Ibid., 341.

can work against racism and towards equity. While there is no one-size-fits-all quick fix to correcting the trajectory of Sunday school curricula away from being racially unaware, I would like to offer some suggestions for curriculum publishers as well as for individual churches.

For Curriculum Publishers

In this research, I came across only one publisher that had commissioned new artwork for all of their materials so that everything from take-home papers to activity sheets to Bible story pictures included racial diversity as well as diversity of skin tone. While quality artwork is costly, this small step in diverse representation of visual material goes a long way to pushing against a white habitus. Representation, while important, should only be one of multiple steps publishers take. Another important step publishers should take is to intentionally increase the diversity of curriculum writers as well as hiring an editor whose sole job is to ensure that curricula competently addresses issues surrounding racism, diversity, and justice. Finally, publishers should not shy away from conversations about race and racism, even in curriculum targeted for young children.

Individual Churches

Churches cannot and need not wait for publishers to make needed changes in curriculum to address the underlying currents of a culturally white spirituality. One of the most powerful and effective moves churches can make towards becoming more racially aware is to sit down with people of color in their churches or in their communities and ask for honest feedback about their experiences in church. Churches should not only be ready to listen but also be ready to learn and take direction from people of color on how to cultivate a spirituality that is more representative of the diversity of God's people rather than white culture. Another step individual churches can take is to increase the representation of diverse bodies and voices in décor, supplementary curricular materials, and leadership. Finally, those in children's ministry should not simply rely on the curricular materials for how to understand, teach, and present Bible stories and lessons. Children's ministry leaders and volunteers should listen to and read from speakers, pastors, and authors of color in order to gain broader, non-white perspectives and understandings of spirituality and the Bible.

CHAPTER 14

BECOMING A SOUL FRIEND

Spiritual Direction with Children

LACY FINN BORGO

———— ┤├ ————

Nine-year-old Jonathan chewed his fingernails and lingered just a bit behind me as we walked into the Holy Listening room together.[1] He looked at the white blanket peppered with green leaves with interest, but he was especially curious about the collection of colorful boxes and bags that lined the edge. "What are these for?" he asked. I explained that in Holy Listening, our spiritual direction ministry with children, "There is a lot of listening. I will listen to you, and you can listen to you, and we both can listen to God. These can help us listen." With a nod of his head he began to explore the colorful bags.

It was the season of Advent, so during Holy Listening, Jonathan and I played with the nativity toys. These wooden manipulatives of Mary, Joseph, shepherds, kings, an angel, and livestock would be the vehicles through which Jonathan heard how his story and the story of God's Son are woven together. As my particular set of wooden manipulatives did not have an "inn," Jonathan and I first began by taking blocks and crafting an "inn," which we called a hotel. Jonathan led, and I followed. As he directed me to hold and place blocks, together we raised a sturdy, two-story design.

---

1. All of the names of the children and their identifying details have been changed to honor the confidentiality and privacy of the children and their families.

Then, using simple language and wooden manipulatives, I told the story. This story began with a woman, Mary, who was going to have a baby and traveling a long distance. "She has to say, 'Oh, my back!'" Jonathan added. This resonated with Jonathan, as his mother had had a baby a few months earlier. "How about you play Mary?" I invited. Jonathan agreed, and we continued. Joseph was with Mary as they asked to stay at the hotel. But since there were no rooms available, the manager of the hotel said they could stay where he kept his animals, in something like a barn. Jonathan limped the wooden Mary behind Joseph. Again, this part of the story was familiar to Jonathan.

I was meeting with Jonathan at Haven House, which is a transitional facility for homeless families. Jonathan knew what it was like to have no place to lay his head. We moved the Mary and Joseph pieces to the makeshift barn and added a wooden baby Jesus.

After telling the story, I invited Jonathan to play it again. He could tell it any way he wanted. In his telling, he was Joseph trying to find a place for Mary. He knocked at the hotel, asking for a room, and then moved Mary to the barn. His face showed the confusion and sadness he must have felt throughout his own story. For several minutes he played his story, woven within the story of God's Son. In one telling, the angel kicked people out of the hotel and made room for Mary and Joseph—an honest response from a boy who was very recently homeless. On his final iteration of the story, all the animals spoke, becoming a welcoming presence to Mary, Joseph, and Jesus. Listening to the words he gave the animals, I could hear his longing to connect, his longing to be wanted, his longing to belong.

On many Wednesday afternoons, I can be found at Haven House in Olathe, Colorado, practicing spiritual direction with children. Abigail was six years old, had Down syndrome, and came to Holy Listening for only ten minutes each week. In her very determined way, she entered our sacred space, plopped herself down on our white blanket, picked up our battery-powered candle, and touched the plastic flame. "God loves you and God loves me," she repeated in a sing-songy tone, touching the flame and touching my forehead over and over. "Now you say it," she said. I said the same back to her: "God loves you and God loves me," touching the flame and touching her forehead.

Annalise, a seven-year-old girl, also came to Holy Listening. For two months she lived at Haven House with her mother and brother. It was the longest time she had lived anywhere. Before Haven House, the family was traveling from Wal-Mart parking lot to Wal-Mart parking lot, trying to outrun her abusive father. Annalise came to play with the Good Shepherd manipulatives; she listened attentively as I told the simple, short story of the Good Shepherd. Then she took the toys and played out her own anxieties, the lion eating the sheep and the shepherd helpless to save them. These are the honest questions that she has for God. In the safety of spiritual direction, she could speak her questions through play to a listening person and to the God who loves her and cries her tears with her.

EXPERIENTIAL KNOWLEDGE

Before we wade much farther into spiritual direction with children, perhaps we can ground our discussion in experiential knowledge. Pause for just a moment and find a large piece of paper and a pen or pencil. Take a deep breath, breathing in an awareness of God's presence with you, and then ask the Spirit to speak to you, revealing to you what you need to know about God's movement in your life when you were a child. Place your pen or pencil in your non-dominant hand, and draw an example of an early experience of God. You may think back to your first understanding of God. It may have occurred at church, in nature, with grandparents, or any myriad of persons or places. Take your time. Allow this memory to come back to you gently, without force. Notice what thoughts and feeling are stirred up with this drawing. Perhaps this drawing will be fodder for conversation with God; perhaps this drawing will touch on some deeper longings or understandings. In any case, keep it near as we discuss spiritual direction with children.

LONGING FOR CONNECTION

William A. Barry and William J. Connolly, Jesuit spiritual directors and experts in the field of direction, define spiritual direction as, "help given by one Christian to another which enables that person to pay attention to

God's personal communication to him or her, to respond to this personally communicating God, to grow in intimacy with this God, and live out the consequences."[2] God's personal communication with human persons begins with longing.

I live on a small hobby farm in Western Colorado. We have horses, chickens, dogs, cats, and goats. When a mama goat is getting ready to have her kids—baby goats—she prepares. She paws the ground like she is making a nest. We might see her rub her abdomen against a tree to move the kid into place, and she might even stretch, doing a funny sort of goat yoga—a downward-dog-meets-cat-pose—to move her young near the birth canal. One particular spring, I noticed that a mama goat does one other remarkable thing. It was just the two of us on a chilly spring night, and I could tell her time had come. To my surprise, about twenty minutes before the baby was born, she began to hum or sing a soft bleat with her lips closed. It wasn't like a cry, as if she was in pain; it was soft and soothing. She continued this singing throughout her labor and the delivery. When the baby was born, she nuzzled the new kid, licking it clean and still singing until—and this is what really struck me—the new kid sang back. There was no other sound in our tiny shed for the next few minutes as mama and baby sang to one another very tenderly. In this way, she marked that kid as hers, and that kid knew its mama's voice and called back.

Every human enters this world looking, reaching, desiring, aching—in a word, *longing*—for connection. Developmental psychologists tell us that everyone comes into the world this way. They tell us that even within the womb, a baby is connecting with the mother's voice, the mother's smell, and even with the mother's heartbeat. After we are born, we search our parents' eyes for connection. When our parents smile, we smile back. An infant's smile doesn't mean the same as an adult's. Infants are not pleased or happy; they are mirroring the adult in an effort to connect. Although this intense desire to connect is an attempt at physical survival, it is also a part of human psychological and spiritual survival.

This longing for connection is woven into every person. From the moment we take our first breath, we are governed by this longing to connect. My first memorable example of this early human longing was when my daughter

2. William A. Barry and William J. Connolly, *The Practice of Spiritual Direction* (San Francisco, CA: HarperCollins, 1986), 8.

was born. As soon as she was placed in my husband's outstretched arms, she grabbed his finger. I am told this is a Palmar grasp reflex. The intense longing to connect is even wired into our reflexes. Not only are humans wired *for* longing, we were created *from* longing. "Before I formed you in the womb I knew you," says Jeremiah (Jer. 1:5). The psalmist reminds us, "You created my inmost being" (Ps. 139:13). Paul explains it to us in Ephesians: "For he chose us in him before the creation of the world" (Eph. 1:4). Every child you know has been longed into existence. In fact, Zephaniah tells us that God sings God's own song of longing over every one of us (Zeph. 3:17).

God, who needed nothing else to be whole, whose joy was complete before one ounce of creation, longed for you. We human beings long from a place of brokenness, but God, who is whole and holy, longs from a place of abundance and joy. Every child you know has been longed into existence, and from that place, they also long for God. Just as we are hardwired to seek connection with our caregivers, we are hardwired to seek connection with God. When we are young children, what we believe about God is formed mainly from our interactions with our parents.[3] We are not whole, we are not complete until we are connected to God, so that hardwired longing pulses in our hearts and minds and bodies, constantly urging us towards connection. From our very beginnings, the Spirit has been reaching for us.

FINGERPRINTS OF GOD

There are three primary touch points for our longings: goodness, beauty, and truth. Whenever we engage one of these three, we hear the song of God like the baby goat heard his mother's song. These three touch points are woven into the tapestry of the world around every human person; God has been singing and will continue to sing the song of truth, beauty, and goodness to each child. These touch points resonate in the human spirit and open our eyes to our own longing for God.

---

3. There is not space for the much-warranted longer discussion that is due on how our initial picture of God is formed. But in summary, our first understandings about God are shaped from the dominant parent in our lives. This is where we associate security and safety. To be certain, this changes throughout our journey. Further, there is ample evidence that the Spirit often intercedes in ways far beyond the adults in our lives in ways marked by the mystical to reach toward the child. God's longing and love cannot be bound and often evades adult understandings.

So just what are goodness, beauty, and truth? Christian philosophy professor Dallas Willard defines truth as "whatever in fact is real." He goes on to say, "A statement or idea is real when it corresponds to a spiritual or material reality."[4] Truth is authenticity; it is what is real. While children enjoy enlivened imaginations, they also know what is indeed real. They know when an adult really wants to get to know them and when an adult is patronizing. They know what real love and real caring look like. And they know down to their very DNA what real connection feels like.

"Beauty," Willard tells us, is "goodness made manifest to the senses."[5] While adult notions of beauty might bring to mind great works of art, children see the beauty in everyday things. Children can observe and receive the beauty of a ladybug on a summer day; children can savor the beauty of a plump blueberry or the carefully painted illustrations in their favorite book while sitting on the lap of someone they trust. Each of these is an invitation from God to connection. They alert the child's soul, inviting him or her to connect with the One who longed them into existence.

Would you indulge me one more time? Place your pen or pencil again in your non-dominant hand. Think back as far as you can, back to when you were a child. Allow your heart to search your memory and find one encounter with goodness, beauty, or truth—something that appeals to our senses, encourages us to connect with God, something authentic and real. Hold that memory with gentle hands, following the lead of the Spirit. Then take your time and draw that memory. As you fumble with your non-dominant hand, allow your critical self to relax and savor the memory of God's fingerprint on your life.

For example, I remember being at my grandparents' convenience store/ deli in West Texas when I was about four years old. This little store was centered between machine shops and pipe yards in the West Texas oil field industry. Hardworking and no-nonsense oil field workers piled in during the breakfast and lunch runs, most of them with a kind, gentle word for my four-year-old self, who wanted so much to help in the family business.

Around eleven every morning, a blind man named Blondie Duncan arrived at the store for a lunch date with me. A bit before he arrived,

4. Elane O'Rourke, *A Dallas Willard Dictionary, 2nd ed.* (Elane O'Rourke, 2016), 275–276.

5. Dallas Willard, Chapel Talk at Westmont College, Santa Barbara, CA, September 12, 2011, www.youtube.com/watch?v=XzzzH9z0SRE.

I helped prepare the sandwich I knew he loved—pimento cheese. I got his Hawaiian Punch and favorite chips ready. I waited expectedly for him to come through the front door. At the first glimpse of his cane, my heart jumped. I knew that the goodness that passed between us fed something deeper than my belly. I have no memory of what we talked about, but I have a distinct memory of the goodness of being valued by another. This encounter helped to shape and form what I believe about God, what I believe about the world, and maybe most miraculously, what I believe about myself. That's the experience I had when I drew my memory. After you draw yours, share your story with someone you trust.

These invitations from God are not limited to what is good, beautiful, and true. These invitations from God also look like wonder, as in *I wonder why it only snows in winter* or *I wonder why kittens are born with their eyes closed.* God's invitation sometimes takes the form of mystery, a posture of grateful acceptance in the presence of the irreducible. Young children don't struggle against mystery. They know that they don't know.

Awe is another fingerprint. Many children experience awe when they stand in front of a Christmas tree, or see fireworks, or when they are out in nature, at a music concert, or at an art museum.[6] Awe can look like goosebumps, raised eyebrows, or a dropped jaw. Awe feels like magic and invites us to reverence. A child's tears are also an invitation from God, for God is always with the broken-hearted. There is something deep in us that yearns for connection when we feel pain, whether emotional or physical.

These invitations can be found in nature and in the ordinary spaces and places of our lives. The Religious Experience Research Unit in Wales conducted a longitudinal study and found that as adults looked back on their early experiences of God, they recalled experiences that fell into many categories, including these.[7] They told stories of goodness, beauty, wonder, authenticity, mystery, death, and tears. They describe these experiences as drawing them to the divine; these were "thin places" where they knew that God was with them. Indeed, for some, these early experiences helped to revive their faith later in life. I wonder how their connection to God might

---

6. Andy Tix, "Nurturing Awe in Kids," *Psychology Today*, posted Sept 21, 2015, www.psychology today.com/us/blog/the-pursuit-peace/201509/nurturing-awe-in-kids.

7. Edward Robinson, *The Original Vision: A Study of the Religious Experience of Children* (Oxford: Religious Experience Research Unit Manchester College, 1977). The book is short and worth the read.

have grown if they would have had someone to hear, to acknowledge, and to encourage their life with God?

SPIRITUAL DIRECTION WITH CHILDREN: TO HEAR, TO ACKNOWLEDGE, TO ENCOURAGE

Spiritual directors who work with children are listening for signs of these fingerprints of God as they listen to children, so that they can help the children open and savor these gifts. In the absence of an awareness of goodness or beauty, the director helps children connect with God in their pain and their sorrow, which may, at the moment, be their only truth. Directors help children savor their experiences of God by reflecting back what they hear and asking questions that help the child to hear themselves and to hear God. And directors encourage listening for more invitations from God, expectantly wondering with the child where God will meet them in the future.

Neurologically, when spiritual directors help children reflect on their experiences, they are helping to lay down a neurological footprint in their brains that will enable them to see God's movement in the future and to reflect on it. South African pastor and spiritual director Trevor Hudson reminds us that we do not learn from our experiences, we learn from our reflection on our experiences.[8] Spiritual direction with children is the opportunity to help a child reflect on his or her experiences. The three movements of hearing, acknowledging, and encouraging a child makes this possible.

THE 5 PS OF SPIRITUAL DIRECTION WITH CHILDREN

While the purpose of spiritual direction with children is similar to the purpose of spiritual direction with adults—to help another recognize and respond to the movement of God in their life—there are some distinctions. I call these distinctions the 5Ps: play, power, projection, pray, and pronounce.

---

8. Trevor Hudson, *A Mile in My Shoes: Cultivating Compassion* (Nashville, TN: Upper Room Books, 2005), 69.

PLAY

Generally, a child's life with God is hidden. This is because most adults do not speak the primary tongue of childhood anymore. Play is the mother tongue of children. Children will play out their joys and their sorrows, and they will play out their conversations with God. A spiritual director who works with children will need to relearn play as a way of communication.

POWER

A spiritual director will also have to learn how to level the power differential in the room. The driving need to please and give "right" answers and to defer to adults has been stamped deeply into children; therefore, in order to hear and see the real child, power will have to be mitigated. One way to do that is to sit on the floor with the child; another is to empower the child to lead the conversation.

PROJECTION AND PRAY

Projecting a child's thoughts and feelings while observing and creating art is another way to invite the inner life of the child out into the open. Through sculpture, watercolor, or blocks, children tell their stories.

They also use these materials to connect with God, to pray. As children have not yet split the self, warring their mind or spirit against their bodies, they pray not with bowed heads and still bodies, but they pray with all the aspects of their selves. They will want their bodies, minds, emotions, all of their parts, in on the connection. This can look like playing their prayer using manipulatives. This can look like painting their prayer using watercolors; it can look like using bubbles and blowing their prayers.

While we might see the hiddenness of the inner life of the child as a drawback or negative aspect, it is really the most gracious hand of God, for adults who see too much will be tempted to control. We are tempted to over-function and grab for ourselves the role of the Spirit in spiritual direction rather than fostering a space for the child to connect firsthand with the Creator of the universe, who longed them into existence.

Again, to ground our discussion in your own experiential knowledge, reflect on a strong emotional event that happened when you were a child. Go back to the paper with your two previous drawings and add another. Begin by allowing yourself to be centered in the Spirit: take a deep breath, breathing in God's presence, peace, and protection. Gently allow the Spirit to bring to mind a strong emotional event from your childhood. It could be something quite difficult that you have not worked through, or it could be something with less "heat" that you have already spent some time on. Reflect on where God was in your emotional event. How do you know God was there? What was the texture and character of your feeling? Finally, how might that moment be different in your memory if an adult in your life could have deeply listened to you and helped you see what was already there—God's loving presence?

PRONOUNCE

The last P in spiritual direction with children is to pronounce. At the end of a spiritual direction session, a director will bless the child. It is very rare to find a space where children are counted as whole persons and accepted just as they are. Spiritual direction can be just such a space. When children are offered the freedom of a nonjudgmental listening partner, a person who can notice the movement of God in them, they themselves can learn to see the fingerprints of God woven in their own soul and surroundings.

A SAMPLE SPIRITUAL DIRECTION SESSION

Walk with me through a spiritual direction session with a child at Haven House. Logan had been coming to spiritual direction every week for six weeks. As we walked through the door together, we entered the space at the same time so that both Logan and I owned the space. I did not hold an authoritative hand over him; we were co-pilgrims on this journey. While I did hold a few boundaries with Logan—care of the items we use, keeping the rhythm of our time together—this was Logan's time, and we were attending to his life with God. So he was in charge. He was the authority on his own life.

We sat down together on the white blanket dotted with green leaves, and Logan took the battery-powered candle and turned the light on. "This reminds us that God is with us," Logan said. I nodded my head. The rhythm of the spiritual direction session has taken hold in his heart, and he knows what the light represents. Then he began to look through the collection of *Jesus and Me* art images.[9] These images, drawn by Jeanette Fernandez, depict children in everyday circumstances of life: gaming, reading, playing outside, and at school. They also depict some common feelings of children: loneliness, fear, abandonment, comfort, and peace. Logan made his choice and placed his image on the mini-easel next to the battery-powered light. Our blanket and the items on it, including ourselves, were all part of an altar where we could say, like Samuel, "Speak Lord, for your servant is listening."[10]

There are a number of ways that our session could flow from this point. A child may want to choose three Holy Listening stones to tell his or her story.[11] Or the child may want to play out the story of the Good Shepherd or create art. Logan chose the Holy Listening stones on that day. Each stone is about the size of a half-dollar and has simple, nonsensical symbols drawn in permanent marker. I proposed, "You can choose three stones that tell a story about when you knew that God was with you. Or you can tell a story about a strong feeling you felt this week. Or you can choose stones that help you tell a story about something good, beautiful, or true that happened to you." Children long to be listened to, and spiritual direction is primarily a practice in listening and asking questions, not for information or general curiosity. Instead, a very few sparse questions or statements are given to invite the child to unwrap their experience a little more. Questions/statements like, "What was that like for you?" "That sounds very sad," or "Can you help me to understand what you mean?" Logan chose three stones and told the story about the light that was streaming through his window when he woke up and how that light reminded him that God was near. He also told the story of how he felt angry on the playground at school.

While listening, the spiritual director is attentive to the whole person of the child, listening not only to words and actions but also to the language of the heart. In addition, the spiritual director is listening to the movement of the Spirit, and when the moment of authenticity and vulnerability is

9. Jeannette Fernandez, www.etsy.com/shop/JesusandMeArt?ref=search_shop_redirect.
10. 1 Samuel 3:10.
11. "Holy listening stones are a tool to help children put their feelings, thoughts and insights into words. They also help adults remember to listen to what children express." Leanne Hadley, Holy Listening Stones, docs.wixstatic.com/ugd/221cbf_37dd908676244c59ac3046757fcc48d1.pdf.

in the air, an invitation is offered: "Would you like to talk with God about that?" On this day, Logan noticed before I did. "I'm ready to use the finger labyrinth to pray," he said. There are endless ways children can respond to God's invitation to connect; today Logan wanted to use the finger labyrinth.

In spiritual direction with children, we use the finger labyrinth to engage the conversational rhythm of a life with God and to get our bodies in on our prayer life. As the child's finger traverses the twists and turns of the labyrinth, moving toward the center, the child talks with God. When they arrive at the center of the labyrinth, they are invited to take three deep breaths and allow themselves to be still and silent and listen toward God. When they feel they are ready, they begin to move their finger towards the exit, and while they are moving, they are not talking, but listening for what God has to stay to them. Children report hearing God say, "I love you," or "I am with you." Children also report sensing God's presence or a shared feeling that God was with them, rather than God's voice. Logan shared that God said, "I am with you," at the playground.

At the end of our time, I took a tube of clear but sweet-smelling lip balm that has been relabeled as "Blessing Balm," and asked if I could draw a cross on the back of his hand.[12] I ask each time, knowing that Logan's body belongs to him. Logan reminds me, "God is like the Blessing Balm. Sometimes I can't see God, but sometimes I can get a 'smell' of God if I'm paying attention." Children, like adults, can't always see God, but they can learn to pay attention to the fingerprints of God, who longed each of us into existence and walks with us in our everyday lives.

In this short chapter on spiritual direction with children, I hope I have cast a vision of spiritual direction. I hope that you have touched your own childhood experiences of God and that those will lead to more conversation with God. I hope that a longing to attend to the inner life of a child has stirred within you, and if so, that you will take the next step to learn to listen a child to life.[13]

---

12. Leanne Hadley, "Reflections on Being a Hospital Chaplain to Children," First Steps, Stepping Up to Wholeness Conference, Grand Junction, CO, May 2013.

13. A full treatment of spiritual direction with children can be found in my book *Spiritual Conversations with Children: Listening to God Together* to be published in the Spring of 2020 by IVP. I also teach a class on Spiritual Direction with Children through the CompanioningCenter.org.

CHAPTER 15

THE SACRED PLAYGROUND

Play and a Child's Faith

MIMI L. LARSON AND SHIRLEY K. MORGENTHALER

||

Within religious education, play is often undervalued as a serious means of learning, as we comment that children are "just" playing. In the church, play activities are utilized as time-fillers or as a reward that enables children to let off steam after we do the "real work" of religious education and teach in a traditional sense. There is a tension between the serious nature of faith development and the idea that play is *just* an enjoyable and recreational activity.[1]

By undervaluing play, we lose the truth that play is a place of discovery where children are free to explore and express themselves. Play is a common childhood experience and is the primary vocation of the child,[2] encouraging the development of the imagination and a significant tool for meaning-making. Early childhood educators such as Montessori and Froebel also believed it was a place for learning, and Elkind asserts that play "is the dominant and directing mode of learning" for young children.[3]

---

1. Note: Early conversations around this topic included Jeffrey B. Keiser, M.A. We appreciate the input he had towards this work.

2. Marcia J. Bunge, "The Vocation of the Child: Theological Perspectives on the Particular and Paradoxical Roles and Responsibilities of Children," in *The Vocation of the Child*, ed. P. M. Brennan (Cambridge: Wm. B. Eerdmans Publishing Co, 2008), 50.

3. David Elkind, *The Power of Play: Learning What Comes Naturally* (Boston, MA: DaCapo Lifelong Books, 2008), 7.

As a joyful activity, play enriches a child's emotional, social, physical, and cognitive development.

Play is also a transformational activity. Within the action of play, children bring their lives, questions, fears, and determinations, which are "mirrored and transformed" in child's play.[4] Froebel, in his discussion of childhood, states that play "is the highest expression of human development in childhood, for it alone is the free expression of what is in the child's soul."[5] If that were the case, we would expect God to be on high alert. It is not much of a stretch to say that God is active in a child's play.

Play also prepares the child for his or her future development. As Froebel discusses in his seminal work, *The Education of Man*, "the spontaneous play of the child discloses the future inner life of the man,"[6] which is a spiritual activity. Bodrova and Leong argue that play "prepares the child's mind for the learning tasks of today as well as future tasks that humans cannot yet imagine."[7] Researchers suggest that play can nurture a child's understanding of faith and can be a "means of discovering one's spiritual potential."[8] Play encourages exploration and enables a child to ask "what if?"[9] This exploration opens a child up to possibilities, to things that are larger than life, to miracles, and to an omnipotent God.

Within Christian education, we feel a tension to ground a child in the gospel, to explain and teach the foundations of faith from a young age. We also know that play impacts both the life of the mind and the life of the body. If play is such a transformational activity and an expression of the soul, as Froebel suggests, can play also be a form of spiritual development? What if play, instead of being an activity to fill time and keep children occupied, becomes a place and an activity where children are able to comprehend ideas and understandings, not just in their heads but deeply in their souls,

---

4. G. P. Stone, "The Play of Little Children," in *Child's Play*, eds. R. E. Herron and B. Sutton-Smith (New York: John Wiley & Sons, 1971), 1–2.

5. S. S. F. Fletcher and J. Welton, *Froebel's Chief Writings on Education* (London: Edward Arnold & Co., 1912), 50.

6. Friedrich Froebel, *The Education of Man* (Mineola, NY: Dover Publications, Inc., 2005), 55.

7. Elena Bodrova and Deborah J. Leong, "Adult Influences on Play: The Vygotskian Approach," in *Play from Birth to Twelve: Contexts, Perspectives, and Meanings*, 2nd ed., eds. Doris P. Fromberg and Doris Bergen (New York: Routledge, 2006), 167.

8. Donald Ratcliff, "The Use of Play in Christian Education," *Christian Education Journal* 6, no. 2 (1985): 26.

9. V.G. Paley, *A Child's Work: The Importance of Fantasy Play* (Chicago: The University of Chicago Press, 2004), 92.

and in turn, it becomes a means of developing and nurturing the faith or spirituality of a young child? Is there a sacred element to play that we are missing or undervaluing in the church today?

UNDERSTANDING PLAY

Describing play is a challenging task.[10] Many scholars have tried to define play, but at the same time they acknowledge the difficulty of doing so.[11] There are many different forms or types of play: solitary, parallel, group, dramatic, fantasy, exploratory, manipulative, games with rules, just to name a few. While pleasurable, play is not just a leisure activity but also a "crucial dynamic" for a person's cognitive, physical, and social-emotional development.[12] Play usually does not have an agenda but is intrinsically motivated.[13] Play is founded in freedom.[14] It is voluntary and must be nestled within an atmosphere of trust,[15] for in play, a child steps out of ordinary life and time to explore and create. While this may appear unstructured or without purpose, play is also understood as a "purposeful activity for a child."[16] Friedrich Froebel believed that children learned best through play, as it is an avenue for discovery and understanding.[17]

Because physical activity enhances brain function and cognitive

10. Our goal, in this chapter, is not to define play or talk about its developmental understanding. For this, we refer to other studies. Our goal is to look at how play contributes to a child's spiritual development.

11. Anthony D. Pellegrini, *The Role of Play in Human Development* (New York: Oxford University Press, 2009).

Brian Sutton-Smith, "Play as a Parody of Emotional Vulnerability," in *Play and Educational Theory and Practice*, ed. Donald E. Lytle (Westport, CT, Praeger, 2003), 3–18; Brian Edmiston, *Forming Ethical Identities in Early Childhood Play* (New York: Routledge, 2008).

12. Elkind, *The Power of Play: Learning What Comes Naturally*, 4.

13. Barbara P. Garner and Doris Bergen, "Play Development from Birth to Age Four," in *Play from Birth to Twelve: Contexts, Perspectives, and Meanings, 2nd ed.*, eds. Doris P. Fromberg and Doris Bergen (New York: Routledge, 2006), 3.

14. Nindyo Sasongko, *"Homo Ludens* Revisited: A Theological Inquiry into Being Human from the Perspective of Javanese Children's Play," *Toronto Journal of Theology* 30, no. 2 (2014): 307–18.

15. D. W. Winnicott, *Playing and Reality* (New York: Routledge, 2005).

16. Lev Vygotsky, "Play and its role in the Mental Development of the Child," *Psychology and Marxism Internet Archive*, 1933, www.marxists.org/archive/vygotsky/works/1933/play.htm, 17.

17. "Comparison among Froebel, Montessori, Reggio Emilia and Waldorf-Steiner Methods— Part 2." *Spielgaben: Smarter Play Smarter Child*, Spielgaben, November 5, 2013, spielgaben.com/ comparison-froebel-montessori-reggio-waldorf-part-2/.

processing,[18] the movement involved in play also encourages cognitive learning. The creativity of play encourages neuron connections within the brain. Doris Fromberg, in *Play and Meaning in Early Childhood Education*, writes, "Enriched educational experiences create stronger structural connections and pathways within the brain."[19] Play, as a holistic experience, not only engages the mind but also engages an individual's emotions. Implicit learning involves our emotions on a deep level, and by activating our implicit learning, we are learning more than just what is being taught.[20]

PLAY AS A PROCESS OF MEANING-MAKING

Play is also a tool that children utilize to make sense of their world. The creative process of play combines what is known in the real world with a pretend world beyond what is known, so that children are able to work out new understandings and meanings. Utilizing their imaginative abilities, children take something ordinary and, in turn, experience it in an extraordinary way. They create connections and accommodate information to make meaning with what they encounter. While a young child may only be wearing an old bathrobe, for that child, it is a robe fit for a king. A blanket over a table becomes, in imaginative play, a royal tent built for this king. Children act on questions, wondering how this king lives. Does a king hide in his tent or go into battle for his people? And what happens when the king's enemy is a giant as big as Goliath? These self-created experiences with blanket tents and royal bathrobes are not just a fantasy for children to find pleasure in. It is real to them. And once they are done exploring these ideas in play, they come back to the real world with new understandings. It is here, Elkind contends, where children learn best,[21] for what is learned in play will be stronger and last longer than what they are told, for example, in a traditional Sunday School lesson.[22]

18. David A. Sousa, *How the Brain Learns*, 3rd ed. (Thousand Oaks, CA: Corwin, 2006).

19. Doris P. Fromberg, *Play and Meaning in Early Childhood Education* (Boston, MA: Allyn and Bacon, 2002), 29.

20. Sousa, *How the Brain Learns*, 239–240.

21. Elkind, *The Power of Play: Learning What Comes Naturally*, 7.

22. Stuart Brown with Christopher Vaughn, *Play: How it Shapes the Brain, Opens the Imagination, and Invigorates the Soul* (New York: Penguin, 2009), 102.

Play provides a safe place for exploration. In play, children bring together both their emotions and cognitive understandings. According to Edmiston, "[T]he emotional and physical safety of play worlds provide children with spaces where they can feel competent and capable while choosing to explore whatever aspects of life interest them."[23] In play, children stop for a moment and choose to investigate a question, a possible solution, or a different ending. How scary was that giant? Does the king have the courage to fight Goliath himself? And if the king chooses to fight Goliath, who is the hero of the story? Is the hero of the story a powerful God or an earthly king? Play engages the emotions, and by having emotions engaged, rational learning is strengthened. The safety of the play world provides children with the courage, space, and freedom to understand something in a new way. Play provides guidance and the scaffolding needed for children to move from a prior understanding to a new meaning. In this instance, scaffolding implies the presence of an adult, but it requires the child to be in charge of the learning. In the Zone of Proximal Development (ZPD), the teacher becomes an assistant, helping guide the child-initiated learning. Bodrova and Leong contend that "play provides support at the highest levels" of the ZPD,[24] where the fundamental needs, desires, and questions of the child are asked, affirmed, and explored.

Play does not just encourage concrete learning, but also encourages the development of symbolic thinking. Edmiston contends that, in play, children can think abstractly and create symbolic meaning because a child's "attention is more on the meaning of things and actions in imagined worlds than on the actual objects and movements in the everyday."[25] Play, then, is foundational for abstract thought and symbolic thinking,[26] where children can leave behind reality and enter into a fantasy world where symbols and imagination reign. That imagination can take the child into a symbolic world where a bathrobe becomes a kingly royal robe, a blanket becomes a tent, and a child-size chair becomes a throne. This is the beginning of symbolic thinking that is developed within play.

But play is not just a solitary experience. Play can also be a relational process

23. Edmiston, *Forming Ethical Identities in Early Childhood Play*, 101.
24. Bodrova and Leong, "Adult Influences on Play: The Vygotskian Approach," 168.
25. Edmiston, *Forming Ethical Identities in Early Childhood Play*, 11.
26. Pellegrini, *The Role of Play in Human Development*, 24; Bodrova and Leong, "Adult Influences on Play: The Vygotskian Approach," 169.

that encourages intimacy, enculturation and socialization,[27] development of interpersonal skills, instillation of cultural understandings, and bolstering of mirroring behavior. When a child is engaged with another person, especially an adult, play encourages attachment and fosters a sense of trust. When a child plays with another, this social play "nourishes the roots of trust, empathy, caring, and sharing."[28] It is in this playful interaction with another that a transformational relationship develops between self-awareness and the awareness of others, along with their feelings, thoughts, motives, and desires.[29]

As families and faith communities seek to enculturate children in the faith, play provides the means for children to observe and imitate others on the faith journey. Have you ever observed a child playing house or office, dressing up in adult-type clothes or carrying a purse or backpack in imitation of a parent? Children observe and imitate in play, working through their understanding of the vignette they are remembering and replaying. Cultural understandings can be bolstered through a child's mirroring behavior. As children play and engage in the process of meaning-making through play experiences, they are integrating new ideas into both their family life and community life.[30]

This mirroring behavior can also be utilized in a child's spiritual development. Through play, a child mimics what is observed in church, working through an understanding of what was noticed. One of the authors' nephews demonstrated this beautifully. When he was three or four years old, he would come home from church and get into his bathrobe, grab a children's Bible, and begin to "preach." This preaching usually consisted of various parts of the sermon, church liturgy, and potluck dinner announcements. He then would grab a Ritz cracker and some juice to serve communion to the family. When that was completed, he would climb up on his toy box to play the "organ" on the windowsill, conducting the choir, nodding when they need to get louder or softer. While adorable to watch, this child's play was serious business for him. He was working hard to make sense of what he experienced

---

27. Winnecott, *Playing and Reality*, 135; Elkind, *The Power of Play: Learning What Comes Naturally*, 145.

28. Brown, *Play: How it Shapes the Brain, Opens the Imagination, and Invigorates the Soul*, 197.

29. Doris P. Fromberg, "Play's Pathways to Meaning: A Dynamic Theory of Play," in *Play from Birth to Twelve: Contexts, Perspectives, and Meanings*, 2nd ed., eds. Doris P. Fromberg and Doris Bergen (New York: Routledge, 2006), 161.

30. Ruth Paradise and Barbara Rogoff, "Side by Side: Learning by Observing and Pitching In," *Ethos: Journal of the Society for Psychological Anthropology* 37, no. 1 (2009): 102–38.

in church, integrating new understandings and information with his current knowledge. Through play, a child's understanding of faith can deepen.

Play is not only a social activity but also an intrapersonal process that supports identity formation and fosters agency. A child's creativity is nurtured in play where each individual is free to do what he or she wants to do when he or she wants to do it. The self discovered within this creative act is deeply rooted in our identity, for, as Brown says, "the self that emerges through play is the core, authentic self."[31] As a therapeutic activity, play is the expression of the soul where words fail. Play thus becomes the language of a child's thoughts. In play, a child is able to try things out, for there is no threat to one's physical or emotional well-being. As Brown again points out, "We are safe precisely because we are just playing."[32] Because there are no consequences, either long-term or short-term, a child can practice and rehearse life.[33]

Self-motivated play helps to develop a child's agency and the ability to determine his or her own mind and own beliefs. Through play, a child makes hypotheses, tests those hypotheses, meets success or failure, and proceeds to retest and revise based on the results. Play is the vehicle through which a child develops his or her own set of beliefs and understandings, and is where the child's faith takes root inside the soul.

Play behavior also shapes future development[34] as it accommodates a child's activities into their thinking. As children play, they are engaging in a learning process that encourages meaning-making, socialization, and identity formation. These acts of exploration, discovery, and wonder are also essential aspects in the development of faith.

PLAY AND A CHILD'S
SPIRITUAL DEVELOPMENT

Childhood should be a time when one can learn and practice the faith.[35] The act of play assists in this quest because it prepares a child for personal

---

31. Brown, *Play: How it Shapes the Brain, Opens the Imagination, and Invigorates the Soul*, 107.
32. Ibid., 34.
33. Ibid., 32.
34. Pellegrini, *The Role of Play in Human Development*, 34.
35. Bunge, "The Vocation of the Child: Theological Perspectives on the Particular and Paradoxical Roles and Responsibilities of Children," 46.

growth, transformation, and for potential spiritual awakening.[36] Play provides the child with the opportunity to explore the Christian faith and discover his or her spiritual identity. Through this exploration, the child learns not only about God and biblical stories, but also shapes and forms understandings of God, self, and salvation.[37] Play is a faith formation activity, one that engages the known and moves toward the exploration and discovery of the unknown.

It is here where play nurtures spiritual identity. We are holistic individuals—physical, cognitive, emotional, social, and spiritual beings. Play provides a place where we can engage in the biblical story through all these identities. We think through different aspects and understandings as we try out ideas in our play. We also explore our emotions in play. We rage with anger or dance with joy without any significant consequences for expressing those emotions. In spiritual play, children engage in a holistic exploration of the biblical story where they discover their place within that story.

Play also provides a non-threatening space to answer life's questions. What might be difficult to articulate in the everyday world is much easier to probe in an imaginary world. Through the lenses of play, a child can magnify a concern or desire and explore the consequences of these ideas. In a pretend world, his or her thoughts, fears, or concerns can be projected onto a hero or a monster, and this idea can be investigated and studied in a non-threatening environment from outside oneself. In this, the scary thought or situation is made smaller, and the child becomes bigger than the problem. And as part of a child's faith community, we are given a window to observe their play and assess what they believe or are endeavoring to understand.

Within this play exploration, the spiritual gift of hope is also encouraged. While we have been redeemed, we still live in a broken world. There is a tension between the already and the not yet realized. Play helps us understand hope, that yearning for something different while living in reality. As Edmiston states, "being playful hints at, and makes reference to, the possibilities of other ways of being, other parallel worlds where we could have different lives."[38] We live in a world of violence, trauma,

36. David Elkind, "The Role of Play in Religious Education," *Religious Education* 75, no. 3 (1980): 291–93.

37. Sasongko, "*Homo Ludens* Revisited: A Theological Inquiry into Being Human from the Perspective of Javanese Children's Play," 370.

38. Edmiston, *Forming Ethical Identities in Early Childhood Play*, 9.

and sexual and physical abuse. These are the harsh realities of a sinful and broken world. In a child's imagination, he or she can create a world where good triumphs over evil, wrong is made right with a snap of a finger, and any other undesirable circumstance can be diverted. Here, play is not just a frivolous activity, but also a serious theological endeavor. For faith, according to the author of Hebrews, is the confidence of what we hope for and the assurance of what we do not see (Heb. 11:1). In a child's play, this imaginary place is an expression of the soul's desire, the desire for a better world where what we hope for can be achieved. In play, we are not escaping reality, but nurturing a faith in God who promises a new world where there is no more pain or death (Rev. 21).

NURTURING FAITH THROUGH A
SPIRITUAL PLAYGROUND

So with all this in mind, how do we encourage a child's faith formation through play? As shown above, play is a wonderful opportunity for spiritual growth and discovering one's spiritual potential. By intentionally utilizing play for spiritual formation, a child's spiritual identity is nurtured, spiritual rituals are understood, and a child's moral development is deepened.

So what does a spiritual playground actually look like? Some churches in England and Sweden have created a portable play church, a cupboard-like structure containing child-size vestments, communion elements, and different seasonal church items that stands somewhere in the church sanctuary. By "playing church" or other spiritual rituals within the worship experience with adults, children can explore understandings and make meaning of their experiences. A crèche-like structure can be established in a classroom with simple dress-up clothes and stuffed animals so children can reenact the nativity story. An imaginative storytelling approach, like Jerome Berryman's Godly Play,[39] can foster a child's imagination and allow him or her to experience the mystery of God.

To begin planning for a spiritual playground, think about your favorite place to play as a child. What was the environment like that encouraged you

---

39. Godly Play is a method that nurtures a child's spiritual development. For more information, see godlyplayfoundation.org.

to enter in and to play? What was needed to encourage your imagination to thrive? What does a space contain that encourages a child to explore and play well? The foundation for a spiritual playground demands freedom. Children must be allowed to explore, self-select, and have space to figure out their own understandings. A spiritual playground requires space and is supported through guidance but is killed by over-structure. For many children, it requires a feeling of solitude and silence, even within a noisy and active classroom. It may require a nook that is out of the way and suggests the safety to explore.

Along with the foundation of freedom, a spiritual playground requires the support and encouragement of your ministry leadership. It is important to assess your own and your ministry's attitude toward play and learning. What might need to change or be adapted in your context so that you can create a space for a child to explore his or her soul and Christian identity through play? This is not always an easy task. Remember, we often see play as a time filler or a recreational activity. A child's spiritual play must have the support of the leaders in charge. The key here is to make sure that parents, teachers, and ministry leaders understand that play is an intentional activity for learning.

The structure for a good playground includes appropriate equipment for children that enhances their imagination without restricting their exploration. Thus, you want to design your context to create different spaces for play. What activities can you facilitate that nurture a child's play and exploration? What equipment do you need? Scarves and bathrobes can be utilized for dress-up. Blocks and simple toys can be utilized as manipulatives for play. Look for simple games or toys that can encourage a child to explore a biblical story. The goal here is to foster and support imagination and play, so spaces are well-equipped in order to encourage exploration without restricting imagination.

BECOMING THE TEACHER IN A SPIRITUAL PLAYGROUND

One of the biggest challenges to utilizing play as a strategic means for formation is intentionality. The atmosphere of a spiritual playground must balance intentionality with freedom. The teacher has to understand that a spiritual playground is a different way of being with children. It requires trust, wisdom, and vision.

Imagine yourself teaching the story of David and Goliath to a group of young children. After telling the biblical story, you offer the children playthings and allow them to engage and explore at their own pace, their own inclination, and their own ability. How many means of engagement should you offer? If you provide only one set of play materials, you have not provided enough. Children must have choices to explore. There have to be at least two or more different, yet related, activities for them to choose from.

In the instance of the David and Goliath story, the materials in one space might include two or three slingshots with soft-sponge stones and a target board or a figure of Goliath that reaches the ceiling for aiming the stones. Here, children can imagine what it might have been like for David to come up to a giant and how God used David to kill Goliath. Another space might include a roll of inexpensive paper, a picture of Goliath, and a measuring stick to discover how tall he really was. Another picture of David, in correct proportion to Goliath, should be in this same space. Yet another space might include vests to become suits of armor, flat cardboard shields, and small cardboard spears. Several sets of this military garb could help children discover the armies around David and Goliath. A dramatic play station could have a blanket tent with a child's size chair for a throne, two different sizes of plastic armor, and a robe. A child could engage with this vignette alone or in group play, discovering different understandings of Saul and David. An additional dramatic play station could include two groups of army men, a Ken doll, and a small action figure. By playing with these toys on a table, a child can have Goliath (the Ken doll) stand among the Philistines and Israelites (the army men) with David (the small action figure) crying out, "I come against you in the name of the Lord Almighty, the God of the armies of Israel!" (1 Sam. 17:45).

All of these choices can be available to the children with no rules about where to start or how many choices to engage. The teacher's role is to simply introduce each space or center, citing possibilities of what could happen there. After those introductions, the teacher becomes an assistant, a benevolent observer, and a pray-er over the children's play.

Choice means we trust the exploration process, and we trust that God can enter into whatever choice a child makes. We trust that through play, the child's soul will be enlarged and nurtured. If we do not provide choices, we are manipulating the child. We are controlling his or her play and have removed the freedom of exploration and wonder. Without real choice, the teacher is making play so controlled that it actually ends up no longer being play.

The act of trust in play requires the adult to trust God, the child, and the power of play to shape an individual. To trust in God, the teacher must believe God is active in the life of the child. If we believe God is engaging with his people, leading, encouraging, and shaping a person's faith, then God is active in a child as much as he is in the life of an adult. The second part of trust is that the teacher must trust the child. We trust that the child is engaged in play and working out his or her understandings. In this experience, we are trusting the process that children are actually making meaning through play. We trust that there is a serious part to play.

Coaching children in a spiritual playground also requires wisdom, which is an essential trait a teacher must possess. The adult must know when to ask a guiding question and when to be silent, allowing the child to self-discover. When is it important for an adult to step in and participate, and when is it important to step back and observe but not be directly engaged? This wisdom requires the adult leader to be present and active but not controlling and domineering. This is not the time to be holding a cup of coffee and "watching the children." For the adult to be engaged in the child's ZPD, that adult must be emotionally alongside the child, and at times, also physically alongside the child, encouraging the child to discover and learn for himself or herself. As children act and play David and Goliath or Noah and the flood or Jesus' baptism, the questions, comments, and even silence of the adult leader within the ZPD support a child's wondering, feeling, questioning, and thinking. For the child to learn beyond herself or himself, the adult must be present to lift up that child to new possibilities and new ways of thinking. This lifting up is then taken into the child's soul for pondering and wondering for the entire week.

Suppose the story for the week is Jesus and the Lost Sheep. You may choose to tell the story with flannel figures on a flannel board and then have the figures available for retelling the story. Another space could include a small bale of straw (readily available in October for Halloween decoration!), a small stuffed lamb, and a pile of sticks in which the lamb can get lost. The child needs a bathrobe or long scarf in which to be Jesus, who goes to look for the sheep. If your learning and exploration space is large enough, this space could also have some sort of fence for the sheepfold, possibly made out of three or four chairs laid on their sides to make each side of the fence. This space will allow the child to become the shepherd looking for the sheep, or to hide and become the lost sheep. Finally, a space for drawing the story is always a good idea. Plain paper and markers are best for this drawing space. The only equipment needed is a child-size table and two or three chairs. Once the teacher introduces the possible activities that can take place in those spaces, that teacher again becomes the benevolent observer and the coach for the child's ZPD, engaging with a question or a nod or a few minutes of playing with the child.

Lastly, vision is essential in creating a spiritual playground. The adult must have vision for a child's faith formation through play and then have the ability to set up an environment where a child can enter in and play with God. The adult's task is to establish a setting that encourages thought and meaning-making in young children while they play. This can be done by creating situations that allow the child to explore understandings, engage in wonder, or reenact a story. The teacher's role is to provide guided, open-ended questions, drawing ideas out of children as they play.

These play ideas are just a few unique ways to help support a child's ability to discover. A rich, soulful play environment must also have the presence of adults who are active but not domineering, asking questions but also silent, and trusting in God, the child, and the play experience. As Froebel suggests, the inner spiritual life of a child should be nurtured through play that is "independent yet supported by the whole."[40]

CONCLUSION

Curiosity, imagination, and wonder are all natural instincts of a child. Through play, a child takes these skills and uses them to make sense of the world, to figure out how things work, to gain abilities and habits for

40. Friedrich Froebel, *Friedrich Froebel's Pedagogics of the Kindergarten, Or, His Ideas Concerning the Play and Playthings of the Child* (New York: D. Appleton and Company, 1909), 28.

life, and to mirror the behavior of those around him or her. Through the uninhibited action of play, a child opens himself or herself up to learn, to observe, and to absorb the world. Children are holistically active in experimentation through play and not just passive observers. As they courageously enter into life through play, children are patiently making meaning of life, not forcing instant answers. They are "willing and able to wait for meaning to come . . . even if it comes very slowly, which it usually does."[41]

This intentional yet patient process of play is a key ingredient for spiritual transformation. Transformation is not the accumulation of information, but a purposeful process of changes in ideas, behaviors, and understandings, and it requires time and a sacred space. Just as the metamorphosis of a caterpillar into a butterfly requires time in a chrysalis for development and life change, so an individual's spiritual transformation requires space, time, and action in order to come to life. A spiritual playground provides this space and activity to nurture such transformation and to give strength to the soul of the child.

41. John C. Holt, *How Children Learn* (New York: Pitman Publishing, 1967), 184–85.

The Future of
CHILDREN'S
SPIRITUALITY

CHAPTER 16

CASTING A VISION FOR THE FUTURE

MIMI L. LARSON & ROBERT J. KEELEY

This book is, in large part, a reflection of the 2018 Children's Spirituality Summit. As the summit was coming to a close, we asked the question "So what?" What do we do with all the information on children's spirituality that was learned and discussed? Our hope is that this book has captured many of the ideas shared at the summit, bridging the gap between theory and practice, with the goal of equipping ministry leaders as they nurture the faith of children. We believe that, as a field, we are ready to take some new steps. What discussions should we be having that were not represented? What is on the horizon for those of us who care about children's spirituality?[1]

IMPROVING OUR MINISTRY METHODS

As methods change and adapt with time, our view of children as empty vessels, waiting to be filled with our understandings, is evolving into a vision of ministry *with* and *by* children. To embrace this new paradigm, we need to listen carefully to the children we are with and invite them into a growing awareness of God. We should be asking questions such as:

---

1. We solicited input for where the field of children's spirituality needs to grow from the authors of this book as well as the leadership board for the Society of Children's Spirituality: Christian Perspectives.

- What does it mean for the adult who walks alongside a child?
- How can we best embrace a reciprocal learning relationship with children?
- How can we empower children to lead?
- As we engage with one another, what can adults gain from a child's unique perspective?
- How is our spiritual development strengthened by childlike activities such as play, exploration, and wonder?

The answers to these questions may require a new posture for those of us working with children. There are already strong hints that we should be doubling down on our efforts to support a child's faith in both the Christian community and in the home. Intergenerational ministry that enhances and deepens not only a child's spiritual experience, but the spiritual experience of all involved, seems to be a particularly fruitful path.

Secular research is showing us the importance of childhood in terms of a person's health and development.[2] If this is true for our holistic development, it is safe to assume this is also true for our spirituality. Yet the church and the academic institutions that support ministry continue to focus on adults and teens as the main arenas for spiritual formation. We need to invest in those who work with children, educating and equipping them well to engage in children's spirituality. It is also vitally important that ministry leaders and academic institutions make children's spirituality a priority, seeing childhood as a significant sphere for spiritual growth.

GAINING CULTURAL INTELLIGENCE

In any church, the culture in which we live affects our ministry. As noted in the book, *Resilient Ministry*, "Cultural intelligence includes the ability to discriminate between cultural preferences and biblical imperatives."[3] We believe there are several areas in which the field of children's spirituality must grow with respect to cultural intelligence.

---

2. "Plastic Brains: Catching Them Young," *The Economist*, January 5, 2019, 7–8.
3. Bob Burns, Tasha D. Chapman, and Donald C. Guthrie, *Resilient Ministry: What Pastors Told Us About Surviving and Thriving* (Downers Grove, IL: IVP Books, 2013), 147.

UNDERSTANDING GENERATIONAL CHARACTERISTICS

As John Roberto pointed out in his chapter, it is important to understand the unique needs of upcoming generations. As they grow, children will be engaging with a variety of issues that can be best addressed with a spiritually rich and biblical worldview. We need to anticipate and respond well to issues in our culture that both directly and indirectly impact a child's spiritual development, asking questions such as:

- How is a child's spirituality impacted by trauma and loss?
- What are the ways perseverance (a theological term for resilience and grit) can be developed in a child?
- How can we engage the issues of sexuality from a Christian perspective?

These discussions should probably start with a better understanding of identity development in children.

THE IMPACT OF DIGITAL TECHNOLOGY

Digital Technology is shaping how our culture engages in every aspect of life, including education and communication. This has huge implications for everyone's spiritual development, especially children who don't remember an environment that was not technology-rich.

- How do we engage with children who are accustomed to multiple screens?
- What are the ways technology hinders a child's spirituality?
- Can technology be used to enhance spiritual formation?

VALUING THE BROAD RANGE OF CHRISTIAN TRADITIONS

To engage well in a discussion of children's spirituality, it is important to value the different perspectives of our brothers and sisters from other Christian traditions. This is the essence of the Children's Spirituality Summit—people from many branches of the Christian faith coming together and dialoguing about our practice regarding children's spirituality. The richness of diverse contexts, the variety of theological backgrounds, and the differences in practice can all inform our understandings of children and their spirituality. To do this well, our engagement should be steeped in an attitude of grace and humility, of openness to a different idea and receptiveness to something new. This doesn't mean we accept everyone's beliefs and practices, of course, but we seek to gain understanding from one another so that we can go back and engage well in our particular context.

THE NEED FOR MORE RESEARCH

About ten years ago, Bob had a conversation with another leader in the field of children's spirituality. They discussed the need to move the great ideas discovered in research down to the people—to get into the actual practice of the church. While this is still a need, we also find ourselves back at a crossroad of needing more research. It is important for the academy to continue deepening our understandings and make a renewed effort to speak into the church and its practices. The field of children's spirituality needs more study, and research on the issues impacting children and our ministry with them falls in three areas.

DEVELOPMENTAL THEORY

For years, the field of spiritual development has followed a developmental stage theory approach and has relied heavily on cognitive development. While John Westerhoff has challenged this approach in past years,[4] we continue to wonder how developmental stage theory helps and/or hinders our conversation about spiritual development. Should spiritual development follow a developmental stage theory approach like cognitive, psychosocial, or faith development theories have? What other directions should it take?

THEOLOGICAL FOUNDATIONS

The field of children's spirituality also needs to have a stronger theological foundation regarding children and our ministry with them. We are grateful for the work presented in this book as well as the work of

---

4. Westerhoff challenges these ideas in his seminal work John H. Westerhoff III, *Will Our Children Have Faith?* 3rd ed. (New York: Morehouse Publishing, 2012) as well as his article John Westerhoff, "Formation, Education, Instruction," *Religious Education* 82, no. 4, (1987): 579–591.

Jerome Berryman[5] and Marcia Bunge,[6] yet the field of children's spirituality continues to lack a strong foundation regarding how children are viewed, both theologically and historically. As Lawson and Harwood challenge us, the church must grow in its understanding of children and how we can nurture their faith. Could an exploration of the early church fathers or the Reformers help us in this understanding? Could a vigorous theological discussion shape how we think about God's views of children?

SIGNIFICANT AND INTENTIONAL METHODOLOGY

In our introduction, we promised that this book would be both theoretical and practical, calling us to hold the tension between strong research that challenges us to think well about these issues and the real-life, practical applications of ministry. While in recent years there have been small studies on how children experience God and make meaning of those experiences,[7] there is a need for more phenomenological research with children that will equip the church to better understand how children experience God and make meaning of those experiences. What methods encourage a child's love of and relationship with God? Are the methods utilized within the local church effective towards nurturing a relationship with God and a deeper understanding of him?

CONCLUSION

Our children and the generations that follow have many challenges before them, challenges that we did not have when we were young. As we described in the introduction, the field of children's spirituality continues to need people who think well about these issues and have real-life experiences in making things work in ministry. Our prayer is that this book has equipped those in ministry for exactly this call. May our children and children's children grow in their love of God.

---

5. Jerome W. Berryman, *Children and the Theologians: Clearing the Way for Grace* (New York: Morehouse Publishing, 2009).

6. Marcia Bunge, ed., *The Child in Christian Thought* (Grand Rapids, MI: Eerdmans, 2001).

7. See Catherine Stonehouse and Scottie May, *Listening to Children on the Spiritual Journey: Guidance for Those Who Teach and Nurture* (Grand Rapids, MI: Baker Academic, 2010); and Mimi L. Larson, "Making Meaning of God: The Faith Experiences of Preschool Children," in *Story, Formation, and Culture: From Theory to Practice in Ministry with Children*, eds. Benjamin D. Espinoza, et al. (Eugene, OR: Pickwick Publications, 2018), 86–98.

AUTHOR BIOGRAPHIES

HOLLY CATTERTON ALLEN is Professor of Christian Ministries and Family Science at Lipscomb University in Nashville, Tennessee. Her books include *InterGenerate: Transforming Churches through Intergenerational Ministry* (ACU Press, 2018); *Intergenerational Christian Formation: Bringing the Whole Church Together in Ministry, Community and Worship* (InterVarsity Press, 2012) with Christine Ross; and *Nurturing Children's Spirituality: Christian Perspectives and Best Practices* (Cascade, 2008). Dr. Allen has chaired the board for the Children's Spirituality Summit, as well as the task force that convenes InterGenerate, a conference that focuses on intergenerational ministry.

LACY FINN BORGO teaches and provides spiritual direction for the Renovaré Institute, for the DMin. in Spiritual Direction at Fuller Theological Seminary and at Portland Seminary. Dr. Borgo provides spiritual direction for adults through GoodDirtMinistries.org and provides spiritual direction for children at Haven House. She is the author of *Life with God for Children: A Curriculum for the Spiritual Formation of Children* and *Good Dirt: A Devotional for the Spiritual Formation of Families*, both of which can be found on her website. Her forthcoming book, *Spiritual Conversations with Children: Listening to God Together* will be released in the Spring of 2020 through IVP.

ERIK W. CARTER is Cornelius Vanderbilt Professor of Special Education at Vanderbilt University. His research and teaching focuses on effective strategies for supporting inclusion and valued roles in school, work, community, and congregational settings for individuals with disabilities and their families. Dr. Carter is the author of numerous articles, chapters, and books, among them is *Including People with Disabilities in Faith Communities: A Guide for Service Providers, Families, and Congregations* (Brookes Publishing, 2007).

KAYLEE R. FRANK recently graduated from Lipscomb University, where she received her Bachelor of Arts in Children's Ministry. She currently teaches in Metro Nashville Public Schools as a corps member in Teach for America. Ms. Frank is grateful for the research opportunities she had as an undergraduate student, which allowed her to gain a deeper understanding of how spirituality can foster resilience in refugee children.

ADAM HARWOOD is Professor of Theology occupying the McFarland Chair of Theology at New Orleans Baptist Theological Seminary, where he also directs the Baptist Center for Theology & Ministry and edits the *Journal for Baptist Theology & Ministry*. Dr. Harwood is also the author of *The Spiritual Condition of Infants* (Wipf & Stock, 2011) and co-editor of *Infants and Children in the Church: Five Views on Theology and Ministry* (B&H Academic, 2017).

MARVA HOOPES serves as the Christian Education Specialist teaching in the department of Bible, Theology, and Ministry at Malone University in Canton, Ohio. Dr. Hoopes previously held the position of children's pastor for twenty-six years in the Evangelical Friends denomination, has served as missions pastor, and has been a curriculum consultant and writer for four different curriculum companies. She has also participated in leadership on the regional and national Christian education boards of Evangelical Friends.

ROBERT J. KEELEY is Professor of Education at Calvin University and Visiting Professor of Faith Formation and Discipleship at Calvin Theological Seminary, where he also serves as the director of distance learning. Dr. Keeley is also the author or coauthor of *Helping Our Children Grow in Faith* (Baker, 2008), *Celebrating the Milestones of Faith* (Faith Alive Christian Resources, 2009) and *Dear Parent: A Guide for Family Faith Formation* (Faith Formation Ministries, 2019).

DANA KENNAMER serves as the Associate Dean of the College of Education and Human Services and professor and chair of the Department of Teacher Education at Abilene Christian University. Dr. Kennamer's publications include *Along the Way: Conversations about Children & Faith* (ACU Press, 2015), *Let All the Children Come to Me: A Practical Guide to Including Children with Disabilities In Your Church Ministries* (David C. Cook, 2013), and *I Will Change Your Name: Messages from the Father to a Heart Broken by Divorce* (Leafwood Publishers, 2007).

MEGAN LARRY is an undergraduate student at Lipscomb University in Nashville, Tennessee. She will graduate in 2020 with a Bachelors degree in Education and Children's Ministry. Ms. Larry has enjoyed blending her two areas of study through researching how spirituality helps children foster resilience.

MIMI L. LARSON serves as the Children's Ministry Catalyzer for Faith Formation Ministries, a ministry for the Christian Reformed Church in North America, and teaches in the Department of Christian Formation and Ministries at Wheaton College and in Educational Studies at Trinity Evangelical Divinity School. Dr. Larson has also authored various chapters and articles on children's faith formation and has developed curriculum for various organizations, including Big Idea/Veggie Tales and Faith Alive Christian Resources.

KEVIN E. LAWSON is Professor of Educational Studies at Talbot School of Theology, Biola University, where he also serves as editor of the *Christian Education Journal: Research on Educational Ministry*. Dr. Lawson is the editor of *Understanding Children's Spirituality: Theology, Research, and Practice* (Wipf & Stock, 2012) and co-editor with Adam Harwood of *Infants and Children in the Church: Five Views on Theology and Ministry* (Broadman & Holman, 2017).

SCOTTIE MAY is Associate Professor Emerita of Christian Formation and Ministry at Wheaton College, Wheaton, Illinois. Dr. May is coauthor of *Children Matter* (Eerdmans, 2005), and *Listening to Children on the Spiritual Journey* (Baker, 2010); she contributed to *Perspectives on Children's Spiritual Formation: Four Views* (Broadman/Holman, 2006), and *Children's Spirituality: Christian Perspectives, Research and Applications* (Cascade, 2004), as well as chapters and articles in other resources.

SHELLY MELIA is the Associate Dean of the Graduate School of Ministry at Dallas Baptist University. She also serves as Associate Professor and Program Director for the Master of Arts in Children's Ministry and Family Ministry. Dr. Melia has authored chapters in *Preschool Christian Education* and *Children's Christian Education* (Christian Leadership Publishing, 2015). She is a Licensed Professional Counselor specializing in children and grief.

SHIRLEY K. MORGENTHALER is Distinguished Professor of Curriculum, Language and Literacy in the College of Education at Concordia University, Chicago. Dr. Morgenthaler is the editor of the *Lutheran Education Journal* as well as the author of *Right from the Start* (Concordia Publishing, 2001) and co-editor of *Story, Formation, and Culture: From Theory to Practice in Ministry with Children* (Pickwick, 2018).

TREVECCA OKHOLM is an Adjunct Professor of Practical Theology at Azusa Pacific University. She also serves the church as a ministry coach, family ministry consultant, and trainer for *Wonder & Worship* models of faith formation. Ms. Okholm has authored *Kingdom Family: Re-Envisioning God's Plan for Marriage and Family* (Cascade, 2012), as well as various chapters and articles on family ministry and children's faith formation. She is a certified Christian Educator in the Presbyterian Church, USA.

JOHN ROBERTO is on the leadership team of Vibrant Faith Ministries. He works as a consultant to churches and national organizations, teaches courses and conducts workshops in faith formation, and has authored books and program manuals in faith formation. Mr. Roberto's latest books include *Faith Formation with a New Generation* (LifelongFaith Associates, 2018), *Families at the Center of Faith Formation* (LifelongFaith Associates, 2016), *Seasons of Adult Faith Formation, Reimagining Faith Formation for the 21st Century* (LifelongFaith Associates, 2015), *Generations Together*, and *Faith Formation* (LifelongFaith Associates, 2010).

ED STETZER holds the Billy Graham Chair of Church, Mission, and Evangelism and serves as Dean of the School of Mission, Ministry, and Leadership at Wheaton College as well as Executive Director of the Billy Graham Center. Dr. Stetzer is a contributing editor for *Christianity Today*, a columnist for *Outreach Magazine*, and Founding Editor of *The Gospel Project*. He has authored a number of books, most recently, *Christians in the Age of Outrage* (Tyndale Momentum, 2018).

KAREN F. WILLIAMS is a Book Publishing and Religious Education Consultant. She has a diversified career in book publishing and children's Sunday school curriculum and is the author of *Sending up My Timber* (Upper Room, 1999) and *Lights, Drama, Worship!* (Zondervan, 2003). Dr. Williams also wrote an award-winning play, "Black Women Walking" (Best Play Award, Atlanta Black Theatre Festival, 2018).

HENRY ZONIO is a Sociology Ph.D. candidate at the University of Kentucky. His research intersects child development, social inequalities, spirituality, and education. Mr. Zonio is a regular contributor to *Children's Ministry Magazine* and author of a chapter entitled "'Is That a Mom and Dad Church?' Children's Constructions of Meaning Through Focus Group Interviews" in *Researching Children and Youth: Methodological Issues, Strategies, and Innovations* (2017).

SUBJECT INDEX

age of accountability, 48–49

awe, 211

baptism, 42, 43, 45, 48

Baptist Church, 43

beauty, 220

belonging

  acceptance as aspect of, 77

  being known as aspect of, 76, 87

  being needed as aspect of, 80–81

  being welcomed as aspect of, 75, 91

  dimensions of, 71

  friendship as aspect of, 79–80

  importance of emphasis on in

    children's ministry, 70, 71

  need for in children with disabilities,

    71, 81, 82

  presence as starting point for, 73

  reenvisioning family as way of

    fostering sense of, 103, 103n. 4

  reflection tool for fostering, 72

  sense of as coping mechanism, 108,

    117, 139, 142

  sharing our stories as way of fostering

    sense of, 107, 108

Bible, the. *See* Scripture

Bible-time museum model, 33

biblical literacy, 34

Bloom, Benjamin, 189, 192, 195

Bloom's taxonomy, 189–92, 194, 200

blue laws, 104

BY period, 37

Catechesis of the Good Shepherd, the,

  176

catechetical schools, formation of, 23

catechism, 43, 45

childhood death, treatment of by God,

  42–43, 44

children

  age of accountability of, 48–49

  awareness of racial differences among,

    58, 58n. 21, 59, 202, 203, 213

  and awe, 221

  and beauty, 220

  capability of for spiritual walk with

    "God, 45–46

  church membership of, 42–43, 44

  common behaviors of after

    experiencing trauma, 131–32

  death of, treatment by God in the

    event of, 42–43, 44, 49

  disabled. *See* children with

    disabilities

  discussing race with, 58, 59–60,

    61–62, 67

  as examples of faith, 46, 48

  fully owned faith of, 46–47, 49–50

255

SCRIPTURE INDEX